EPIC MEXICO

Epic Mexico
A History from Earliest Times

TERRY RUGELEY

University of Oklahoma Press : Norman

Publication of this book is made possible through the generosity of Edith Kinney Gaylord.

Library of Congress Cataloging-in-Publication Data

Names: Rugeley, Terry, 1956– author.
Title: Epic Mexico : a history from earliest times / Terry Rugeley.
Description: Norman : University of Oklahoma Press, [2020] | Includes bibliographical references and index. | Summary: "A concise and comprehensive history of Mexico from its ancient origins to the twenty-first century."—Provided by publisher.
Identifiers: LCCN 2020007866 | ISBN 978-0-8061-6707-7 (paperback)
Subjects: LCSH: Mexico—History.
Classification: LCC F1226 .R84 2020 | DDC 972—dc23
LC record available at https://lccn.loc.gov/2020007866

The paper in this book meets the guidelines for permanence and durability of the Committee on Production Guidelines for Book Longevity of the Council on Library Resources, Inc. ∞

Contents

Illustrations

Figures

Illustrations

Maps

1

First Peoples

Precontact Civilizations from Earliest Times to 1519

A few hundred miles north of the Isthmus of Panama, just south of a huge waterway that gathers from the melting snow of the Rocky Mountains and runs eastward through desert scrub, lies a land that has consistently beguiled and confounded human expectation. Brilliant, beautiful, troubled, gifted, with more facets than a fistful of diamonds, it is a place with an impossibly distant past, an epic land where moments of mayhem and carnage have punctuated long epochs of peace. Its inhabitants have known the landscapes of their existence by many names: Mayab, Teotihuacán, Zempoala, Pátzcuaro, Aztlán, Chapultepec, and finally and collectively, in a word that rolls off the modern tongue as if it had always been there, Mexico.

As with so many places throughout the world, Mexico's geography has played the central role in shaping human culture and society. North America's vast central plain reaches southward past the Rio Grande, into the semiarid Mexican states that stretch from Sonora east to Tamaulipas. Only tough natural plants like cactus, agave, guayule, and hardy, deep-rooted grasses can survive here. The profoundly arid Sonoran Desert may appear a wasteland to outsider, but in fact it teems with highly specialized forms of life: insects, birds, reptiles, and mammals that thrive on the land's hidden resources.

As in the United States, two inland mountain ranges run parallel to the coasts: an older and far more eroded eastern Sierra Madre and the younger and more rugged western range of the same name. These mountains provide the catchment for seasonal rivers on which peoples like the Yaquis, the Mayos, and the Tarahumaras depend for survival. Along the Pacific coast, the shifting of Pacific and North American tectonic plates far beneath the earth's surface has rendered Mexico, especially in the south and southwest, susceptible to earthquakes, exactly the problem that plagues modern west-coast cities in the United States like San Francisco.

South of the Tropic of Cancer, the arid high plains give way to a zone of more dependable rainfall. The vegetation gradually becomes more exuberant. Along the upper part of this region lies a thin zone known as the Trans-Mexico Volcanic Belt; it runs westward from Colima, passes through the heart of the country, and extends all the way to the Veracruz coast. Mexico's highest mountain is found here: the Pico de Orizaba rises to a majestic 18,491 feet. A mere 500 feet shy of that, the famous volcano Popocatépetl (smoking mountain) keeps watch over Puebla and Mexico City. Locals know Popocatépetl as Don Gregorio, a living being of petulant rumbles, a personified force who demands periodic ceremonies in order to behave himself. Still, volcanic birth is hardly confined to the prehistoric past. As recently as 1943 an entirely new volcano, named for the nearby village of Parícutin, erupted out of the cornfields of Michoacán.

In the belt's center the converging eastern and western ranges form a protective bowl around the Valley of Mexico, known in precontact days as Anáhuac (close to water). At an elevation of some 7,000 feet, the valley enjoys a cool to temperate climate, with average high temperatures around 70 degrees Fahrenheit and lows of 33 degrees in the winter to 50 degrees in the summer. In precontact years the vast Lake Texcoco formed in the valley's center; it grew from both saline and freshwater springs, but over time the lack of drainage heightened its salinity. From circa 1000 BCE onward, this valley has been the center of human existence in Mexico, with the richest agriculture and the densest populations.

Between the mountains and the oceans lie two long coastal strips of *tierra caliente*, the "hot country," so different from their upland counterparts. These seductive lands offer all the fecundity that the altiplano denies: all the fruits and aromatic plants, the brilliantly colored birds and elusive jaguars, the hot afternoons and temperate evenings, and the irresistible lure of the seashore. Firs and hardwoods give way to palms and to indigenous fruits such as mamey, papaya, and zapote—bananas, lemons, limes, oranges, and pineapples all being colonial introductions.

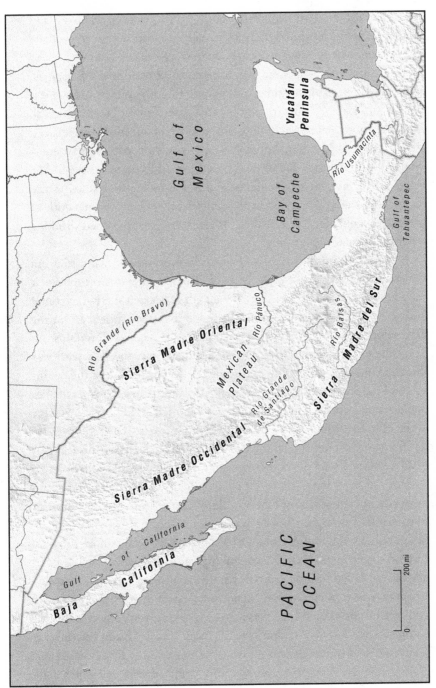

Topographical map of Mexico. Map by Erin Grib Cartography.

Mexico also has two peninsulas, both departures from the mainland geography. To the southeast, Yucatán actually began as an entirely separate landmass located in that vast waterway that we call the Gulf of Mexico and the Caribbean Sea. Essentially a huge, flat limestone shelf, over the course of eons it gradually floated westward, rotating counterclockwise as it went, until it collided with and became part of lower North America. Every now and then momentous events happen in out-of-the-way places, and so it was in Yucatán. Approximately 65 million years ago an enormous meteorite struck the northern coast; in addition to raising a dust cloud whose ensuing winter doomed the heat-loving dinosaurs, it also fragmented the upper layers of the limestone, creating the network of distinctive sinkholes (*cenotes*) that for centuries have provided drinking water for human populations.

A second peninsula, that of Baja California, juts downward from the southwest coast of North America. Far narrower than Yucatán, it stretches approximately one-third the length of Mexico and is a region of both geographical variety and immense biodiversity, particularly in the days before hunting and ranching made their incursions. Mountains run along the eastern coast, while grasslands and desert, together with vast shoreline, predominate at lower altitudes. The waters between the peninsula and the Sonoran mainland, a deep body alternately known as the Sea of Cortés and the Gulf of California, contain such interesting marine life as the Humboldt squid, known to fisherman as *diablo rojo* (red devil) for its ability to flash red and white colors; and the blue whales, those largest of all mammals, who come there to carry on their outsized courtships.

Mexican rivers mostly flow out of catchments in the central mountain ranges and downward to the coasts. Many of the waterways have courses too steep and precipitous to be navigable. The largest network actually lies elsewhere: the Usumacinta-Grijalva system of what is now Tabasco. Its twin rivers originate in the western highlands of Guatemala and wind devious and flood-prone courses before converging near modern-day Frontera. Mexican civilization began just west of the Grijalva, but after 400 BCE it moved elsewhere, leaving the southern wetlands as a zone of comparatively low population, then as now, and by historical times it was an isolated wilderness cut off from the more culturally advanced and densely populated altiplano. Mexico thus imitated neither Egypt's delta culture nor China's vast system of human-controlled irrigation.

Northern rivers, meanwhile, are seasonal, like those of the western United States. They form out of melting snow or seasonal rains and disappear altogether for parts of the year. The longest river of all, the Rio Grande (or as it is known in Mexico, the Río Bravo) offers a case in point. Originating from the spring melt-off of the snowpack of the southern Rockies, this nearly nineteen-hundred-mile-long body of water could become utterly torrential in spring but could shrivel to nothingness by the end of summer. Today sapped by damming, irrigation, and urban water usage, its flow seldom even reaches the Gulf of Mexico. Those beholding this muddy trickle, heavily militarized with walls, concertina wire, and closed-circuit cameras, will have a difficult time believing that human beings once had to tie ropes to themselves, rather in the style of alpinists, in order to cross without being swept away. In those days this waterway could be truly *bravo*: wild.

Enter the Human Race

The first and most inescapable fact regarding Mexico's human presence is its age. Civilization here was ancient long before the first buckle-shoed Englishman set foot on the banks of the Chesapeake estuary. Alternative and often crackpot theories notwithstanding, most scholars adhere to the theory first proposed by the Spanish Jesuit José de Acosta in 1588: namely, that the peoples of the Americas migrated here from northeast Asia. Some thirty to forty thousand years ago, colder temperatures brought more ice, lowering ocean levels some fifty feet. This in turn allowed for a prolonged migration period into the American and Australian continents as people traveled in search of game animals. By 15,000 BCE temperatures and ocean levels rose once again, cutting these two worlds off from Eurasia and Africa.

The migrants traveled southward, leaving as they passed the distinctive Clovis-point arrowheads they used for bagging such game as camels, horses, wooly mammoths, and the lumbering, overgrown armadillos known as glyptodons. They reached the Valley of Mexico by 23,000 BCE. Fifteen centuries later these early migrants had made it all the way to Tierra del Fuego on the southern tip of South America, and by the time of European contact, early humans had occupied all but the most inhospitable parts of the Western Hemisphere.

Early peoples of Mesoamerica struggled against a set of limitations so severe that the rise of huge and complex civilizations seems improbable. The area had no beasts of burden: no horses, no cattle, no donkeys, not even such domestic stalwarts as pigs or chickens. (The peoples of ancient Mexico had only turkeys, first domesticated around 3000 BCE, along with a hairless dog, ugly but lovable, known as *xoloitzcuintli*). There was only one work animal in these parts, and it traveled on two legs.

Neither did early Mesoamericans enjoy the use of metal. While the Old World entered a bronze age as early as 5000 BCE, Mesoamericans had no such options. They mastered the arts of working gold and silver, both soft and easily mined and smelted, and produced a certain quantity of copper trinkets from western Mexico or else imported them from the region of Panama, but they nevertheless lacked the ability to make bronze, for Mexico's vast and yet-undiscovered copper deposits lay far to the north, in extremely arid conditions and far from the centers of human settlement. Nor had Mesoamericans unlocked the secrets of iron. This left only such materials as stone, wood, bone, and shell.

Last, and somewhat more inexplicably, Mesoamericans never developed the wheel. The only known exception is a child's pull-toy from the Veracruz region, a ceramic deer mounted on a wooden board. Some scholars have hypothesized that the technological lacuna resulted from a lack of beasts of burden, but we have to wonder whether ancient peoples would not have benefited from pulleys, handcarts, and potter's wheels. Collectively, these deficiencies meant that all labor had to be done using only human muscle and with materials far less efficacious than in other parts of the world.

How then did early Mesoamericans accomplish so much with so little? They discovered that some rocks were harder than others and used flint and chert to quarry softer materials such as limestone and *tezontle* (basically a solidified form of volcanic froth, complete with air bubbles). They learned to use sand to grind stones to their desired shape. For spear tips, arrowheads, and cutting tools they preferred a smooth black volcanic stone known as obsidian. It could be flaked to an extremely sharp edge: though easily chipped, it was lethal while it lasted.

Of all their discoveries and innovations, none surpassed agriculture, and more specifically, the domestication of corn. Primitive hunters did their work only too well, and as the herds of game animals slowly disappeared, hunter-gatherers were forced to search for alternate food sources. Between 30,000 and 2500 BCE, humans learned to use a number of wild seeds and grains, including amaranth and cactus fruit. They also discovered a wild grass called *teocintle*, the distant ancestor of modern maize. The original version of this plant consisted of a relatively short cob of grain and a disproportionately large germination tassel, the latter being useful for catching pollen in the wild. But thousands of years of human manipulation resulted in the plump, grain-filled cobs that maintain life, along with a decreased need for natural reproduction. The oldest known human use of teocintle comes from a cave in Tehuacán, Puebla, but actual cultivation may have begun along the Balsas River, somewhat to the south of that point, between 8000 and 7000 BCE. Corn spread to South America during the subsequent millennium. By 2500 BCE it had started on its travels into the rest of North America. Dozens of regional varieties exist, all suited to particular soils, climates, and seasons, and it is hardly surprising to find corn gods wherever human beings settled.

Then as now, Mesoamerican farming depended on a highly reliable yearly weather cycle. From October through May, a dry season allowed for harvests and plantings, while a rainy season of June through September, usually manifesting itself as intense afternoon downpours, provided the water for agriculture. Following this cycle, the farmer identified an area of overgrown land and in February or March slashed the vegetation to the base; then, after that vegetation had dried sufficiently, he set fire to the remaining bramble. This fire had the twin effect of clearing the land and also adding a certain amount of nutrients, in the form of ash, to the soil. At that point the farmer walked through the field, poking shallow holes in the soil with a digging stick; into these he planted seeds of corn, beans, and squash, the so-called "three sisters." The corn grew high, the squash covered the ground, and the beans filled the middle. After a minimum of weeding and maintenance, the family harvested and dried the corn and beans in the fall. Properly boiled and ground, corn became the basis of the tortilla; combined with the beans, it formed a complete protein that provided the basis of life for millions of human beings.

While it may sound primitive by the standards of modern green-revolution agriculture, this system of farming—known variously as slash-and-burn, swidden, or *milpa* farming (the latter is the old Nahuatl term)—is actually highly efficient in terms of calories produced per calories expended. Put simply, the farmer gets a lot of food for not much work. But it does entail some limitations. Burned fields produce high yields for one or two years, but without the benefit of deep plowing, the soil plays out thereafter, and the farmer must allow it to return to fallow as he farms elsewhere. Land quality varied immensely: some areas recovered fertility in a few years, while in rocky places like the Yucatán Peninsula the process could require tend or fifteen years. Milpa farming therefore requires constant mobility. That fact, in turn, meant that ancient Mesoamericans had little need for the concept of private property, since the agriculturist might not rework a given field in his lifetime. What did matter—and what would pit milpa farmers in a relentless battle against nineteenth-century reformers—was free access to public land.

Even as they were developing their great grain baskets of corn, ancient Mesoamericans also domesticated and cultivated tomatoes, tomatillos, pumpkins, green beans, cacti, and multiple varieties of squash. They learned to season their dishes with herbs such as epazote. (Another flavoring herb widespread in modern Mexico, the cilantro leaves that grace so many tomato sauces, actually came later, from India.) Similarly, the Mesoamericans knew nothing of such plants as wheat, barley, rice, garlic, coffee, or sugarcane, which all arrived in the wake of Europeans.

Tillers of this ancient world also learned to value the chile, known for the mouth-burning capsicum that nature had given it as a means of warding off predators. Humans domesticated chile sometime between 6900 and 5000 BCE. It became a Mexican mainstay and went on to conquer the world, redefining the diets of places such as India, Africa, and Korea (the latter boasting the world's highest per capita consumption). Chile does everything: it aids digestion, retards the decomposition of food, is loaded with vitamins, and above all tastes delicious. Over a dozen major varieties exist in Mexico today, the hottest being Yucatán's chile habanero, used in innumerable regional recipes but also, given its extraordinary firepower, exported for the manufacture of antipersonnel gas.

From the second millennium BCE humans had also learned to harvest the seeds of the tropical cacao tree. Originating along the Amazonian river banks, the plant traveled northward by means of natural transmission such as birds, until it found a home in what is today Tabasco, one of Mexico's hottest and wettest provinces. The pods that mature trees produce in abundance contain the bitter, tarry seeds used in making chocolate. But no sweet confections for these hardy peoples: they drank cacao without benefit of sugar, milk, or marshmallows. They typically preferred to dissolve it in a suspension of corn and water, enlivened it with chile or pepper, and poured it from one container to another until it developed a thick frothy head. Cacao grains became the closest thing to money that Mesoamericans ever possessed. When Christopher Columbus first reached the mainland, somewhere off the coast of modern-day Honduras, he found cacao traders carrying their wares in enormous canoes and noticed that when traders dropped a cacao grain, they desperately bent to recover it, "as if they had lost an eye."

Finally, ancient Mesoamericans also cultivated, and appreciated, the agave plant. Over a hundred varieties exist, all distinguished by the long, tough leaves known as *pencas*, which store the plant's water as a way of surviving Mexico's harsher and more arid regions. Long before Aztec times, people learned to use the agave for medicine, and that knowledge survives in our own use of aloe vera for soap, shampoo, and skin cream. They employed its tough inner fibers for ropes and cords and discovered that the pencas' sharp points made excellent sewing needles. But more than anything, they learned to ferment its juices into a milky, lightly alcoholic beverage known as *pulque*, a beverage that formed a mainstay of the rural diet well into the twentieth century. For well over fifty years rapid modernization and the commercial beer industry relegated pulque to déclassé shadows. But this heirloom drink has recently made a comeback and now delights connoisseurs from all walks of life. Don Pulque, a citizen from the most ancient of times and endowed with the most impeccable Mexican credentials, has at last reclaimed his seat at the table.

With agricultural surplus came the need to store food against future need. Archaeologists have found Mexico's oldest known ceramics along the bay of Puerto Marques, just south of Acapulco, dating from sometime around 2440 BCE (considerably later than the earliest known Japanese and African clay pots of 11,000 BCE). Because Mesoamericans never developed the wheel, they manufactured their vessels using the coil method, in which long strands of clay are spiraled on top of one another, then smoothed to perfection. Distinctive styles sprang up everywhere, from the crudely baked pots of northwestern seminomads to the Mayas' delicate, fine orangeware.

Two children stand beside an abundance of agave. Like the cactus, the drought-hardy agave provides an important human resource and offers a habitat for innumerable forms of wildlife. From precontact times to the present, the people of Mexico have used it for food, fiber, medicine, and needles. Most importantly, they extract *miel de agave*, the liquid that forms the basis of pulque, a hearty alcoholic beverage. Courtesy of the New York Public Library.

As in so many peasant societies, gender dictated the basic division of labor. Men farmed, hunted, and built the homes; women did virtually everything else. For most females vast stretches of life consisted of boiling and grinding corn and patting out the dough to form tortillas. Marital unions began as soon as the young man could farm and the young woman could bear children. And while the royalty of the great Mesoamerican kingdoms often enjoyed the privilege of polygamy, bonds among the commoners almost always consisted of one man and one woman, joined for the brief duration of their hard lives.

A People Summon Their Gods

If Mesoamerican cultures demonstrated a strong continuity of ideas and material culture, they also experienced regular cycles of change over the course of their long existence. First, a powerful urban center would emerge, founded by dynamic, creative people intent on extending their power over neighbors near and distant. However oppressive, imperial peace allowed commerce to flourish; over time the outlying communities matured, while the old center peaked, then declined. Eventually imperial power would collapse altogether: sometimes as a result of attack by some rival, on other occasions through such natural disasters as drought. The old peace disintegrated, and after a period of chaos a new ruling city-state would emerge.

The first such cycle centered around a people we call the Olmecs, the Western Hemisphere's oldest identifiable civilization. Although recent years have seen enormous strides in this particular field of archaeology, questions about the Olmecs still outnumber answers and doubtless always will. What the Olmecs really called themselves, what language they spoke, where they came from, and whether they even saw themselves as a single people: those answers remain beyond the reach of modern understanding. They appeared at least as early as 1500 BCE in the southern Gulf Coast area that today constitutes the states of Tabasco and southeastern Veracruz. Their settlements formed along the fringes of the Grijalva-Usumacinta river network, in places such as San Lorenzo, Tres Zapotes, and La Venta, areas whose warmth and water allowed for an annual double-cropping of corn.

Like all early peoples, the Olmecs depended on the mercy of natural forces, which led them to posit unseen spiritual beings whose inscrutable whims they tried to appease through ceremony and sacrifice. Human agency was the only causal model they possessed. Just as other early peoples such as the Sumerians and the Egyptians had done, they therefore conceived of those gods as being in some ways similar to themselves, only with far vaster powers. Individuals who mediated between humans and gods gradually evolved into a ruling class. Those same rulers even took on the attributes of divinity, a fact that Olmec artists indicated by giving their likenesses the features of a jaguar with fangs and angry gaze.

Among the deities the Olmec worshiped were two beings who eventually became an axis of religious experience for almost all Mesoamerican people. A seated dwarf with a headdress of swirling clouds gradually evolved into Tlaloc, the rain god whose all-important gift required some form of blood sacrifice: water for water, as it were. Over time Tlaloc assumed the essential features of two enormous goggle eyes and a gaping, hungry mouth, and his cult reached as far away as the Pueblo cultures of Arizona and New Mexico and Mogollon settlements in Texas's Hueco Tanks region just outside of El

Paso. Zapotecs knew him as Cocijo; Mayas called him Chaac. Alongside their rain dwarf the Olmec worshiped a divine crocodile that over the centuries morphed into Quetzalcóatl, a feathered serpent that brought culture and promised rebirth to a crushingly limited humanity. Why a feathered serpent? Doubtless, as in the epic of Gilgamesh, the god's iconography owed to the serpent's ability to shed its skin, thereby giving the impression of renewing its own life. Precontact peoples also associated Quetzalcóatl with the planet Venus, the third-brightest object in the heavens and a traveler of the night sky that also heralded the dawn.

The Olmecs bequeathed further gifts to later Mexico. Among other things, they fostered a base-twenty number system, the practice of ritual blood-letting, an architectural style known as *talud tablero* (pyramidal slopes intersected with horizontal cornices), and an emphasis on the four cardinal points as the basis for aligning human construction. Though ignorant of gold, the Olmecs treasured a green mineral called jade. It came from only a handful of remote locations, principally the Motagua River valley of Guatemala. Extremely hard, it could with patience be wrought into beautiful shapes and polished to a glossy exterior. Jade working became one of Mesoamerica's greatest art forms. Artisans could produce sculptures the size of a grapefruit or pendants and rings of high symmetry or even delicate creations like pins and drinking straws. Like the gold and silver that native artisans learned to work prior to 1492, jade had a feature greatly prized in this world where almost everything consisted of perishable materials: it endured. Even the most carefully constructed home of pole and thatch will rot, and even the tallest of stone temples eventually sink back into the ground, but the glorious, green luster of jade art pieces still sparkles three thousand years later.

The Olmecs also claim two of early Mesoamerica's greatest intellectual achievements. Dedicated watchers of the night sky and the passage of days, they used a calendar system that to us suggests the turning of intermeshed gears of different sizes. Each gear connected with the others through the various cogs representing each day; eventually the gears return to their starting point, and a new cycle begins. In addition to marking months and years, the Olmec calendar also allows an absolute dating system that takes as its starting point August 11, 3114 BCE, thus allowing archaeologists to correlate so-called "long count" dates to their exact counterparts in the Western calendar centering around 0 CE.

The Olmecs also created the first and only precontact system of writing in the Americas. They used twin columns of glyphs, some ideographic and some phonetical and grammatical, that were read left to right and top to bottom. This particular system reached its height many centuries later, during the Classic period of Maya civilization, but its origins actually lie with the ancient Olmecs, whose reliance on perishable material like wood and bone meant that relatively few samples of their writing have survived.

Olmec influence spread far and wide. Their trade goods penetrated into western Mexico, to places like Guerrero, but also as far south as El Salvador in Central America. Meanwhile, a similar growth took place along the edges of Lake Texcoco in the Valley of Mexico. Settlements such as Tlatilco and Cuicuilco, building on the surpluses of organized agriculture, developed raised platforms that eventually grew into more permanent public constructions. By 100 CE these communities had cults of the dead, as evidenced by the large quantities of ceremonial objects found in burial sites. Whether these customs developed from Olmec imports or whether the various cultures somehow shared in the creation of a region-wide civilization remains uncertain.

Whatever the exact means of trade and transmission, early Mesoamerica's achievements dramatically enhanced the ability of humans to alter the environment to their own advantage. Peoples prospered and centers grew; their temples rose up like tiny Towers of Babel, stone expressions of purpose and permanence. And, as always, the point of origin declined: by 400 BCE the core Olmec culture had exhausted itself, and Olmec ceremonial construction ceased, but the seeds of this *ur*-society had by now rooted themselves throughout Mesoamerica and became the basis of a remarkable burst of social growth, technical innovation, and artistic creativity. By 200 BCE modest hamlets, once outliers to the Olmec world, had grown into substantial centers. The Classic era had begun.

In the Time of Marvels:
The Classic Period, 200 CE to 900 CE

The chief nucleus of that millennium-long era was the Valley of Mexico, which had been gathering strength since Olmec times. It witnessed the birth of one of the ancient world's great urban centers, Teotihuacán, located approximately thirty miles north-northeast of what is now Mexico City. Settlement here began as early as 150 BCE, contemporary with places such as Cuicuilco. But around 100 CE that latter center declined, apparently unable to complete with its increasingly powerful northern neighbor. Moderate construction in Teotihuacán continued until around 100 CE, when a boom began that lasted for the next century and a half; much of that growth probably came from in-migration by peoples throughout the Valley of Mexico. During this time Teotihuacanos constructed the great pyramids devoted to the Sun and Moon. The city's greatest phase came in the years 350–550 CE, during which time the population peaked at 350,000 making it about a third the size of Rome but built lacking the latter's advantage of metal, wheels, or beasts of burden. It was during this final phase of construction that the city achieved the layout seen today, with the addition of the vast Avenue of the Dead and the Temple of Quetzalcóatl at its southern end.

Teotihuacán's wealth owed to a combination of natural resources, artisanry, and trade. The city's location allowed it privileged access to the obsidian deposits of Hidalgo state's Sierra de las Navajas. In those days the immense lake of Texcoco—partly saline, partly freshwater, and now largely vanished—lay not far to the west, and its natural springs provided the drinking water necessary for the urban population. The area around the city contained significant clay deposits essential for pottery, along with the basalt and volcanic tezontle used in construction.

Equally important, Teotihuacán's geographical location made for quick and direct access to the Gulf Coast and the Valley of Mexico. Teotihuacanos drew in goods from the entirety of Mesoamerica, their merchants protected by an army that allowed a certain amount of upward mobility for those who chose to join. So great was the urban demand for goods both basic and luxurious that artisans from such faraway places as Oaxaca settled there in ethnic barrios, where they churned out wares without having to worry about transportation costs. Teotihuacán grew so powerful that it intervened in cultures as far away as Yucatán, as evidenced by the archaeological remains of Acanceh, close to Mérida, and in northern Guatemala, where it exerted a strong influence over the great city of Tikal.

Much of Teotihuacano culture remains a mystery. We do not know what language they spoke or what became of the vast population following the city's later decline. But they did leave evidence of their beliefs in the form of murals. Their artists employed various mineral combinations to produce reds, yellows, greens, blues, and blacks. Painters covered their stone walls with an even stucco surface, then sketched the outlines of the intended images; after that, they covered over their work with an extremely fine layer of slow-drying clay that kept the surface moist as they applied colors. They illustrated scenes of both supernatural power—mainly the Feathered Serpent and the rain god Tlaloc, both derived from the earlier Olmecs—but they also depicted daily activities: farming, dancing, and playing the ball game.

Teotihuacanos, together with the cultures that came before and after them, made music a part of their lives. Precontact musicians used two types of instruments: percussives (ranging from drums and rattles) and wind, the latter created from such natural materials as clay, bone, or seashell. Variations of these two groups accompanied most ceremonies, but unfortunately we know next to nothing about the actual nature of the music itself. As in much early music, melodies probably built around a pentatonic scale. The Spanish brought a radical revolution in musical concepts; the earliest ethnomusical recordings, all made at least four centuries after contact, reveal a strong internalization of medieval European songs and dances. Those same recordings suggest a sensibility that prized continued repetition and a slow evolution of basic rhythms and musical phrases, a kind of pre-Columbian Philip Glass. But the fact remains that most of what passes today as the "music of indigenous Mexico" is, however interesting and accomplished, a fanciful creation.

Teotihuacán also dealt in another of early Mesoamerica's great innovations: clothing and textiles. Modes of dress varied considerably according to climate and level of material development. But in central Mexico, at least, with its mild summers and chilly winters, cotton, woven on the trusty backstrap loom, provided the fabric of choice. By now Mesoamerica had developed a repertoire of natural dyes for their clothes, such as the red produced by crushing the cochineal bugs that lived on prickly pears, a pursuit that would become the second-most lucrative industry of the late colonial period. The tough fiber from henequen and other forms of the agave plant provided more functional threads for sacks and ropes, while the upper crust enjoyed the privilege of accessories made from animal skins (rabbit or jaguar, for example), elaborate feathers, and jewelry that was limited only by the artist's imagination. The city offered merchandise unimaginable in simple and remote settlements, and as the signs on the old country stores used to say, if you didn't find it here, you didn't need it.

But the good times could not go on forever. Secondary cultures gradually grew up under the pax teotihuacana, and as they asserted their own power and autonomy, the old imperial center lost its relevance. So, too, the city's agriculture may also have fallen victim to one of Mesoamerica's periodic long-term droughts. Teotihuacán entered a decline after 550 CE and was intentionally burned and abandoned sometime around 650. Gone were the extravagant ceremonies that once graced its platforms and temples; instead, for many centuries the sun and moon became the sole witnesses to this testament of genius, hubris, and fallen grandeur.

This silent megacity, with its colossal pyramids, spacious avenues, and stunning murals, fixed itself forever in the Mexican imagination. The Aztecs visited its ruins in the fifteenth century and carried out the first tentative explorations. They concluded that only gods could have inhabited this mysterious dead city and in fact gave it the name Teotihuacán: "the place where gods are made." The late seventeenth-century polymath Carlos de Sigüenza y Góngora made some preliminary explorations here as well. At the turn of the twentieth century, Leopoldo Batres led some of the first major restorations, and President Porfirio Díaz himself toured Teotihuacán with foreign dignitaries during Mexico's centennial celebrations of 1910, only months before the coming revolution. Modern Mexican archaeology cut its teeth on scientific studies here, attracting such luminaries as Manuel Gamio and Jorge Acosta. Efforts to penetrate the secrets buried within the Pyramid of the Sun continue into the twenty-first century. This home city of the gods remains the most visited archaeological site in Mexico, an ancient wonder of global appeal.

Maya Peoples

While Teotihuacán extended its power across the altiplano, an equally impressive civilization was taking shape in the area to the east and south of Olmec country. We find earliest evidence of distinctly different people as early as 800 BCE, mostly raised house-mounds in low-lying areas of what is today northern Belize. Four centuries later certain core cultural elements had jelled; the Maya civilization was born, and from it came some of the greatest achievements of the precontact New World. It spanned Mesoamerica's Formative (2000 BCE–200 CE), Classic (200–900 CE), and Postclassic (900–1519 CE) periods and survives today in innumerable forms.

Few civilizations have been as mesmerizing, or as mythologized, as the Mayas. Variously tagged as a race of philosopher-kings, a collection of bloodthirsty barbarians, a mighty empire, the descendants of biblical figures, and even the protégées of ancient astronauts, the Mayas in fact answered to none of these descriptions. Rather, they rose by carrying Olmec innovations to greater heights. Faced with environmental limitations, they developed techniques for wringing surpluses from the delicate subtropical forests of southeast Mesoamerica. They resisted political unification like a pox and elevated the warring city-state to an art form.

Rather than being bastions of equality, Maya societies took on a profound stratification in which an immense base of commoners supported a privileged elite. Leadership presumably emerged from the need for defense or else to mediate between the many gods that Mayas believed controlled the fortunes of their lives. Following the Olmec model, the nobility almost immediately identified itself with those gods (a near-universal practice among early peoples). Almost all of the great Maya artifacts found in archaeological museums today reference either the vast supernatural forces that governed life or the god-kings who somehow spoke with and tamed those forces.

Like the early Greeks—a people similarly divided by provinces and rival city-states—the Mayas appeared to have entertained diverse and often conflicting accounts of the world's origin. The *Popol Vuh* (literally, "common book"), a body of Quiché Maya legends and chronicles, tells that a council of gods, inscrutable and remote, summoned the world out of nothingness. Their early attempts to create humanity failed for lack of a suitable raw material. In the chaotic struggle between good and evil divinities, a pair of hero-twins named Hunhunapú and Ixbalanqué eventually defeat the death gods, confining them to creepy caverns, and thus make the world safe for humanity. At this point the divine council tries making humans out of corn, a smashing success on all counts. Classic-era vases also tell the story of a jaguar god slaying a primordial reptile-fish monster, whose blood in turn became the ocean surrounding the Maya world. Human beings, the story ran, lived on the back of a giant turtle or crocodile that floated on endless waves.

Maya artistic creations, and particularly those of the Classic period, rank among the finest anywhere. They experimented in all available mediums, including ceramics, sculpture, painting, and drawing. Classic-era ceramics are instantly recognizable for their polychrome designs: cream on ocher, with lines in black. Treatments ranged from royal portraiture to whimsical scenes of strange animal beings. No minimalists, Maya artists filled empty space with organic, curling designs often supplemented with written words (in the form of glyphs), a far cry from the chunky sculptures and highly angular pictorial styles of the later Aztecs. At the same time, Mayas shared Teotihuacán's passion for murals. In the greatest of these, the illustrations found inside a temple at Bonampak, Chiapas, the artist actually painted himself into a small corner of his elaborate creation, like a pre-Columbian Rembrandt. Even in 790 CE, ego was ego.

One pursuit that obsessed the Maya was their ball game. Similar to our own soccer, and in all likelihood an Olmec creation, the game's idea was for teams to force a ball into the territory of their opponents. However, this was not the more forgiving, inflatable ball of modern times, but rather a solid mass of *hule*, or tree rubber, and considerably more dangerous. Players could only strike the ball with their forearms or waists, both of which required the heavy padding seen in paintings and sculptures. Much nonsense has been written arguing that victors enjoyed the privilege of being sacrificed, but in reality most contests were simply for sport; in certain places and moments captured enemies may have been forced to play, only to be defeated and executed, but those would have been the exception, not the rule. Court designs varied: most are lined by sloping sides that would have returned the ball to the center court, while viewers sat above them; but in the largest of all Mesoamerican ballcourts, that of Chichén Itzá in Yucatán, high vertical walls line the court, rather like a squash court. The huge stone rings that hung from the tops of those walls would have formed too difficult a mark for this sort of play. Getting the ball through them was apparently a sort of "extra point," an accomplishment that allowed the skillful (or lucky) player to go into the stands and demand the spectators' jewelry. Whatever the exact rules and true origins, the ball game won popularity throughout Mesoamerica. Places such as

Cantona in Veracruz state include "kiddie courts" for beginners, the ancient equivalent of Little League baseball.

Maya peoples carried earlier innovations to new heights. Compared to the scanty examples of Olmec writing, the growing Maya centers were virtual printing presses. Glyph writing, partly ideographic and partly phonetic, adorns everything from conch shells to immense public monuments. Like the Sumerians and Egyptians, the Mayas had no use for writing as a means of fixing some objective truth. Rather, literacy served the ruler of the moment. Almost all existing glyphs from this period retell the great deeds of the nobility: their births, their ascension to power, and their glorious victories in battle. Among the most common themes is the commemoration of blood-letting ceremonies in which highborn men and women perforated parts of their bodies with a stingray spine. The individual lost enough blood to enter into a hallucinatory state in which he or she had a vision of an ancestor, thereby validating their noble status. It is highly doubtful that acts of literacy ever inched far beyond the domain of this tiny elite and their privileged lives. Nor is there much evidence that reading and writing served such quotidian functions as journaling, note-taking, or corresponding, although writing on material such as paper would hardly have survived for twenty centuries in this relentlessly hot and humid region.

Despite its high propaganda content, the surviving corpus of Maya writing allows epigraphers to reconstruct entire dynastic successions in such places as Palenque. One fact that clearly emerges from both written history and material artifact is the centuries-long rivalry between two supercenters: Tikal and Calakmul. The former stands in what is today Guatemala's northernmost province, the Petén. The latter lies deep in the forests of southern Campeche state, in Mexico, where it was discovered by chicle tappers in the 1920s. Calakmul was the largest of all Maya cities, although today it remains only partially excavated and restored. As if enmeshed in some pre-Columbian cold war, these two giants squared off in a series of attacks and counterattacks between 537 and 744 CE, each power drawing to it a series of client cities. Initially Calakmul, in alliance with the immense center of Caracol (located in what is now western Belize), held the upper hand; but Tikal eventually reversed its fortunes with a stunning victory in 695 under the leadership of the dynamic young king Jasaw Chan K'awiil. Calakmul did not disappear but instead turned its attentions elsewhere, to trade with smaller centers located to its east.

Rather than inaugurating some thousand-year empire, Tikal's victory heralded one of the most cataclysmic reverses in the history of the entire ancient world. After 800 CE Classic Maya civilization entered a profound decline. Some of that decline may have been a delayed effect of the collapse of Teotihuacán; but just as destructive were the swollen populations, the environmental degradation caused by radical deforestation, and the deleterious effects of a top-heavy social structure that allocated massive resources to an ever-growing and unproductive elite. Maya peoples did not simply vanish, as sometimes portrayed in popular venues. The "collapse" of an ancient city simply means that elite activities such as ceremonial construction came to an end. People continued to inhabit the region, albeit at a less complex level of social organization. Still, the extent of the cataclysm should not be underestimated. For whatever combination of reasons, the cities of the one of the most sophisticated and densely inhabited parts of the world ceased to grow, and life devolved back to peasant subsistence levels. The last known Maya long count date is 909, found in an inscription in Toniná, Chiapas. By 1000 great centers like Tikal, Calakmul, and Caracol were no more.

A Fallen World Recovers:
The Postclassic Period, 900–1519 CE

The end is never really the end. After 900 the Valley of Mexico witnessed a reorganization of power and trade, this time built around the ceremonial center of Tula, located in the present-day state of Hidalgo. Selecting the site based on its access to the important obsidian deposits and water from the seasonal Tula River that drains out of the Valley of Mexico, a people known as the Toltecs gradually extended their influence in all directions. Possibly originating in northern Mexico, they controlled or allied with settlements as far away as Zacatecas, and Toltec trade extended into the Four Corners region of what is now Arizona, Colorado, Utah, and New Mexico, from which they obtained precious minerals like turquoise.

The Toltecs drew on the advances of Teotihuacán culture, including the latter's religion and architecture. However, this new society lacked the innovation and delicacy of its Classic-era forbearers. Its art was derivative and at times clumsy in execution. To judge from surviving artifacts, the Toltecs prized military power and prowess above all else. Their blockish statues depict gigantic warriors with weapons clasped firmly at their sides. Among the most emblematic creations of all precontact Mexico are the great south-facing Toltec warriors nicknamed Atlanteans, fifteen-foot-tall basalt sentinels that stand guard atop the Temple of Tlahuizcalpantecuhtli (house of the morning star).

Toltec peoples treasured the legend of a semidivine leader named Topilztín Quetzalcóatl. The story runs that his enemies connived to make him drunk and that in that condition he had sex with one of his own daughters. Unable to live with the shame of his act, he built a raft of serpents and sailed away to the east, promising to return someday. This legend likely had its basis in a power struggle in which a leader associated himself with this most quintessentially Mesoamerican deity, only to be ousted in some sort of coup. However, the Topilztín Quetzalcóatl story has also spawned no end of interpretive mischief. Even today many people wholeheartedly accept the old misconception that the Aztecs failed to defend against incoming Spanish conquistadors because they thought that Hernán Cortés was in fact this same deity, returned at last to the land of his birth.

But all military empires meet their end. Sometime in the mid-1100s a prolonged dry period struck the entire region stretching from north-central Mexico into the Four Corners area far to the north. Great population centers such as New Mexico's Chaco Canyon disintegrated. Tula itself came under increasing pressure from the seminomadic northern peoples it so greatly feared: the so-called Chichimecas (hunting people)—in reality a composite name for a variety of north-central ethnicities—bested the Toltec armies in a series of engagements. Surviving Toltecs abandoned Tula around 1150 and migrated farther south, where their culture disintegrated into rival bands. Nevertheless, the image and the reputation of this warlike culture survived, above all in the imagination of the later Aztecs, who held up the Toltecs as a race of wise men and their center of Tula as a kind of vanished utopia.

Meanwhile, Maya culture caught a second wind. Even as the tropical forests reclaimed old centers of the southern lowlands, new city-states had begun to spring up in the riverless northern half of the Yucatán Peninsula. Raid-fed agriculture remained the basis of life, but for drinking water people drew from the vast limestone sinkholes known as cenotes (from the Maya *tsonot*), probably formed as the result of the Chicxulub meteor impact, or else they collected rainwater in voluminous underground storage tanks called *chultunes*. While diverse building styles coexisted, the most defining style was the Puuc (hill range), so named because its greatest centers, places such as Uxmal and Labná, are found in a low-lying hill country that runs through the peninsula's center. Puuc architecture features elegantly carved abstract motives and corbeled arches.

Ironically, the best-known of these new cities is the least Maya in terms of art and architecture. Little consensus exists regarding the actual history of Chichén Itzá, located in central-north Yucatán. It had prospered for centuries as a minor outlying center, but sometime around 750 it began a visible transformation that followed the trajectory of central Mexican culture. Some evidence points to foreign invaders, the Itzá peoples, who originated from a place called Xicalango along the Tabasco-Campeche coast. Oral history in the form of the *Chilam Balam* document, a poem of history and prophesy set to paper after the coming of the Spanish, tells of the intrusion of a culture that area Mayas considered crude and disgusting. Surviving mural fragments also appear to suggest an attack via the seacoast. Beyond that, however, all is mystery. Modern archaeologists have grown skeptical of an invasion by either Putún or Toltec peoples and instead argue that northern Mayas themselves began their city's dramatic makeover. In this telling, the "Toltec invasion" may have been part of a pan-Mesoamerican attempt to copy Classic-era designs, an early version of retro refashioning. Whatever the actual nature of events, at some point Chichén Itzá and other northern cities began a concerted campaign of adopting central Mexico styles; inhabitants shucked their abstract Puuc designs and instead opted for the three-footed cacao vessels, the warrior columns, the sloping talud tablero architecture, and the feathered-serpent imagery of the altiplano.

Chichén Itzá's club-wielding rulers grew rich off the trade in salt from the north coast, the greatest concentration of this essential resource in all of Mesoamerica. Stretching from central Mexico into the Caribbean, the city's commercial network dwarfed all competition, and Chichén's affluence and power remain written on every building. Within the confines of their wonderous city they created ancient America's largest ballcourt, a sweat bath, and a market of hundreds of warrior-columns that held up a roof of perishable materials, now long vanished. Like other Postclassic

The enigmatic figure known as Chac-Mool has become emblematic of northern Yucatec Maya culture, but the representation actually derived from artistic conventions of central Mexico's late Classic era. The eccentric French archaeologist who invented the name "Chac-Mool" tried to take this particular piece out of the country in the 1860s, but President Benito Juárez intervened at the last minute. Courtesy of Tulane University Latin American Library.

Maya centers, the city was built somewhat inland from the coast, doubtless as a hedge against invaders, and like other Yucatec Maya cities it featured raised, paved footpaths known as *sacbé* (white road) to connect it with key points like ports and the immense salt farms. One road stretched north to the city's port of Isla Cerrito, while another reached eastward to Cobá and Tulum.

Chichén Itzá's demise is as elusive as its origins. The city entered a decline around 1000 CE; new construction ended, and although its military and commercial power endured, that too disappeared in the following century. The southern Puuc cities had already ended, abandoned as a result of a series of crippling droughts—and possibly from the damage inflicted by Chichén Itzá's own monstrous dominance. This in turn would have limited the volume and variety of trade goods in which Chichén dealt. Northern Yucatán's flagship power was never completely abandoned, but its days as the colossus of the southeast had ended.

The Postclassic Maya world turned into a shifting series of alliances among various centers, including Uxmal and Mayapán. The latter was in fact an intentional miniature of Chichén Itzá, complete with a Toltec-style central pyramid and a domed astronomical observatory (or something that resembled our modern conception of one). The last attempt at some sort of political unity came with the Mayapán league, but that too collapsed somewhere around 1440 as Maya cities returned to doing what they did best: namely, fighting with each other. When the Spanish arrived in the first half of the sixteenth century, they therefore entered a deeply fragmented world peopled by cultures whose better days lay behind them.

During the era of contact, Europeans found Postclassic Maya society all the more baffling because Maya political clout lacked a clear geographical base. Mayas had at least two forms of authority: a village-based chieftain known as the *batab* (possibly "he who wields the hatchet") and above him, the *halach uinic* (true man), who governed areas beyond his town of residence. But the halach uinic's power did not necessarily align with a designated territory in the way that, say, the governor of Arkansas's authority is restricted to the state of Arkansas. Rather, his power depended on a series of personal ties of loyalty with batabs who for whatever reason found the alliance favorable; these subordinate allies might live far away and could be separated by areas with rival loyalties. This sort of checkerboard arrangement made it extremely difficult for the first conquistadors and friars to impose a European-style system of authority based on conquered territory.

Foremost of Kingdoms

Beginning in the mid- to late 1200s, Mesoamerican society once again pulled itself out of entropy and decline. This latest reorganization was based on the emergence of a powerful new empire based in the Valley of Mexico. Its people called themselves the Mexica, but because they claimed to have come from a homeland called Aztlán (the place of the heron), they are known widely, if somewhat erroneously, as the Aztecs, or "the people of Aztlán." While the long-standing interpretation situates that mythical homeland in the northwest, possibly in present-day Sinaloa, little evidence substantiates this claim. The Mexica loaded up on self-serving mythologies, and almost everything they asserted about their origins must be taken critically. In all likelihood Aztlán was one of those mythical points of origin that early peoples so often claimed; a more prosaic explanation is that the Mexica came from an area just outside the Valley of Mexico, possibly what is today southern Guanajuato, and no more than a hundred miles from Lake Texcoco itself. Their departure from their original homeland undoubtedly owed to the general dislocation of peoples following enormous drought in the twelfth century.

According to this same mythology their tribal deity, a certain Huitzilopotchli (hummingbird on the left), commanded them to wander until they saw an eagle perched on a cactus and devouring a serpent. They supposedly encountered this image at Chapultepec (hill of the grasshopper), which lay on the southeastern coast of the Valley of Mexico's great salt lake. Whether this story captured a real event or was mere poetic embellishment, the Mexica arrival was real enough, and it presented new challenges for this itinerate people. In 1300 the Valley of Mexico sheltered one of the most densely inhabited places on earth, and its land was hardly available for the asking. Other *altepetls* (city-states) of Nahuatl-speaking peoples then dominated affairs around the salt lake, particularly the Tepanec people of Azcapotzalco (at the anthill). The Mexica originally insinuated themselves into the picture by hiring themselves out as mercenaries. But within a short time they transformed themselves from a collection of egalitarian clans to a stratified hierarchy whose organization gave them strength. And as that strength grew, and as patrons and allies began to fear their own soldiers of fortune, the Mexica found it expedient to relocate to an island located in the middle of the lake.

Here they built what was to become the seat of their great empire: Tenochtitlán, or "the place of rock and cactus." Finding it too small to accommodate their growing needs, the Mexica reclaimed land from the lake by sinking tree-trunk piers into the mud and heaping earth and

No one ever said that pre-Columbian deities were lovable. The great statue of Coatlicue, mother to the Mexica's tutelary spirit, Huitzilopotchli, was discovered in 1790. Serpents form her belt; human hands and skulls hang from her necklace. The goddess keeps watch today at Mexico City's Museo Nacional de Antropología. Courtesy of the Library of Congress.

refuse around and on top of them. *Chinampas* (which were smaller islands of reclaimed land) allowed for intensive agriculture. On top of this expanded territory they constructed their new home, complete with canals that allowed for canoe travel from one point to the next. The central plaza boasted massive ceremonial constructions that included houses for the emperor and a dual temple to Huitzilopotchli and Quetzalcóatl. Two enormous aqueducts brought fresh water into the island, while marketplaces allowed for the trading of goods. Finally, the Mexica connected their city to the land through a series of long, narrow causeways, but they prudently inserted gaps covered by planks that could be removed in times of threat, rather like the drawbridge over a castle moat. Impregnable by the conditions of the time, Tenochtitlán became the largest city of the Americas, with an estimated population of two hundred thousand at the moment of contact, far larger than anything than the Spanish conquistadors had ever seen.

Ever in search of ways to strengthen its hand, Tenochtitlán formed a triple alliance with two other altepetls. Texcoco lay to the east of the great salt lake and was ruled by a series of kings that included the wise and cultured Netzahualcoyotl (coyote who fasts), famous as a poet and a collector of art and rare animals. Tlacopan (flat ground) lay on the lake's west side, just below Azcapotzalco itself. In time, however, Tenochtitlán grew to dominate this three-way partnership.

At the top of this growing juggernaut stood the *tlatoani* (he who speaks), for he did the talking while others listened. Like the rulers of so many other premodern people, he bestrode his world like a god incarnate. He commanded all endeavors of the society: chiefly its political decisions, its military actions, and its religious preoccupations. Beneath him stood a nobility known as the *pilli*. While hardly of the godlike status of the tlatoani, they nevertheless shared his privileges of polygamy, slaveholding, and private landowning.

Commoners lived far humbler lives. The so-called *macehuales*, a term Spaniards later applied to all indigenous peasants, shouldered the burdens of both empire and daily life. Boys learned farming by working with their fathers, while they trained in the arts of combat at neighborhood schools. They became adults as soon as they were able to raise corn. Girls learned to make tortillas and to maintain a household, and they married as soon as they could bear children. The leaders of this warrior society preached to the commoners that a special place in the afterlife awaited men who died in battle and women who perished in childbirth: incentives for doing the difficult work of empire. Unlike the nobility, macehuales were expected to maintain the same monogamous relationship for life.

To help feed the massive population of Tenochtitlán, the Mexica required the services of an immense transportation system. Human porters known as *tlamemes* freighted most of the materials on their own backs, using a tumpline across their foreheads to better distribute the weight, with each man carrying some fifty pounds. The Mexica also used large canoes capable of holding a thousand pounds of goods and crew. Under these conditions, the city's causeways and its surrounding lake were hives of continual activity, ancient equivalents of the huge trucking systems that feed Mexico City today. (Incidentally, the tlameme system far outlived the Mexica empire. Human porters may have carried less weight than mules, but they moved far more quickly through challenging and at times vertical terrain. Tlamemes remained a fixture in Mexico through the nineteenth century.)

While the Mexica did not employ a written language, and while they and their fellow precontact societies did not use books as we understand the term, Mesoamerican peoples did produce a series of complicated, bound illustrations known as *códices* (the singular form being *códice*, or codex). Some were written on animal skin, but the majority consist of thick, handmade paper. A total of nineteen of these works have survived into modern times: four are housed in Mexico and fifteen others reside in various European repositories. In the case of the three Maya códices, at least, written words accompany the illustrations. Six others come from the Mixtec peoples of Oaxaca, while the remaining ten are from either the Mexica or other Nahuatl-speaking peoples. They record such topics as history, biography, the intertwined pursuits of astronomy and astrology, and in the case of works like the Codex Boturini, the Mexicas' obsession with the route of the travels that eventually brought them to their island-capital. These visual manuscripts possibly served as mnemonic devices to help a special class of interpreters whose job it was to memorize the lore and learning of their people.

For all their many achievements, the Mexica will always be remembered, and without fondness, for their devotion to the cult of heart sacrifice. They believed that the world had been created and destroyed four times—by winds, jaguars, earthquakes, and flood, successively—and that they now lived in the time of the Fifth Sun, in which their petulant deities might tire of them at any moment and wipe clean the earthly slate once more. The only way to mollify the gods and assure that the sun would rise again was to offer continuous heart sacrifices. Priests led a prisoner, stupefied with narcotic plants, to the top of a temple and stretched him face-up over a large stone; there, four of the priests spread out his limbs, while a fifth cut out his heart with an obsidian dagger. The latter process would have required the last and longest two minutes of the victim's life.

Other peoples had done the same, but the Mexica, flush with military triumph and a seemingly unending supply of prisoners of war, carried the ceremony to new levels. We do not necessarily have to believe that, as one of their accounts holds, they sacrificed ten thousand people in a single day. As with the thirty-foot-tall kings of India's ancient Brahminic sagas, huge numbers propelled a narrative technique for driving home an idea with listeners. The point is that the Mexica did indeed sacrifice large numbers of victims over the course of their imperial careers and saw nothing wrong with the practice.

Mexican expansion reached its height in the second half of the fifteenth century, when their armies pushed into most of what is today Oaxaca, establishing control of lands formerly under the domain of the Mixtecs. But there were two important holdouts. Far to the west, in the region of Lake Pátzcuaro, the Purépecha peoples (or, as the Spanish called them, the Tarascans) built Mesoamerica's second-largest kingdom, based around the city of Tzitzuntzan. Diverse ethnic groups had inhabited the area since Olmec times, but sometime around 1300 a *cazonci* (Purépecha for "leader") named Tariácuri launched a campaign of conquest and unification; his heirs finished the job. In 1478 the Mexica king Axayacatl launched a full-out invasion, but this overweening tlatoani stretched his supply lines too thin, and his army of 24,000 men suffered a humiliating defeat that dampened further dreams of westward expansion. Meanwhile, the Mexica had yet to defeat the Nahuatl-speaking altepetl of Tlaxcala, just north of Puebla. Geographically smaller than the Purépecha empire, its rulers proved vastly more skillful in the business of Spanish-era political alliances and emerged as one of the most successful and autonomous of indigenous communities within New Spain.

For all its might, then, the armor of the great Mexica empire concealed fatal chinks that Europeans exploited to their own advantage. A huge percentage of Mesoamericans resented the tribute-hungry Mexica and were only too happy to cast their fortunes with anyone who promised to defeat them. The Tlaxcala altepetl in particular was determined to preserve its independence and eventually provided the true shock troops of the Spanish conquistadors.

Surveying the grand sweep of Mesoamerican cultures from earliest times to 1519, one is struck by the magnitude of their accomplishments. Olmecs, Mayas, and others succeeded brilliantly in that greatest of all challenges: abandoning the hunter-gatherer existence for the pursuits of agriculture and the crops that they so patiently and systematically refined help feed the world's population today. Their languages and vocabularies survive today. Mayas in particular excelled at mathematics—probably in relation to astronomical divination—and independently developed the concept of the number 0. Everywhere Mesoamericans created art whose power and magnificence remain undiminished and continue to inspire further creativity. And they began the superlative and globally appreciated Mexican cuisine.

For all their differences with the Spanish, who were soon to arrive as conquistadors, the ancient Mesoamericans—and the Mexica in particular—shared a great deal with the newcomers. Both were warrior societies that had risen by and for the expansion of territories. Men heaped up fortune and prestige by their ability to bring victory in battle, and the passion for those victories fed on itself, luring more and more hopefuls into the business of conquest. Once a conquest society begins, its political and psychological dynamics are difficult to stop, for the leader of the moment immediately becomes vulnerable to the frustrated expectations of the people below him. As Robert Clive said of Britain's great trading company in India, "To stop is dangerous, to recede ruin."

Both Spain and Tenochtitlán featured hierarchical societies with assigned differences of power and privilege. Throughout the entire world, virtually all early peoples who had developed complex civilizations operated on the idea of a semidivine leader qualitatively different from other men. Immediately beneath him stood a nobility who shared many, if not necessarily all, of his special attributes. Next came a huge peasantry, and beyond them a world of subject tributaries. Under these terms, powerless people paid up to powerful people in the form of goods and services. (Europe, of course, had coinage by this time.) Inequalities had to be reinforced constantly, lest anyone forget or be tempted into doubt. Differently ranked people lived in separate areas; they operated under different marriage laws; they ate different foods and in different quantities. The societies upheld sumptuary laws whereby people of rank wore special clothing such as purple cloaks or jewelry or feathers as opposed to tunics and sandals.

Both Mexicas and Spaniards had embarked on large-scale modifications of their environments. The Mexica did so from the safety of their island-capital. The Spanish, as we shall see, created a society marked by profoundly unequal land ownership built around a network of cities and castles and instituted a ranching system that privileged grazers over farmers.

Finally, both inhabited worlds were defined by religious sensibilities. At one level religion functioned as a state ideology, for it explained why the world had come to be and why the social order had to exist in the form that people knew it. To avoid muddying or questioning those explanations, both Europeans and Mexicas had priests who answered questions, resolved doubts, performed ceremonies, and pointed the way generally. But beneath the level of ideology lay another layer of religion, one that would prove far more enduring (and often endearing): popular religion, as practiced in the worship of those spirits who look after the home, the village, and the fields. Popular beliefs have little to do with grand questions of national destiny. Rather, they address the daily concerns that trouble most people, such as love, luck, fertility, health, and warding off hexes. And in the case of Mexico, those spiritual forces, like the many solid achievements of precontact America, remained a vital part of the scene long after Huitzilopotchli and his dagger-bearing priests had been shown the door.

2

Colonial Crown Jewel

Spaniards and Indigenous Peoples,
1519–1690

Mexico's other great heritage, the people and culture of Spain, had an equally complicated past. Originally a mixture of Romans, Celts, and a Germanic people known as the Visigoths, Iberian civilization succumbed to the great Islamic wave in 711 CE. The Berbers, or Almoravids, of northern Africa brought with them advanced Middle Eastern ideas about architecture, irrigation, and metallurgy, as well as Greek and Roman classical knowledge that had been lost to Europe. For centuries Jews, Christians, and Muslims lived together, but as the Baghdad Caliphate weakened after 1100, Christian monarchs stepped up attempts to retake their lost peninsula. The Reconquista molded Spain in its own image: a warrior people with hyperdeveloped codes of chivalric honor and conduct.

Monarchs there were, but they remained weak. The actual business of defeating Muslims fell to private warlords known as *caudillos*. Such a man raised an army and equipped his soldiers, and with the blessings of the king to whom he pledged loyalty, he won back territory for Christianity; in exchange the king granted him back much of that the property as a personal feud (a kind of land grant). To his infantrymen, or *peones*, the victorious caudillo awarded rights to settle on that feud, where they took up the role of vassals. This process was known as *encomienda*, or "entrusting," and it converted Spain into a society of powerful landowners. Ambitious men dreamed of becoming *encomenderos*, or recipients of these feudal rights; they fought to own property, not to scratch its parched surface with rickety, mule-drawn plows. The ceaseless series of battles and grants ended in an arrangement whereby less that 5 percent of the population controlled virtually all the arable land, very much in the cut of the late Roman republic. It was a system of landowning and its attendant values that the Spanish carried with them wherever they went.

In reality, few things held the Spanish peoples together. The language that we today call Spanish was in fact one regional version among many: Castilian, the language spoken in the central province. Since their marriage in 1469, the monarchs Fernando of Aragón and Isabel of Castile had labored to encompass the entire peninsula within their shared kingdom. But varied regional cultures and languages persisted, as they do to a lesser extent today. More than anything, it was the Catholic faith that bound Spaniard to Spaniard, just as it had imposed a tenuous degree of unity across Europe after Rome's fall in 476 CE. And because Iberian Catholicism matured in the warlike climate of the Reconquest, it assumed a harsh, exclusionary tone. Its followers pledged to convert or eliminate anyone of another faith. This crusading and intolerant tone also became a Spanish hallmark in the New World.

A Collision of Peoples

The Reconquest had very nearly concluded when Spain first arrived in the Caribbean on October 12, 1492. Within twenty years the newcomers' presence decimated the native populations through brutality, forced labor, culture shock, disruption of native farming, and above all the unwitting introduction of diseases to which the natives had no natural immunity. Little by little, enterprising settlers began to push out from the islands to the mainland in search of new slaves and riches. A 1518 expedition led by one Juan de Grijalva skirted the Gulf Coast from Yucatán to Veracruz and in the process picked up rumors of a vast kingdom the locals called Culua, located in the uplands to the west. Grijalva actually made contact with a Mexica delegation; he returned to Cuba with one of its members to serve as a translator for future operations. For his troubles the explorer suffered an arrow wound to the chest, but the news he brought back sufficed to whet Spanish ambitions.

Among those attracted to the possibilities of lucre by conquest was Hernán Cortés (1485–1547), an Extremaduran trained in law but with more of an eye to extralegal chances. Cortés rounded up a band of some four hundred men, including numerous individuals of African descent, and absconded from Trinidad, Cuba, with unauthorized ships and supplies. They reached what is today the city of Veracruz on Easter Sunday 1519. While skirting the southern coast Cortés had picked up the services of a slave girl, the capable Malintzín (also known to history as La Malinche), who became his interpreter, mistress, and partner in conquest. This pitifully small band of Spanish adventurers seemed doomed to failure, but in fact they enjoyed four important advantages. First, Europeans brought with them a repertoire of war technologies that native peoples simply could not match. Toledo steel had no rival in the world, and a man with a steel sword will defeat a man with a club every time: the latter has to raise his weapon to strike, leaving him vulnerable to a fatal thrust. Of equal importance, Spaniards had horses, creatures the Mexica had never seen before, that were as terrifying to them as Hannibal's elephants had been to the ancient Romans. Mounted conquistadors had little difficulty skewering a frightened native infantryman. Spaniards also possessed arquebuses: primitive guns that, if wanting in terms of marksmanship, dealt pain when directed at assembled warriors. Add to these advantages the various technologies of sail-powered ships, written communications, large attack dogs, and lengthy European experience with siege engines.

Second, the tlatoani commanded a massive army, but he could only wield it during the dry season, when its macehuales-soldiers took time away from their fields. This left a six-month window of vulnerability, which hardly mattered when fighting other Mesoamericans, since opponents operated under identical constraints. But those limitations turned into weaknesses on contact with the Spanish, who conducted warfare on a year-round basis.

Third, the conquistadors also prospered from their introduction of harmful microorganisms. Because the natives lacked contact with the domestic animals that often serve as disease vectors, they had no immunity to measles, whooping cough, smallpox, or even such basic infirmities as cold and influenza. Wherever Europeans went in the New World, their invisible pathogens obliterated the natives and left whole peoples open to easy conquest.

Finally, Hernán Cortés exploited the advantages of indigenous politics: namely, the vast ocean of hatred many harbored toward the tribute-hungry

Mexica empire. After establishing military superiority in direct combat, he convinced altepetls such as Tlaxcala that an alliance with Europeans offered a golden opportunity for revenge against an enemy that had threatened and humiliated other Mesoamericans for decades. As the conquistadors advanced toward Tenochtitlán, then, they marched beside a far larger contingency of Tlaxcalan warriors. It was a trick that later conquistadors repeated to great success. Meanwhile, political dynamics favored Cortés in other ways as well. Mexica society, like so many early civilizations throughout the world, oriented itself around an absolute ruler, an individual who kept one foot in the smoky world of the gods and whose word was law. In exactly the way that Alexander the Great had only to defeat the king of Persia to take over the latter's vast empire, Cortés mostly depended on a bold strike at the top and not on a grueling series of battles to the last man.

Along the way he left no doubt in his allies' minds of his own power as he "discovered" a supposed Mexican plot in the city of Cholulá and ruthlessly massacred its inhabitants. The Mexicas, meanwhile, toyed briefly with the idea that this was the returning Quetzalcóatl come to claim his own, but the Mexicas were also rational men of the world and quickly sized up the Spaniards' all-too-human nature. On November 8, 1519, when the conquistadors at last arrived at the outskirts of grand Tenochtitlán, they found themselves dazzled to speechlessness. The city exceeded anything these men of Spain had ever seen, and as participant and chronicler Bernal Díaz later reminisced, "Gazing on such sights, we did not know what to say, or whether what appeared before us was real."

Uncertain and vacillating, Moctezuma tried to buy the Spaniards off with a regal welcome then send them on their way. But the sight of urban opulence, and especially the emperor's treasures of gold and silver, kept the conquistadors glued in place. Cortés batted down suggestions that he leave and as a precaution took the emperor as "guest" in his own quarters—in other words, as a hostage against fortune. The conquistador bought off a Spanish force sent to arrest him, but in his brief absence one of his lieutenants, Pedro de Alvarado, had panicked and perpetrated yet another massacre, this time of Mexica priests and warriors who had apparently assembled in one of the plazas for nothing other than a religious ceremony. Cortés thus returned to a city in which anti-Spanish anger approached fever pitch.

On the evening of June 30, 1520, Cortés and his soldiers and allies attempted to sneak out of the city, but this lumbering multitude of men could hardly travel in secret, and the enraged Mexicas came after them in hot pursuit. Trapped on the narrow causeways, the conquistadors suffered huge losses, and according to legend Cortés later sat weeping under a tree in the coastal village of Tacuba, mourning his losses in the so-called *noche triste*, the "night of sorrow." But the reverse was temporary. Cortés rallied his forces, obtained supplies and reinforcements from the coast, and imposed a terrible siege over the city. It was at this point that microorganisms came to his aid. Prior to fleeing Tenochtitlán, the Spanish had left smallpox, and within the space of fourteen months, the great metropolis was reduced to a charnel house. On August 13, 1521, with his subjects dying all around him, Cuauhtémoc, Moctezuma's nephew and the last tlatoani, rowed out onto the lake—either to escape or, in more romantic tellings, to surrender—and soon fell into the hands of the triumphant Spanish. The greatest empire in Mesoamerican history had fallen in less than two years.

For a brief time the reputation of Cortés outshone all others, but for this conquistador there was no second act of triumph, only fruitless searches for nonexistent kingdoms, together with exhausting struggles to defend his own seigneurial rights as a feudal lord. In 1524, when one of his most trusted lieutenants, Cristóbal de Olid, repudiated his authority and proclaimed himself governor of the Captaincy of Gracias a Dios (modern-day Honduras), Cortés led a two-year campaign of subjugation. As they were en route through the jungles and rivers of southern Mexico, his prize captive, Cuauhtémoc, the last ruler of the Mexica empire, fell under suspicion of plotting an escape. Cortés tortured him by burning his feet but was unable to extract a confession. He hanged Cuauhtémoc and two fellow nobles, then trudged on to Honduras, where he discovered that Olid himself had already died of natural causes. Having accomplished nothing except to traverse a jungle that soon consumed any vestige of human presence, Cortés returned to Spain, where he died fighting in defense of his emoluments in 1547. Meanwhile, his former lover and companion in conquest, Malintzín, perished in 1529 in one of the epidemics that followed the Spanish like a malignant odor.

It fell to lesser men to bring the peripheral parts of Mesoamerica under Spanish control. Between 1524 and 1536 Nuño de Guzmán, former bodyguard to the king of Spain, subjugated the Purépecha empire and other parts of western-central Mexico using tactics that made Cortés himself appear a humanitarian. For later generations Guzmán left behind the city of Guadalajara and a reputation for unbridled cruelty. At the same time Francisco de Montejo, a lieutenant from the original conquest, obtained a patent to subdue the Maya peoples of Yucatán, Tabasco, and Honduras. There he learned a painful truth: fragmented villages and tribes actually present a more daunting mark than great empires, the latter requiring only the capture of the maximum leader. Between 1526 and 1544 Montejo launched one inconclusive campaign after another, often employing as leaders his son and nephew—both of whom, to the lasting confusion of historians and general readers, were named Francisco de Montejo. The Yucatecan campaign only succeeded after epidemic disease decimated the peninsula and when key centers opted to ally with the newcomers. It had cost more Spanish lives and treasure than the conquests of Mexico and Peru combined and yielded little more than bushels of corn, beeswax, and the occasional processing plant for indigo, a blue dye derived from a grass common to tropical and subtropical regions.

It soon became apparent that Montejo's work had fallen short. Independent Maya communities located in what is today northern Belize and Guatemala continued to nettle Spanish hegemony as late as 1690. The most elusive group of all, the Lacandones, paddled the isolated rivers of northern Guatemala and southern Chiapas and Tabasco well into the twentieth century, their lands shielded by near-impenetrable forests of mahogany. Legends notwithstanding, the Lacandones were almost certainly not remnants of Classic Maya civilization but rather the detritus of those who had escaped Spanish conquest by fleeing into these remote territories. Maya culture lived on in varied forms postconquest and continues into the twenty-first century.

Laying the Bricks of New Spain

The first decade of Spanish rule over Tenochtitlán amounted to sheer chaos. The Spanish king, Carlos V, had prohibited the granting of encomienda, fearing both a repeat of Caribbean devastation and an overly powerful encomendero class. But Cortés inaugurated what was to become a long tradition in the history of Mexican governance: "I obey, but I do not comply."

The conquistador reiterated his absolute loyalty to the crown but then explained that he had no choice, given the demands of the men who had sacrificed and achieved so much under his command. The ocean was deep and the king far away, and encomienda rights thus flowed liberally. This first generation grew rich on a windfall of tribute. For the only time in history, Indians had surplus to give because epidemic diseases had momentarily thinned out the adolescents and the elderly; under normal circumstances work-age Indians would have had to support these largely unproductive people. Nor did high-level support for the encomenderos endure. With the great civilizations of Mexico now mostly subdued, Spain lost interest in its daredevil conquistadors and cosseted them with rights and privileges only to the degree necessary to keep them quiet. After a failed attempt to abolish encomienda altogether in 1542, the Crown eventually succeeded in limiting the privilege to the lifetime of the first heir, with encomienda rights persisting somewhat longer in outlying fringes of the colony.

The explorer yields to the bureaucrat. Unlike its island colonies, Spain managed to impose a reasonably stable, balanced form of government over its mainland colonies. At the top of that order stood the king, naturally. A mere two years prior to the beginning of Cortés's enterprise, the grandson of the Catholic Monarchs (Fernando of Aragón and Isabel of Castile) inherited the throne: young, lanky, speaking little Spanish as a result of his youth spent in the Netherlands, he became Carlos I of Spain but preferred his other title, Carlos V of the Holy Roman Empire, a loose confederation of Europe's (mostly German) principalities. He and his successors of the House of Hapsburg ruled Spain and the Americas for the next two centuries.

But neither Carlos V nor any other Spanish king ever set foot in the New World; nor did the young man immediately recognize the discovery's importance. Wholly absorbed in continental affairs, he initiated the practice of naming a figure known as the *virrey* (viceroy) to serve as his representative in Mexico. That office's first occupant, tapped by Carlos in 1535, was the pliable Antonio de Mendoza. "Do nothing, and do it slowly," he liked to counsel. Aware that radical changes only threatened to disturb Spain's tenuous hold on its new territories, he dedicated himself to constructing a new order that altered only slightly the Mexica world, while guaranteeing as much privilege and wealth to the Spanish conquistadors and settlers as possible.

Mendoza and his successor viceroys governed sluggishly but not autocratically. By the 1540s an overseas bureaucracy had taken shape, one that prevented settlers from assuming too much power or committing too many abuses. Many of the actual decisions fell to a body known as the *audiencia*, an institution that blended judicial and legislative powers. It consisted of Spaniards with legal training, and while the viceroy presided, he did not actually vote. In terms of budgeting, viceroys had to work through a form of exchequer: then as now, money required extra oversight and accountability.

Even as the viceroy and *oidores* (judges) debated, many of the decisions of colonial life remained in the hands of a European body known as the Consejo de Indios. Charged with overseeing all things relating to the Americas, the Consejo waxed and waned in power over the years: weak in times of a strong king such as Felipe II, dominant when paired with Felipe's more indolent successors. In sum, a form of checks and balances did exist. The concept lacked a written theoretical basis, but the Spanish shared the opinion of the ancient Chinese legalists that people are basically no good and that if left to their own devices will almost certainly do wrong. Thus arose the confusing body of New Spain's many different authorities and their poorly defined and often overlapping jurisdictions.

In theory, at least, only *peninsulars*, or Spaniards born in the mother country, could manage colonial governance. The crown considered creoles (*criollos*, or American-born Spaniards) too alien, too independent, and too power-hungry to be trusted. Over time, however, creoles slowly inserted themselves into managerial positions.

Meanwhile, religious matters—not easy to separate from secular political decisions—necessarily involved the opinion of the clergy. New Spain's religious bureaucracy was better trained and organized and more highly motivated than its counterpart of governors and lawyers. In many ways it functioned as a parallel state whose tenacious grip only began to weaken under secular assault in the eighteenth century.

Throughout its long existence, Mexico's Catholic Church remained very much in Spanish hands. In return for extending the faith overseas, the Vatican granted to Carlos V and his successors a privilege known as the *patronato real*, which gave the latter complete control over the designation of churchmen in the Americas, and during the sixteenth century the Hapsburg monarchs used that power extensively. As the first archbishop of New Spain, Carlos chose Juan de Zumárraga, a highly educated Franciscan of Basque ancestry. The capable Zumárraga arrived in Mexico in late 1532 and until his death sixteen years later dedicated himself to building a church that concerned itself with indigenous welfare but that did not admit native peoples into its priesthood.

Zumárraga's life and policies very much epitomized church attitudes toward the new Christians. At first enthusiastic about evangelizing a people supposedly uncontaminated by the sins of old Europe, many early colonial fathers imagined that Mexico would someday become the true locus of Catholic faith. After all, the native people absorbed Christian teaching rapidly and behaved deferentially toward the powerful newcomers who had almost miraculously done away with Mexica rule. Yet it soon became apparent that conversion was only skin-deep and that the adoption of Jesus Christ did not necessarily put an end to the veneration of rain gods and other moody spirits who had for so long presided over the Mesomerican world.

But it was not the normal church hierarchy, or "seculars," who carried out the arduous task of Christianizing Mexico's Indian people. From the very start that responsibility fell to the regular orders, so called because they chose to live by some special rule, or in the Latin term, *regula*. These orders drew men of talent and a strong sense of spiritual vocation. Despite belonging to the same religion and working toward a common spiritual goal, the secular and regular orders locked horns repeatedly over the years. The Crown used the latter to spearhead the colonization process, relying on their talent and dedication to permit them to learn the indigenous languages and customs and to carry Spanish belief to the village level. But the friars did their work only too well, and as the colony matured, the need for their heroics lessened. One by one the church secularized the parishes of the Franciscans, Dominicans, and Augustinians. The first great age of mission work ended in the late 1500s with the terrible population decline and the consequent loss of evangelizing gusto. Thereafter the initiative belonged to a newer order, the Society of Jesus, or Jesuits, who undertook the particularly arduous task of setting up missions among the seminomadic peoples north of Guanajuato.

The colonial church originally attempted to hold native converts to the same standards as they did Europeans. But the plan went awry. One of the most sensational cases occurred in Yucatán in 1562 when

Two cultures meet in Cholula, in Puebla state. Here the Spanish church of Nuestra Señora de los Remedios, constructed in 1594, sits atop the pyramid Tlachihualtepetl (mountain made by hand). The latter boasts the largest temple base in all of precontact Mexico. Courtesy of the Library of Congress.

a Franciscan named Diego de Landa claimed to have discovered evidence of human sacrifice and pagan backsliding. The indefatigable friar launched an impromptu inquisition that soon got out of hand, resulting in torture-based interrogations and the considerable destruction of native books and idols. Following an investigation by the bishop of Guatemala, Landa was called to Spain to answer charges. A lengthy inquiry absolved him of wrongdoing, and in 1571 he was reinstated as the bishop of Yucatán, but with clipped wings. For in that same year the church formally established a Holy Office (that is, an Inquisition branch) in New Spain, and in a landmark decision indigenous peoples were exempted. Ever after churchmen turned a blind eye to many of the thinly disguised precontact features imbedded in colonial religion, preferring to focus on promoting basic conversion and the suppression of polygamy, homosexuality, and human sacrifice. The concept of Indians as "children with beards" remained a basic theological tenet throughout the colonial period, and bishops quietly shelved the idea of creating a native priesthood. Fitful attempts to resurrect the old campaigns of extirpating idols typically happened under some headstrong novice *cura* (priest) and almost always raised so many hackles—among villagers, bishops, and encomenderos alike—that such enterprises died quick deaths.

With the Indian peoples off-limits, the Inquisition in the Americas settled into the role of a vice squad for Spaniards. Despite a deeply entrenched stereotype of tortures and public burnings, the real Holy Office functioned in a less dramatic and far more plodding fashion. Inquisitors spent most of their time investigating people for such offenses as gaming, blasphemy, polygamy, and loose living. Cases could remain under review for years altogether, during which time the life of the accused went on pretty much as normal. The Inquisition also failed miserably as a filter for reading material. Individuals living in places like Mexico City and Lima could find virtually any reading material that interested them. In the eighteenth century the focus of inquisitorial investigations shifted from religious to political heresy. For all its inefficiency New Spain's Holy Office hobbled on until it was finally abolished by the Spanish Constitution of 1812.

The Village Makeover

Beyond the confines of the capital, the first century of the colonial order amounted to the Mexica empire under new management. With Spaniards thin on the ground, native life reconstituted itself in ways strongly resembling precontact antecedents. A number of factors help explain the continuity. In the altiplano and elsewhere, Mexican indigenous populations vastly outnumbered those of the Caribbean islands and were sufficiently dense to survive epidemics. Their way of life was too deeply rooted to succumb to a handful of decrees. Nor could a few thousand Spaniards impose any radical redefinition of culture. Finally, the clergy mounted a reasoned argument for limiting the power of Spanish settlers, one made all the more persuasive when it coincided with the Crown's own fear of encomenderos grown too wealthy and powerful for their own good. For all of these reasons, the first generations of New Spain's rulers had to let the Indians be Indians.

Above all, that meant respecting the indigenous village. The Spanish strongly equated urban life, however miniature the scale, with civilization. Moreover, religious conversion and tribute collection both required stable, easily accessed populations—the larger, the better. Milpa farming, to the contrary, had an entropic effect. Its practitioners lived in relatively temporary constructions, working the land until its fertility gave out and the farmer had to move elsewhere. In a plan that was to sow infinite confusion, the friars rounded up the inhabitants of far-flung hamlets and relocated them, by force if necessary, into larger and more settled communities. The so-called *reducción* system, which also featured in the colonization of Central America and the Andes, attempted to impose fixity on an extremely fluid system of human habitation. Sometimes the resettlements took root, while others failed as people eventually returned to their places of origin. Some communities ceased to exist altogether, while at other times new ones came into being. These resettlements began early and picked up speed during the mid-sixteenth century as epidemic diseases began to tear into the native communities. Whatever the outcome, it became increasingly difficult to talk about a place of definitive origin for many of Mexico's indigenous peasants.

For those communities that did survive, the reducción system amounted to a kind of apartheid arrangement in which each ethnic and cultural group kept to its own space and hewed to its own norms and responsibilities. The Spanish remained in a handful of European-style cities, principally Mexico City itself, where they recreated their old lives in the so-called *república de españoles*. They tore down indigenous temples and used the stones to build their own homes and churches. Following royal decree, they laid out their streets in a convenient grid pattern quite unlike the often chaotic and twisting alleys of old Europe. They practiced their accustomed religious rites, spoke Castilian, and as much as circumstances permitted continued their traditional diet of wine, olive oil, and wheat bread. Spaniards possessing encomienda rights expected to batten on tribute, but given their well-known propensity to exploit, they were not allowed to enter Indian villages at their will nor to spend the night there. Natives brought tribute to the cities, where they deposited it in designated areas. As so often happens, then, human beings confronted with radically new circumstances made every effort to go on living as they had before.

Something similar applied to the native peoples. Following their conversion to Catholicism (a point discussed at length below), the natives simply resumed what they were doing before 1519. Each community received a grant of land that carried the old Spanish name of *ejido*; it consisted of a block of *tierras* covering approximately one square kilometer. The land in question was both communal and inalienable. Nestled within it was space allotted for what was called the *fundo legal*, the urban center in which the farm families could reside. The village land grant was the single most important document the community possessed: measured off by elders, a priest, and a scribe, and guarded in locked chests, these titles guaranteed that while the community might not grow rich, it would at least survive, protected by cherished papers that in some cases survive today.

European micromanagement of the affairs of hundreds of villages speaking dozens of languages was a practical impossibility. For that reason daily management fell to a council of village elders known variously as the *república de indios* or *república de indígenas*. Each of these organizations included a series of rotating offices named after Spanish counterparts: *regidor*, *alcalde*, and the note-taking *escribano*. Presiding at the top stood a headman who went by many names: tlatoani among Nahuatl speakers, batab for the Mayas, cazonci for the Purépechas, to take the most prominent examples. But the Spanish themselves lumped them together under the name *cacique*, a term they picked up in Cuba, carried with them everywhere, and which survives in modern usage to refer to a local power broker untroubled by such niceties as due process. But those unsavory connotations came later, and for the entirety of the colonial period it was these offices who guarded important papers, oversaw land quarrels, and adjudicated such transcendent matters as who stole someone's chicken or who ran off with someone's wife. To carry out their orders they typically employed a gendarmerie of sorts whose agents were known as *tupiles*. Through the escribano's trusty pen, the repúblicas maintained records, almost always in native tongues, papers that even today open windows into the minutia of village life.

Accompanying this reconstitution of village affairs came another sort of colonialism, a transformation that in the long run sank deeper roots: the spiritual conquest of Mexico. Franciscan friars, soon to be joined by Dominicans and Augustinians, carried out most of the difficult work of contacting native villages, learning their languages the hard way (no digital translators here), and converting the residents to Catholicism. The friars operated through a three-stage process. First came instruction in the fundamentals of this new religion: the divinity of Christ, the warm protection of the Virgin Mary, the litany of sins and taboos, and a generous assortment of Biblical stories, particularly the tales of Genesis. After that the friars conducted mass baptisms in order to assure that those who died would do so in a state of grace, ready for the blessings of the afterlife. The final stage consisted of settling in for the long haul of teaching the intricacies of faith and with them imparting vast amounts of cultural information about Spanish society.

In this last stage the project stumbled. Sons of prominent native nobility, at least, received preferential treatment, receiving intensive education in convents and special schools, and they assumed auxiliary roles that made them pillars of church orthodoxy. But the masses fared differently. The friars were few and the Indians many, and that in turn meant that multiple elements of precontact culture would remain forever imbedded in this colonialized world. When confronted with utterly new circumstances, human beings typically look for some feature that they recognize, and Mexico was no different. Here the natives originally worshipped many gods, so one feature of Christianity that caught their eye was the abundance of saints, spiritual beings who could act as intermediaries between humans and God. But not all saints were created equal. Every village had a *santo patrón*, the patron saint who granted special protection and consideration. Borrowing from European precedent, most Mexican churches boasted a *retablo*: an elaborate display mounted on the wall behind the altar and often decorated in gold leaf. The retablo featured a special niche reserved for the statue of the santo patrón; there the image was displayed.

The new and syncretic Christianity thus made the cult of the saints its centerpiece, and the santo's feast day became the defining moment of the ceremonial year. For the space of a week or so practical endeavors ended, and the village gave itself over to huge celebrations of masses, processions, eating, and binge drinking, all punctuated by another new acquisition, fireworks. Prominent men of the village strove to win prestige—that tireless human quest—by sponsoring the fiesta. And they paid dearly: men who stepped up could incur near-ruinous debts that could take years to discharge. The height of honor came when a *cofrade*, a member of a lay organization known as a cofradía, helped carried the santo in procession through the streets of the village. The actual details of cofradía operations have inspired no end of scholarly writings; for our purposes it suffices to say that those details varied greatly over time and changed in part owing to the opportunities and pressures generated not within the village but rather by the outside world.

Far from causing repugnance, the new religion had everything the Indians liked. Its piety was public, not private, and therefore reinforced communal solidarity. The grand events of its annual ceremonial life showered welcome relief onto the crushing monotony of subsistence farming. It provided a set of mediators who promised to help people with such pressing issues as fertility, health, good luck, and successful crops. It allowed them the opportunity to demonstrate initiative and creativity. Above all, it promised them that somewhere, however high above the clouds, there was a mighty king who held them in equal esteem with the Spaniards.

Certainly the most famous syncretic saint of New Spain was the Virgin of Guadalupe, said to have appeared to a certain Mexica, the recently rechristened Juan Diego, on the hill of Tepeyac outside of colonial Mexico City in 1531. Since that time most aspects of the traditional story have been called into question, including the dates of the visitation, the identity of Juan Diego, the original following of the Virgin, and the origins of the famous cloak bearing her image. Regarding that last point, we know that the church actually commissioned the cloak painting, which was in turn based on images of Spain's own Guadalupe Virgin (hence the name). Key elements of the apparition story do not in fact appear until the seventeenth century. To judge from records of pilgrim visits, the shrine at Tepeyac remained largely a creole cult, while the Virgin as we know her did not gain colonywide prominence until a massive promotional campaign from the 1750s onward. Nevertheless, the fame of the Virgin of Guadalupe eventually transcended documentable origins and has come to symbolize a religion that extends infinite compassion toward both a dark-skinned, colonized people and the white Spanish polity that stood above them. Today the Basilica at Tepeyac is among the most visited sites in the entire Christian world, while people throughout the entirety of the Americas embrace the Virgin of Guadalupe as their protectress.

Meanwhile, lesser-known santos feature throughout Mexico. Yucatán's Virgin of Izamal combines the attributes of an all-caring and all-loving

Christian Virgin with a Maya sun god, and her shrine remains a popular pilgrim destination today. Tabasco's church of Cupilco contains a Virgin supposedly discovered on nearby shores after a shipwreck in 1634. Despite attempts to place her in one church or another, the statue continued to return by its own accord to the retablo of Cupilco, which residents eventually realized was the Virgin's choice for a permanent home. The devotional cults of Izamal, Cupilco, and many others speak of a religion whose roots reach deeper than the strata of early missions.

This cozy tableau of communal lands, public piety, and low-level self-government might have continued indefinitely and without significant complaint. After all, it was what people had always known; and if tribute exactions went up, countervailing benefits like pigs, chickens, livestock, metal, and plows helped improve material life. What rocked the boat was the wave of demographic disasters that began to torment rural Mexico in the mid-sixteenth century. Spread by the very friars who went into the villages to convert souls and improve native life, pathogens like smallpox, measles, typhus, influenza, and even the common cold tore through populations that had had no previous contact with livestock and who had thus failed to develop any immunities. In 1500 the population of what is today Mexico may have stood somewhere around twenty-five million; by 1620 that number had fallen to a mere million, a decline of 96 percent, and no one, neither Indian nor Spaniard, had the slightest idea of why it was happening.

Encomenderos naturally panicked: who was to provide their promised riches, now that Indians' numbers had dwindled? In the 1550s Spain experimented with *repartimiento*, in which an official known as the *corregidor* divided and dealt out Indian workers like a man rationing loaves of bread. But the system provoked massive discontent. Spaniards and Indians alike discovered that these new and unsolicited bureaucrats, underpaid in the Hapsburg tradition, worked the office for their own benefit and were for sale: bidding wars thus ensued for the corregidor's attention. Nor did officials work quickly, for fear of setting precedents they might actually be expected to maintain. The arrangement was centralized, cumbersome, and above all unpopular.

Mexico's settlers found a way around the jam: private estates. The decline of Indian populations suddenly made land available for the taking, and for the first time enterprising Spaniards began to move into the countryside to set up properties that came to be known as *haciendas*. Those who acquired these lands adopted the name *hacendados*. The trail-blazing scholar François Chevalier called them "men rich and power-ful," and while he may have stretched things a bit, the term "hacendado" has ever after been associated with social dominance in Latin America. Such a property absorbed large amounts of land: not so much because its owner needed it for production but rather as a way of leveraging na-tive peoples out of their dwindling villages and onto the estate. A worker who settled there became a *peón*, after the old Spanish term for a foot soldier; in the southeast they were called *luneros*, because in exchange for land and security they did one day of labor a week for the estate: on Monday, or *lunes*. Commercial in buoyant times, the estate limped by, isolated and autarkic, when recession struck. Those estates located close to Spanish populations produced wheat and barley, whereas the remoter versions focused on the traditional corn crop. The peones lived in debt to the estate, although the degree to which debt limited their options varied enormously by time and place.

Colonial haciendas probably lacked the harsher features of their late nineteenth-century counterparts. After all, sluggish markets and low populations worked in the peones' interests. Colonial haciendas were not necessarily profitable, and like modern-day homes they depreciated in value without constant investment and upkeep. But whether cruel or accommodating, the institution had a profound effect on its world. Ha-cendados were not merely employers but *patrones*, miniature lords who assumed a parental role in the lives of the resident workers. The relation-ship between hacendado and peón was a defining feature of this world, a relationship far more intense than that between citizen and president, while the hacienda system stood perpetually on the verge of something akin to European feudalism. By the time the dust settled from the de-mographic shake-up, rural Mexico comprised a trio of institutions: the surviving Indian villages, the haciendas, and the Spanish-style towns. Re-lationships among the three swung from harmonious to resentful and litigious, depending on personalities and circumstances.

In the course of all these changes, the indigenous peoples assimilated not only legal and religions practices but also vast amounts of Europe's material culture. The introduction of metal greatly facilitated the hard work of country life, reducing critical tasks such clearing brush from

Xcanchakán (c. 1842), a typical Yucatecan hacienda, seen here in a sketch by British landscape artist Frederick Catherwood, who accompanied gentleman archaeologist John Lloyd Stephens in his explorations of the region. The architectural style is known as the Franciscan arch, but the design actually has Islamic origins. The hacienda is located outside the town of Tecoh. Courtesy of the New York Public Library.

days to mere hours. In Yucatán two emblematic features of peasant existence—the hammock and the *coa* (a short, curved machete excellent for weeding and general fieldwork)—both came with the Spanish from the Caribbean. Similarly, most indigenous peoples adopted some form of European clothing. The friars had no patience with topless women, however devout and docile, and made certain that females covered up with an embroidered cotton tunic known as the *hipil* or *huipil*, still common throughout Mexico.

In terms of agriculture the Spanish learned more than they taught, since the milpa complex of corn, beans, and squash so perfectly suited this particular environment. The newcomers tasted chiles and tomatoes and never looked back. Wheat and barley became regular crops in the cooler, drier altiplano. Rice, previously unknown in the Western Hemisphere, also settled on the Mexican table, as did fruits such as apples, oranges, lemons, bananas, and melons. Even more revolutionary in terms of peasant household economy, Europe's domestic animals made their appearance: the slow but sure-footed burro, the hard-plowing ox, chickens laying eggs in abundance, and that peculiar version of a poor man's bank, the pig. Given the new presence of goats and cows, the people enjoyed their first access to milk and cheese. Thus were born the many distinctive versions of Mexican artisanal cheese: salty *sopero* and *cotija*, mozzarella-like *oaxaqueño*, and many others beside. In sum, the centuries of colonial rule witnessed the development of the highly varied Mexican cuisines of today.

This was the system that emerged in colonial Mexico: partly a design imposed from above, partly a concession to the enduring realities of indigenous life, and partly inadvertent reactions to unplanned events. Some measure of its efficacy lies in the fact that it endured for so long without serious challenge. Indeed, rural revolts typically came at one of two different moments: either shortly after the conquest, when the strength of the Spanish order remained unclear; or far later, when that order, along with its benefits and protections for the lower classes, had begun to crumble. In the culture of the densely populated villages that lay south of Mazatlán, which formed the core of the New Spain colony, these latter revolts happened almost exclusively during the last third of the eighteenth century, when the Hapsburg moment was giving way to an aggressive new era of colonial exploitation. Between the two moments lay 250 years of relative peace.

A Colonial World

New Spain was to have been a land of stark binary population division: Indian and Spaniard—and no one else. However, nature had other ideas and soon enough muddied the ethnic waters. Spaniards themselves distinguished between peninsulars and creoles, the former occupying all the leading positions and hoarding that undefinable and glorious prestige that Mexicans refer to as *abolengo* (lineage). Creoles, meanwhile, wore a chip on their collective shoulder: they felt themselves the equals of their European counterparts and nursed a heightened sense of honor that was as hard to appease as it was easy to offend. Indeed, the creole became a quintessential figure in early Mexican politics, as men of this description sought by any means necessary to prove their nobility, their virility, and their intrinsic excellence.

Meanwhile, out of the union of Spaniards and Indians came Mexico's most important racial category, the *mestizo* (a person of mixed Spanish and Indian heritage). At times that union was biological, while at other times the individual in question simply borrowed and blended cultural practices. Like Ishmael in the Bible, every man's hand was against him: Spaniards scorned the mestizo, while Indian villagers wanted him nowhere around. But the process of *mestizaje* (racial blending) continued apace, and by the late colonial period mestizos formed the fastest growing of groups, a body of men and women who had to shift for themselves and find a place as their wits and their talents permitted.

Not everyone was Spaniard, Indian, or some combination of the two. During the century of demographic decline, enterprising Spaniards offset the labor shortage by importing African slaves. Warfare among the various kingdoms of western Africa, and in particular the expansion of the Asanti state in what is now Nigeria, had produced a glut of POWs whom customary law condemned to bondage. The Asanti and others had begun to trade their surplus slaves to Portuguese explorers, and these explorers in turn retailed some of their acquisitions to the Spanish. All in all, some two hundred thousand Africans came to Mexico in the course of the colonial period.

Here they met varied fortunes. Valued for their heartiness, their resistance to diseases like malaria and smallpox, and their closer acquaintance with a European understanding of the world, the incoming Africans usually found flight easier than fight. Those determined to escape the toils of slavery ran to remote mountain redoubts to establish *cimarrón*, or maroon, communities. Unions of white men and black women produced *mulatos*, while black-Indian marriages yielded *pardos*. These mixed-race offspring came to outnumber African blacks within a few generations, in no small part because the rebound of Indian populations after the mid-1600s made slavery less cost-effective, and Mexico's participation in the transatlantic trade, while not ending completely, declined to marginal levels. By the twentieth century Mexicans of African heritage had mostly dissolved into Mexico's gene pool. Identifiable Afro-Mexican populations are located mostly in two coastal concentrations: Veracruz (on the Gulf of Mexico); and the Costa Chica of Guerrero, Michoacán, and Oaxaca (on the Pacific coast), all places where the ancient rhythms of sugar cultivation have persisted across the centuries.

As elsewhere in the Americas, African peoples imparted a legacy of vocabulary, music, dance, plant species, agricultural know-how, and other practical skills. African peoples also brought a huge corpus of oral literature that became integral to Mexican society. It is truly astonishing how quickly narratives, folk tales, and sayings spread. To give only one example, African stories about a predacious coyote and a cunning rabbit—probably best known to modern readers as Br'er Rabbit or through cartoon incarnations in the Warner Bros. Roadrunner series—penetrated into the remotest corners of Mexico, so much so that many consider them of Amerindian origin. These stories took their place alongside the narratives of Genesis as integral elements of Mexican oral literature.

The arrival of Spanish culture in Mexico changed gender roles as well—roles that varied greatly depending on one's ethnicity and wealth. Women in indigenous villages remained strongly tied to the demands of survival. They married as soon as they could conceive and spent much of their time in the obligatory activities of raising children and preparing food. Their husbands' constant labor away in the cornfields made women the centers of home life, and they served as vessels of folk knowledge regarding such matters as healing and traditional narratives. Indian women carved out fame as weavers, pulque makers, and petty merchants and found in Christianity an ideology that celebrated their roles as mothers, even as it bid them to be silent on matters of public life.

At the top of the social ladder, Spanish women recreated in their lives the conventions of the old country, albeit with some special twists. In the early colonial period there were relatively few of them. In 1530 females accounted for only 6 percent of total Spanish migration to the Americas; seventy years later that statistic peaked at 20 percent. At no time did European settlers achieve anything resembling gender parity, and men usually established unions, formal or otherwise, with women of Indian or mixed race. That fact merely reinforced the notion of Spanish women as rare and exotic treasures, the trophy wives of old Mexico.

Daughters almost invariably remained under the control of their parents, in whose charge they learned the female virtues of modesty, chastity, and obedience. When they entered adolescence, some women received education in a convent; that did not mean they necessarily became nuns. Rather, these institutions functioned as the boarding schools of the time.

Matrimony was the defining relationship for women. While men typically married after establishing themselves in the world—probably around twenty-five or older—women wed between the ages fourteen and eighteen, as soon as they could bear children. Spanish custom dictated that at the time of a daughter's marriage the family provide her with a sum of money or property known as the *dote*, or dowry; the husband supplemented that with a matching sum known as the *arras*, a custom still recalled in modern-day Mexican weddings where, in addition to the wedding ring, the groom provides a miniature metal box with tiny coins. Should the marriage for any reason be dissolved, both dote and arras went with the woman. If childhood and marriage brought women under male supervision, though, widowhood gave free agency. Widows disposed of their time and property as they saw fit, and colonial records overflow with the businesses and properties of women whose husband had passed on to a better world.

While most colonial women lived relatively scripted existences, a few broke the mold. Catalina de Suárez (1592–1650), also known as the "Nun of Alférez," rejected life as a woman and lived as a male muleteer, fighting duels and charging her way through adventures romantic and otherwise; her cross-gender life inspired plays and biographies in her own lifetime and continues to intrigue a modern age fascinated by those who challenge sexual norms. But certainly the most famous of all colonial Mexican women was Sor Juana Inés de la Cruz. Born to a prosperous creole family in Mexico City in 1648, she demonstrated remarkable scholarly abilities and was able to compose complicated verse and read numerous languages while still quite young. At age nineteen she entered a monastery in order to continue undisturbed in her life of letters. In a brief period Sor Juana produced a remarkable body of poetry and drama, some of which brought her into conflict with church authorities offended by her outspoken criticisms of male domination. She died during a plague in 1695, leaving behind an enormous corpus of literature; what survives is only a fragment of her total production.

Sor Juana aside, colonial Mexico was no great incubator of dynamic new ideas. Europeans remained relatively few in number, while indigenous peasants lacked the means and the motive to pursue philosophy, the mechanical arts, or literary or scientific invention. Most human energy went toward the simple struggle for survival or else to public ceremonial activities often performed in the interest of winning personal prestige. Moreover, such forums as newspapers and popular journals did not exist. Educational training focused overwhelmingly on the static fields of canon and secular law, with a healthy dose of reading and writing fundamentals. Well into the nineteenth century the mysteries of Castilian grammar revealed themselves as they always had, in the ancient guide composed by Antonio de Nebrija in 1492 for the court of Fernando and Isabel, a manual that he not inaccurately styled "the tool of empire." Science and mathematics, meanwhile, did not enter curriculums in any serious way until the late eighteenth century, and even then those disciplines mostly featured in the training of military officers.

The first and greatest intellectual achievement of the colonial period was the transfer of vast quantities of new information between the Old and New Worlds. And while this transfer may have lacked the intellectual fireworks created by the study of quantum mechanics, it nevertheless ranks as one of the most essential learning experiences of the human race. One half of that process, native peoples' adoption and adaptation of foreign culture and knowledge, lacks a chronicler. Within the space of a generation or less, peoples such as Nahuas and Mayas had to absorb large amounts of Castilian vocabulary, legal concepts, clothing styles, plants, animals, and technology. The sheer volume of the inflow made it akin to the arrival of invaders from another planet. Conversely, in terms of its effect on Europeans and other Old World cultures, contact opened astonishing new vistas, a sudden and undeniable awareness that the world was far richer than anyone had ever imagined. Contact with Mexico allowed the Spaniards to acquaint themselves—and ultimately peoples as far away and as disparate as Russians, Koreans, and Africans—with essential knowledge of plants, animals, and technologies that laid the basis for later global development.

Advanced intellectual pursuits remained almost exclusively the province of churchmen. Priests alone possessed the training, the means, the organization, and the spare time to engage in matters of research and inquiry. A major part of their labors was ethnographic. The early friars who evangelized Indian villages also composed the first grammars, histories, and ethnographies of those many peoples. Their writings drip with cultural chauvinism, but in terms of sheer scope and content these works today still command the attention of scholars. Among the most essential studies is Bernardino de Sahagún's *Historia general de las cosas de Nueva España*, better known as the Florentine Codex. A Franciscan and a graduate of the prestigious University of Salamanca, Sahagún (c. 1499–1590) had absorbed the Renaissance focus on human society and culture, and he brought said interests to bear in his twelve-volume study of the Nahuatl-speaking peoples of central Mexico. He labored over the project for forty-five years, always keeping one eye on guard against the Inquisitional scrutiny that his studies of indigenous religion threatened to invite. In the southeast Diego de Landa (1524–79) authored his *Relación de las cosas de Yucatán* in the 1560s. Landa was as talented as an ethnographer as he was overbearing as a bishop, and to this day his brief work constitutes an indispensable source on late Postclassic Maya religion, and in the mid-twentieth century it provided a key to the deciphering of Classic-era Maya glyph writing.

European intellectual curiosity also gave birth to the *Relaciones geográficas*, a sort of Domesday Book composed in the 1570s and 1580s. In this great work Spaniards assembled, within the limits of their knowledge and ability, a multivolume encyclopedia of the peoples and places now under their possession. The Consejo de Indios oversaw the *Relaciones* at the order of Felipe II, who was anxious to establish better justice and firmer metropolitan control over his father's sprawling overseas possessions. Even today this monumental compilation provides essential information concerning the nature of precontact and colonial societies.

On a smaller scale, the impulse to know and explain places like Mexico, the recurring elite fascination with a world that was theirs and yet not their own, outlived the colonial years. The never-to-be-completed process of cultural understanding survives in priests' letters about village affairs, in the reports of district officials, in the endless litany of *memoriales* tabulating the people and products of the land, in the writings of the gentleman historians and ethnographers, and, finally, in the works of those intellectual descendants of Franz Boas, the cultural anthropologists of modern academia. Meanwhile, the great scholarly accomplishments of the colonial period—the monumental works of encyclopedia, history, and natural sciences—still lay in a late colonial future, when the influence of the Enlightenment, selectively chosen to permit both Bourbon regalism and Catholic theology, coaxed works of brilliance from such men as Benito Jerónimo Feijóo and Francisco Javier Clavijero.

Visual arts in the colony initially consisted of a small handful of genres. First, there were those illustrations essential to the ethnographic codices collected by friars like Sahagún. Indigenous artists produced them, and the overall style and sensibility harken back to precontact traditions. Second, the explosion of Catholic churches throughout Mexico birthed a demand for decorative arts, the most eye-catching of which remains the layering of hammered gold leaf over the retablos. The pinnacle of this art decorates the church of San Francisco Javier de Tepotzotlán, constructed in the late seventeenth century as a Jesuit college and today the home of the stunning National Museum of the Viceroyalty. Decorative arts branched into innumerable directions: silversmithing, etched metal, woodworking, and, via Mexico's contact with the Philippines after 1600, sacred images carved in ivory.

Common folk could be artists as well. Our current appreciation of colonial decorative arts includes many material efforts not originally conceived with an eye to the distanced appreciation of a museum, but rather created as devotional items integral to the daily spiritual lives of Mexico's citizens–what today might be terms "outsider art." Among the most charming example is the *ex-voto* (literally, "out of a vow"), an item central to human conversations with God and the saints. When pressed by need or hardships, the troubled individual pledged to carry out some demonstrative public act once a saint had lifted the problem. Sometimes these pledges involved pilgrimages—for instance, carrying the image of

San Antonio from one town to the next—but quite often the lucky in-dividual discharged the debt by creating a painting that illustrated the story and included a text explaining the matter in greater detail. Mexican ex-votos created during the past four centuries run into the thousands, but only a few of the colonial samples survive today, even though some churches exhibit large collections of more recent works. Such paintings show a naive charm unattainable by more academically informed works.

Beyond these genres, the new rulers of this land commissioned portraits that captured their own magnificence, and if that magnificence has ceased to impress, the painters' skill lives on. Perhaps the best-known Hapsburg-era Mexican painter was Cristóbal de Villalpando (c. 1649–1714). Born in the colonial capital, he rose to become head of the painters' guild and completed canvases for the cathedrals in both Mexico City and Puebla; one of his most important works was the cupola decoration of the latter town's Capilla de los Reyes (executed in 1688–89). Villalpando's earlier works invoke the style of Peter Paul Rubens, as their brightly colored fig-ures swirl unbothered by the laws of gravity; later paintings assume a more somber tone. His large workshop produced an impressive corpus, one that comprises some of Mexico's finest contributions to the Baroque genre.

Northward Momentum

From the moment that Cuauhtémoc paddled out into Lake Texcoco in his canoe to surrender, Spaniards had dreamed of yet another great kingdom somewhere to the north. But this kingdom proved as elusive as Atlantis. Cortés himself explored the Baja California peninsula in 1536, nearly drowning in the process, but no kingdoms and no gold ever ma-terialized. In that same year, a certain Álvar Núñez Cabeza de Vaca, ac-companied by a linguistically gifted African slave named Esteban and two other Spaniards, straggled back into Mexico after an eight-year journey straight out of Homer. They were the last survivors of an ill-fated expedi-tion planned to explore the Florida peninsula, where they had found no fountain of youth, only dangers and hardships. Their mishaps had taken them through the southern coasts of North America and then on to Texas, where they won fame as healers and from whence they walked to western Mexico, accompanied by a faithful band of Indian followers. Cabeza de

Vaca and Esteban also brought tales about a city of gold, a certain Cíbola, and in so doing laid the groundwork for Spanish *entradas*, or formally sanctioned expeditions of exploration and conquest, into New Mexico.

Those who journeyed north to explore these fabled cities found only the remnants of a once-teeming culture and people known to those who superseded them by their Navajo name, the Anasazi: "the ancestors of our enemies." Francisco Vázquez de Coronado came this way in his vastly disappointing expedition of 1540–42, trudging to such far-flung places as the Colorado Plateau and central Kansas. But the cities of gold receded into the horizon before him. A half century later, in 1598, conquistador Juan de Oñate established a permanent Spanish presence in Santa Fe de Nuevo México. Native peoples of the region still revile his name for the enormous brutality with which he treated their ancestors. Time was not on Oñate's side: under the rule of Felipe II, Franciscans and other regular orders had managed to increase their power over the high-handed conquistadors of old, and in 1606 missionaries used their influence to have Oñate recalled, leaving them with a power equal to or exceeding that of successor governors.

In the north, as elsewhere, the empire's consolidation depended on some tangible economic benefit. At first very few products of New Spain found a market abroad, mainly because Europeans had yet to acquire a taste for things like chocolate and tobacco. But there was one great exception. The expanding European economy needed precious metals as the basis for its currency. That need became all the more pressing as Europeans embarked on a distinctly one-way trade with Asia, purchasing such luxury goods as silk and porcelain in exchange for silver.

Fortunately for Spain, a series of mining strikes in the mid-sixteenth century established Mexico as a formidable producer of silver: not quite enough ore to rival Peru's great silver mountain of Potosí, but enough to turn mining into the colony's most lucrative industry. In 1546 Spanish miners made their first strike in what is today Zacatecas state. Subsequent discoveries emerged in a broad, rolling area north of Mexico City, a region that stretched from Guadalajara to Querétaro, known as the Bajío. Prospectors naturally worked the upper deposits first but eventually discovered greater lodes, the so-called *negros*, that lay beneath the water table. Only two methods existed for freeing these ores from nature's watery grip. Digging vertical shafts allowed the insertion of pumps to free up mining space, but in the sixteenth and seventeenth centuries hydraulics remained primitive, inefficient, and above all costly. The more effective approach involved digging a sloping, horizontal drain shaft known as an adit, but adits were herculean undertakings that required vast capital, an even vaster labor force, and the political support necessary to procure both.

Native peoples, meanwhile, did not take kindly to these heavy-handed intrusions into a land that had always given them life. Conflict soon erupted, and between 1550 and 1585 the Spanish vainly attempted to subdue irate tribes through a policy aptly named "fire and blood." But honey catches more flies than vinegar, and in the following fifteen years a policy reversal enacting "peace by purchase" accomplished what force could not. As the French discovered in North America, gift-giving lulled native people while allowing Europeans to slowly insinuate themselves. In the course of the struggle the conquistadors founded Saltillo (1577) and Monterrey (1596), both near dependable water sources. These frontier communities prided themselves on their hardy self-reliance and became centers for miners, wheat farmers, and sheep ranchers. New Spain lacked the population and resources to populate the area between its frontier and its metropole, so it settled on a system of missions linked to the capital via roads intersected with military outposts known as *presidios*. On both sides of these trails lay the alluring world of northern Mexico, replete with dust and cacti and glorious sunsets, but also marked by a nagging insinuation of menace always just beyond the horizon.

Northern and western colonization added new variations to the Spanish-Indian relations sketched above. Those ethnicities who lived in the vast arid region north of Mesoamerica survived by combining hunting and gathering with agricultural efforts along seasonal rivers. Small, isolated bands often failed to endure the shock of contact. But larger groups, including the Yaquis, Mayos, and Tarahumaras, learned to incorporate Christian missionary outreach and labor on Spanish properties into their repertoire of survival techniques. They tarried in such places only long enough to reap the benefits and then retreated to mountain redoubts and traditional farming zones as needs dictated. Unlike the indigenous communities of the south, northern ethnicities remained aloof, and their hardscrabble homelands inspired the idea of "regions of refuge" that twentieth-century proponents of mestizo acculturation pledged to eliminate.

The two centuries of northern New Spain under the rule of the House of Hapsburg ended on a downbeat. Expansion beyond the Bajío had come at enormous human and financial costs and had achieved a degree of permanence only by allowing huge chunks of native culture to continue to function as before. Gifts replaced warfare, while in the colony of Nuevo México the Pueblo system of native authority and belief survived despite the Franciscans' fitful attempts to wipe it out entirely. But the whole arrangement teetered on a razor's edge. A series of droughts hit northwestern New Spain in the 1670s; with droughts came famines and Athabaskan Indian raids, plagues that the friars, for all their talk of the Almighty's blessings, were visibly powerless to arrest.

The Santa Fe mission was the first to go. Operating with a cunning and a secrecy the Spanish never dreamed possible, Pueblo leaders organized a revolt that brought together numerous villages. They coordinated the timing of their uprisings by supplying the plotters with knotted cords; one knot was untied each day until the last knot brought them to the appointed time. Their leader, Popé, had been a religious leader prior to the Franciscan ascendency, and he deeply resented his loss of status. In 1680, under his direction, the Pueblos killed or expelled Spanish settlers, and visitors to Santa Fe can still see the marks their machetes left on the ancient church door. With friars and encomenderos driven out, the Pueblo proceeded to desecrate churches, symbolically purging their world of a religion to which they had never truly subscribed. Surviving colonizers made the lonely trek back to old El Paso to lick their wounds.

For over a decade Pueblo culture resumed its independence. But divisions among the villages eventually tore apart their unity, and in 1692 the Spanish, under Diego de Vargas, made a triumphant and entirely peaceful return. To avoid a repeat of the 1680 debacle, Vargas curtailed encomienda rights and halted the more intrusive practices of the friars.

Meanwhile, one other Spanish-controlled domino fell after Santa Fe. The Jesuit order had established a mission presence in western Chihuahua in the 1670s. In the process their often-heavy-handed approach—particularly their tactics of resettling natives and moving their children into Jesuit-run boarding schools for indoctrination—antagonized the Tarahumara peoples. In March 1690 the Indians killed a Jesuit missionary; the revolt quickly spread to other villages. As with the Pueblo Revolt, leadership often emerged among traditional authorities whom the Jesuits had removed from power. And as in the Santa Fe colony, the presence of a virtually autonomous regular order had nettled Spanish secular officials, who were quick to blame their religious rivals for the problem. The governor managed to suppress the uprising by destroying the Tarahumaras' cornfields and livestock, but conflict erupted all over again in 1697 and required a year of brutal counterinsurgency to defeat.

None of this signaled a land of cultural equality, but the concessions sufficed to bring peace and allow a more gradual evolution of nuevo-mexicano society. The reverses of the 1680s had one other effect as well. However temporary, they shook the Spanish and hardened their determination for the eighteenth-century campaign of northern expansion, a campaign with far-reaching effects for later Mexican and U.S. societies.

For any resident of New Spain in 1699, a glance back at the previous two centuries invariably produced mixed emotions. The native peoples had endured the hardships of contact and colonization, but while they had lost enormous portions of their old world, much remained. The time-tested agricultural community had reasserted itself with the same tenacity that had allowed it to endure the rise and fall of so many ancient Mesoamerican kingdoms. Languages like Nahuatl, Otomí, Mixtec, Zapotec, Tzeltal, Tzotzil, and Yucatec Maya prospered, and the scribes of native repúblicas continued to churn out the minutes and the decisions of those tiny, august bodies. Spanish tax and tribute obligations may have weighed on them, but the concept of being rich had never factored in their lives to begin with. True, the friars had come to stay, but the natives succeeded in bending the new religion to accommodate their own needs and expectations. The intricate checks and balances of this new world, its safeguards and protections, endowed it with so much legitimacy that two centuries later, native *campesinos* would risk everything to defend it.

3

Blue Skies, Blood-Stained Land
The Coming of Independence, 1690–1821

Revolution, like charity, begins at home. This applies to the con-
vulsions that tore apart Spain's vast empire in the early 1800s. The
mother country had spent the entire eighteenth century trying to shake
off a crippling economic and intellectual malaise. It partially succeeded
but in so doing brought wrenching changes to Mexico and thereby set
the conditions for the colony's successful movement for independence.

The House of Bourbon Remakes Mexico

Spain's changing fortunes greatly depended on its ruling dynasty. Hapsburg monarchs Carlos V and Felipe II had towered over their world,
but after 1600 imperial power gradually weakened, the result of political
mismanagement, crushing national debt, an excessive dependence on colonial silver shipments, and mercantile practices that guaranteed a market for Spanish goods but simultaneously discouraged innovation. The
decline was everywhere: in the inflation born of too much silver, in the
contracting population, in the peninsula's anemic agricultural output,
and in a uniquely pessimistic and cynical literature whose symbol was
Don Quixote, an impoverished old man trapped in dreams of vanished
glory. In 1700 the last Hapsburg monarch, the physically and mentally
enfeebled Carlos II, died without heir; after a wrenching fourteen-year
European conflict known as the War of Spanish Succession, in 1704 the
crown passed to Philip of France, nephew of the mighty Louis XIV, the

so-called Sun King, on the condition that the two branches of the Bourbon family remain separate.

Philip (that is, Felipe V) and his advisors brought with them a new outlook on government. Bourbon France had selectively adopted large portions of Enlightenment thought, and ruling circles embraced the ideas of efficiency, science, secularism, free trade, and universal law while adhering tenaciously to kingship. Just as the sun governed the solar system, the monarch presided over the social order: Who was to say that this latter arrangement was somehow "unscientific"? Unlike the Hapsburgs, whose patchwork colonies employed different laws for different peoples, Parisian intellectuals championed simplicity and legal uniformity as the superior methods of governance. Spain's new king spent most of his days living the libertine good life, but his technicians, more dedicated to the rigors of public management, immediately began a program to revitalize the empire. Their approach was simple: put the colonies on a paying basis by liberalizing their economies while simultaneously tightening administrative control—above all, tax collection. These initiatives go by the name of the Bourbon Reforms, and they transformed Mexico and the other Spanish possessions.

Liberalization assumed many faces. Spain gradually did away with the cumbersome bottleneck of the Casa de Contratación (which controlled all aspects of trade, travel, and immigration to the New World), so that by 1796 any port within the empire could trade with any other port. The idea was to expand the volume of commerce, while extracting increased profits by means of a simple 7 percent ad valorem tax on all goods. Borrowing from the French model, the Bourbon reformers superimposed a new tax bureaucracy over Latin America, the so-called intendency system. Under this arrangement the crown divided Mexico into a series of large tax districts known as intendencies, each headed by an *intendant* and a string of local subordinates known as *subdelegados*. Manpower came strictly from Spain in order to prevent money from seeping into the pockets of avaricious creoles. True to stated goals, imperial revenues increased; Mexicans now paid more than ever to finance the mother country, and rural villagers found themselves liable to increasingly inflexible collections. Beyond those changes, the intendency organization proved so effective that the intendencies became the templates for the states of independent Mexico, with only minor variations added in the nineteenth (Campeche, Colima, Guerrero, Hidalgo, and Morelos) and twentieth centuries (Baja California, Baja California Sur, Nayarit, and Quintana Roo).

Target areas for development included the Bajío, the area north of Mexico City that held rich silver deposits. The fabled Peruvian silver mines had once ruled the colonial economy, but they lay far away, high in the remote Andes, and had been in slow decline since 1600; the eighteenth century belonged to Mexico. Spanish technicians and capital now moved into places like Guanajuato, Zacatecas, and Querétaro. Using the latest mining technology, these new entrepreneurs sank shafts hundreds of feet deep, often well below the water table but kept accessible through adits and hydraulic pumps. And to help safeguard the reinvigorated silver shipments, from 1770–76 Spain constructed the massive Fortaleza de San Carlos, outside of Perote, Veracruz. This seemingly impregnable structure later served in a number of capacities until being opened to the public as a historical site in 2007.

The colony soon towered as the world's largest producer of silver. Its mineral bonanza turned Pedro Romero de Terreros (1710–81), a poor peninsular boy who came to Mexico as employee of his more successful relatives, into the Conde de Regla, perhaps the richest man in the world in his day and time. He wasted no opportunity to insist that New Spain's government deliver on his privileges of Indian corvée labor, and with that labor he constructed massive new systems of mine shafts and adits that disgorged unprecedented amounts of the treasured mineral. In terms of religious belief, the reclusive Terreros was strictly traditional, and he devoted his fortune to acts of public piety such as founding chapels. He also created one of Mexico's most venerable institutions, a "royal pawn shop" known as the Monte de Piedad, which even today does a brisk trade in family jewels and yesteryear's electronic devices. The Conde once bragged that if the King of Spain chose to visit Mexico, he could provide His Majesty with a road of pure silver stretching from the coast to the capital. This exaggeration spoke a truth: Mexican mining was producing world-class yields, and the men who controlled those yields rivaled the great capitalist robber-barons of later centuries.

Beyond the glittering silver of the mines, New Spain experienced economic growth in a number of other key areas. Its southern provinces produced cochineal, the splendid—and splendidly profitable—red dye made by crushing the bodies of insects harvested from the nopal cactus.

Further to the north large cattle estates generated meat and leather. Sugar continued to dominate the rainy tierra caliente on both coasts, all the more so once the Haitian Revolution of 1791 knocked the world's foremost producer out of business.

Bourbon reformers financed this growth through a variety of means. The larger investors had access to Spanish capital, but those investors were few in number. The many smaller operations relied heavily on funds known as *capellanías*. These were church-controlled accounts, usually set up as bequests on the part of dying laymen and awarded to a particular priest. The latter in turn loaned out money at low interest, using real property as collateral, and in exchange for the interest received the priest celebrated a certain number of masses for the benefit of the original donor's soul. Capellanías seldom generated fortunes, and in almost no circumstances did the holders of loans ever foreclose: in this insecure world, better to receive ongoing small payments than to reclaim some unsellable property. But capellanías greased the wheels of everyday operations and allowed many ranchers or hacendados to improve their property, many merchants to invest in goods that they might sell for profit. The arrangement thrived for over three centuries, only ending with the Liberal revolution of 1850s Mexico.

The reforms also demanded a rethinking of New Spain's defense, a matter made all the more urgent by the Seven Years' War (1756–63). In essence an imperial power struggle between Britain and France, the war was fought principally in North America and the Caribbean. Naval power gave the victory to Great Britain, but not before Spain had entered the conflict on the losing side. Spain had to give up Florida (though twenty years later it regained the territory); it also endured a humiliating, six-month British occupation of the supposedly impregnable port city of Havana. The whole affair shocked Bourbon policy makers. They concluded that if the Americas were to remain in imperial hands, those same colonies would require a better system of defense.

From these concerns came the militias, grandfathers of the often-notorious Latin American armed forces. The idea was to create a series of coastal units commanded by loyal and well-trained peninsular officers but manned at the bottom by American recruits. The latter consisted principally of black and mixed-race volunteers, who obtained privileges such as pay, a spritz of training, and an even smaller spritz of prestige. They also received a coveted right known as the *fuero*, an arrangement whereby they could only be tried in military, not civil, courts. On the Gulf Coast in particular, recruitment focused on the many Afro-Mexican inhabitants, and to make service more attractive officers had to grant such unorthodox perks as allowing the men time off for fishing.

The militias supposedly excluded Indians, since the idea of arming them ran counter to the very essence of colonialism. But in practice officers often found it hard to fill the rosters and ended up quietly incorporating Yucatec Mayas and other non-Spanish speakers as a matter of expediency. Together these improvised legions waited for the invasion that never came—Britain being far more interested in expanding commerce in the Caribbean and North America—but the experience of service gave some members of the lower classes experience with arms and military discipline and injected a sense of self-assuredness that would come in handy a generation later.

Leadership in the militias came from peninsular officers, who were both well trained and unbreakably loyal to imperial interests. These men recruited and trained soldiers, but they also served as the conduits of the Spanish Enlightenment. Military officers were among the few individuals who received advanced education outside the purview of the Catholic Church. They read and wrote with proficiency, understood mathematics and large-scale logistical organization, and learned by hard experience how to conduct diplomacy and public administration. For said reasons they looked down on a rival institution that seemed petrified in its medieval pretensions. The military was the only Mexican institution that would grow under the anarchic conditions of the next hundred years.

The Bourbon Reforms advanced Mexico in many ways. The novohispanos of the late 1700s lived in a world that was more educated; they were aware of its vast geographical scope and great economic diversity, and with that knowledge came signs of true cultural sophistication. But from the distance of three centuries, its negative consequences loom far larger. Now more than ever, New Spain was inundated by peninsular officials intent on collecting taxes and making the colony responsive to royal interests. A question naturally arose in the minds of many: What are *they* doing here in *our* country? The reforms thus awakened the restless spirit of creole nationalism.

Economic quickening also hurt the lower classes, as times of growth often do. To begin with, more people inhabited that world: indigenous campesinos slowly rebounded from the apocalyptic plagues of the

The National Palace in Mexico City, scene of maximal political authority. Built on the site of one of Moctezuma's palaces, it has undergone frequent renovations and expansions over the centuries. The current exterior consists mainly of volcanic tezontle stones, while the interior displays a wealth of murals by Diego Rivera. Benito Juárez died of a heart attack here while reading at his desk. Courtesy of the Library of Congress.

Conquest, and by 1800 the population had swollen to a robust seven million. This growth in turn created land pressures that the Bourbon reformers could not resolve. In almost all places the solutions of the sixteenth and seventeenth centuries fell by the wayside; community land bases could no longer support a younger generation. In addition, stricter taxation, rising property values, and the spectacle of an ever-richer class of peninsulars and creoles set Mexico on the road to social unrest.

Mexicans Rethink Their World

Tax schedules may have come in for revision, but equally momentous was the change of ideas in Mexican society. The eighteenth century witnessed the birth of a movement we call the Enlightenment, which built on centuries of accumulated knowledge and stressed order and reason. In this world the human race improved its lot by understanding and following uniform natural laws. The Spanish rolled out their own Enlightenment cautiously: universal laws and human perfectibility met with acceptance, while the concepts of monarchy, established religion, and social hierarchy remained off-limits. It was within these confines of thought that the Mexican Enlightenment came to be.

The reshaping of intellectual climates requires communication, and to that end the written word offers the most important tool. Mexico City had printing presses since the mid-1500s, and even if the provinces remained far behind (in Yucatán, for example, there was nothing of the sort until 1812), colonials did indeed produce, disseminate, and above all read printed material. Moreover, the existence of the usually lethargic Holy Office did not prevent foreign materials of all sorts from reaching the hands of intellectually curious colonials, particularly in the second half of the eighteenth century.

Mexico also expanded its base of institutions necessary for the advancement of ideas and culture. True, universities had existed here for some time; the Royal and Pontifical University had opened in Mexico City in 1551, and its Puebla counterpart was founded thirty-six years later. But in the latter half of the Bourbon era, they were joined by Guadalajara (1792) and Yucatán (1812), the bases of two modern institutions. That same period also witnessed the emergence of at least two other schools that bestowed long-term benefits. Mexico City's Academy of San Carlos, which opened in 1793, taught, and continues to teach, the European tradition of fine arts. In colonial times it boasted such luminary instructors as its first director, Valencia-born Manuel Tolsá (1757–1816), a polymath sculptor and architect whose works still grace the older parts of the capital. In 1811 the Colegio de Minería (mining college), opened its Tolsá-drafted edifice in heart of the old city. The college offered secular instruction in the fields of math, engineering, and applied sciences: although too late to rescue the sinking empire, it was noteworthy as the beginning of new directions in Mexican education.

Naturally enough, the first wave of enlightened Mexican thinkers came from within the Catholic Church, the only institution whose members enjoyed the time, education, and resources necessary to transcend daily concerns. The natural sciences attracted the most attention, perhaps because they offered the building blocks for other sciences or perhaps because they posed no immediate threat to the social order. In the case of Mexico, Enlightenment scholars also studied archaeology and ethnohistory.

The herald of this new age was the formidable Jesuit scholar Carlos de Sigüenza y Góngora (1645–1700). Born of Spanish parents in Mexico City, he entered the seminary of Tepotzotlán (see chapter 2), where he studied, among other things, the indigenous languages of the colony. In the course of his career he turned his restless intellect to such topics as archaeology, astronomy, geography, and mathematics, and he authored a number of works that document New Spain's society and culture. A commanding figure in the history of the New World's intellectual growth, Sigüenza's greatest contribution lay not in any single doctrine or discovery but rather in showing his fellow creoles how the mind could engage productively in the things of their own country.

Building off the work of Sigüenza, Jesuit writer Francisco Javier Calvijero (1731–87) wrote the ten-volume *Historia antigua de México*, together with a four-volume work on Baja California. The Catholic Church's expulsion of the Society of Jesus in 1767 meant that Calvijero did most of his writing in Italy, but he maintained extensive correspondence with researchers in Mexico itself. Another cleric, José Antonio de Alzate y Ramírez (1737–99) published numerous pamphlets on archaeology, astronomy, and above all meteorology, and founded the *Gaceta de Literatura de México* in 1788. Antonio de León y Gama (1735–1802) was not a priest, but rather a lawyer educated at the Jesuit college of San Ildefonso. While he made his living working for Mexico City's *ayuntamiento* (town council), he wrote seminal pieces on the pre-Columbian past and authored the first analysis of the so-called Aztec calendar (actually not a calendar at all but a massive stone monument to the sun god), that construction workers had unearthed in the main plaza in 1790.

In the person of Manuel Abad y Queipo (1751–1825), an Asturian who immigrated to Mexico and rose to become bishop of Michoacán, Enlightenment thought turned to social matters. Abad y Queipo fiercely criticized the marginalization of indigenous Mexicans and urged land reform and tribute abolition as ways to rectify the problem. Although he decried violent change, his opposition to Spain's conservative reaction of

1815 caused his recall; the former bishop died in prison in Spain ten years later. Admittedly, the number of Enlightenment thinkers here numbered no more than a handful, but their position in the worlds of education, printing, and administration gave them an influence on later generations that far exceeded their original numbers.

It was one thing to dabble in the natural sciences; after all, a few insect collections never hurt anybody. But in the broadening climate of the colonial Enlightenment, the very tenets of theology felt the pendulum swinging away from the dour mindset of the seventeenth century. Religiosity in that earlier period had often conformed to one of two extremes. The first of those had been one of baroque gloom: as if trapped in a lurid Caravaggio canvas, mankind languished as prisoner to the darkness and violence of a fallen world and could only hope for redemption through the divine light of the afterlife. In contrast stood popular religion, with its carnivalesque revelry torn straight from the Middle Ages, only here it was melded with the unmistakable flavor of indigenous beliefs.

The rise of Enlightenment knowledge, together with pressure from the Protestant challenge, nudged the Catholic Church in a new direction. Among church thinkers a new "theology of optimism" began to emerge. Hopes for a better life in this world and the next now twinkled on the horizon. Church art became more cheerful as blue skies chased away inky blackness, and hellfire slowly disappeared from sermons. Meanwhile, a new Catholic current known as Jansenism cautiously adopted some of the Protestant critique. It rejected the old concepts of ostentatious public piety. Devotion, the Jansenists argued, involved inner acts of spirituality, and that meant reigning in the Rabelaisian village fiestas with their prancing costume devils and endless fireworks. It also meant restraining the lavish burials and endless endowment of chapels that rich Mexicans had come to expect. Faith involved a better life, a happier one, but this was a path accessed through sobriety, self-restraint, and private piety, a kind of Puritanism tailor-made for the Hispanic world.

These ideas appealed to many eighteenth-century theologians and worked their way into the sermons of village priests, but they failed to satisfy secular antagonists. Hardly atheists, Bourbon reformers nevertheless disliked rival claimants to power, and they targeted the Catholic Church as a barrier to progress. To that end the Bourbons launched a campaign of secularization. Felipe V and his successor kings resumed the old Hapsburg privilege of patronato real, in this case by simply declining to authorize new transfers of priests to the colonies; the size of the Spanish American clergy consequently contracted by 50 percent over the course of the century. In 1717 the Crown prohibited the foundation of new convents and seventeen years later imposed a decade-long ban on the introduction of regular orders.

The single greatest target of these initiatives was the Society of Jesus. Unlike priests in the far older Franciscan order, the Jesuits had taken no vows of poverty; their order, set up along quasi-military lines and formidable in matters of education and debate, came late to New Spain, but by the mid-eighteenth century it dominated elite education. However, their success proved their undoing. The Spanish Crown continually suspected that the Jesuits' ultramontane policies rendered them disloyal. In 1767, following the Portuguese policy in Brazil twelve years earlier, Carlos III banished the Jesuits from Spain's American colonies. The expulsion stirred up no end of ill will. Prominent Mexicans resented the loss of their educators, and several riots had to be put down by force.

The expulsion of the Jesuits, however unpopular at the moment, came relatively early, and none of the leaders of the later independence movement had a personal memory of the Jesuit presence. But collectively, the changes in Mexico's intellectual climate readied the country for a revolution that few could have predicted in 1750. Devout Mexicans increasingly saw a world of piety and virtue under siege. When the wars for independence wars came, village priests figured prominently as insurgent leaders.

Less controversial than religion, public health was another Enlightenment cause that the Crown could safely champion. The finest moment of the imperial government came in 1803, when Dr. Francisco Javier de Balmís launched a three-year expedition to take the recently developed smallpox vaccination technique (1798) to parts of the Spanish Empire. Methods were crude: Balmís traveled with a series of boys who had suffered a mild case of the disease and used them as a human chain to keep up the necessary pus, passing it from one host to the other. Despite the inherent difficulties of the assignment, the Balmís expedition was the largest of its kind attempted at that time, and it presaged later world-health campaigns by over a hundred years. Public health concerns also emerged in the form of a campaign to stop burying the dead in churches. People of the era widely (if mistakenly) believed that the smell of decaying corpses actually generated disease. The Bourbon officials, men who often found church prerogatives more offensive that the smells in question, seized on public health as a pretext for easing away church control of such life passages as burial. Ayuntamientos began to decree burial in atriums, the large open spaces outside of churches, instead of beneath or behind the interior masonry. Bourbon reformers and killjoy Jansenists notwithstanding, affluent creoles still treasured their traditional form of interment as the highway to heaven and persisted in said burials even as the mid-nineteenth century reforms prohibited them altogether in favor of secular, city-owned cemeteries.

These same trends also revealed themselves in the visual arts. Perhaps artists like Villalpando had overstated the case; perhaps humanity was not enveloped by some crushing darkness. More optimistic tendencies emerged in the works of Miguel Cabrera (1695–1760), Mexico's most important eighteenth-century artist and perhaps the first of his craft to achieve celebrity status. A specialist in the much-loved *casta* (literally, "caste") paintings that adorned so many homes—even as the casta system itself was falling into decline—Cabrera rose to become the court painter of the archbishop of Mexico. At times the figures in his canvases swirl above the ground with Rubens-inspired movement, but at other moments they retain a charming, earthbound simplicity lacking in European counterparts. Significantly, Cabrera was among the first Mexican painters to adopt the portrait genre. His work represents an important if overlooked phase of national art and has enjoyed renewed interest in the twenty-first century.

The Empire Looks Northward

Eighteenth-century Spain also embarked on another campaign, one that was to cast a shadow across later Mexican history: an attempt to shore up and expand the colony's northern frontier. After the great silver boom and the ensuing Chichimeca War of the 1550–1600 period, affairs had settled considerably in the region as disruptive penetration gave way to a hundred years of slow, steady growth. The dust from the Indian revolts of the 1680s and 1690s had hardly settled when authorities received yet another imperial scare: news that the French had established a colony in coastal Texas, near the modern-day city of Victoria, under the haphazard leadership of Robert Cavelier, Sieur de La Salle. Concerned, Spain established a system of missions and presidios reaching into the northern territory, the end point of which was the mission of San Antonio de Béjar, founded in 1718. Thus began the city that was to serve as the nucleus of Spanish-speaking Texas colonization and that until World War II would be the largest Hispanic center in the United States.

But San Antonio was only the beginning. In 1765 the great Bourbon administrator José de Gálvez (1720–87) arrived in New Spain, endowed with the extremely broad powers of *visitador*, an official authorized to enact whatever reforms he saw necessary for strengthening the colony. Gálvez belonged to that class of men who invariably found others to be slothful and incompetent. Energetic to the point of mania, Gálvez set out to reinvigorate New Spain while simultaneously making it more pliable to royal interests. He imposed that trusty tool of imperial soakings, the tobacco monopoly, and raised taxes on a broad number of consumer products. He also oversaw the expulsion of the Jesuits in 1767 and favored peninsulars over creoles when it came to appointments and commercial opportunities. The visitador also lowered the price of the crown-controlled mercury, an element vital to silver refining; this step, together with other encouragements, proved instrumental in boosting yields of silver bullion.

However, Gálvez will always be remembered for his obsessive determination to assert imperial authority over the vast frontier beyond the Bajío. Personally led by the visitador himself, the Spanish established semimilitary colonies in what was then called Alta California, aided by a Franciscan order that was enjoying a second wind following its great missionary work of the 1500s. Spaniards, including Hernán Cortés, had made early forays here; the occasional English pirate weighed anchor in the harbors; while even the Russians, who had worked the northwest coast seeking fishing opportunities and animal skins, had entertained designs. But none of this spotty activity had ever materialized as sustained colonial development. Gálvez set out to change that. This was the beginning of the California settlements and the creation of a Spanish presence there that endured vibrantly until the war of 1846–48 and that has flavored the land ever after. The Franciscans now established such missions as San Diego, San Francisco, and Los Angeles. The order's leader in this campaign, friar Junípero Serra, was something of a throwback to the early sixteenth century. Known for traveling barefoot from mission to mission, he remains a controversial figure in California history because, despite good intentions, his efforts to round up Indians into missions turned those places into veritable death camps. Between 1769 and 1821 the indigenous population of Alta California declined by two-thirds.

At times the pressure of this vast undertaking caused the micromanagerial Gálvez to crack; in such moments he talked seriously of raising an army of monkeys to conduct his frontier Indian wars. But no monkeys came forward, and at Crown insistence the visitador at last returned to Spain in 1771, where he continued to serve in the Council of the Indies until his death fifteen years later, taking a leading role in suppressing populist revolts that swept across South American colonies at that time. José de Gálvez died in 1787, a year before the passing of the king whose interests he had served so unstintingly.

The huge area of Chihuahua (later to become Mexico's largest state) suffered similar problems. Spain had an unrivaled record in defeating indigenous groups but met its match in the tough-as-nails Apache and Comanche bands who roamed the huge area of what is now West Texas into northern New Spain. The various Apache groups had come from western Canada in the fifteenth century and lived by raiding agricultural communities in the Four Corners region, and while some adopted farming, others refused to abandon their lives as warriors. The Comanches, meanwhile, controlled an enormous swath of the Great Plains stretching from central Texas into Kansas, and they benefited from that territory's abundance of horses and bison. To ward off attacks and maintain some sort of presence, in 1778 Spain created a new administrative region called Provincias Internas. It homesteaded Spanish-speaking settlers with the promise of land, money, and tax exemptions; in return the settlers had to organize into frontier militias, keeping muskets always loaded and handy. The policy worked reasonably well, but in addition to holding off Apaches and Comanches, it also created a hardy class of sharpshooting frontiersmen who valued their autonomy and whose hostility to Mexico City fed directly into the revolution of 1910.

To the northeast the fear of French incursions led to a more successful version of the California project. In 1748 soldier-turned-impresario José de Escandón (1700–70) launched colonization in the territory of Nuevo Santander, an entity that he would govern for the next twenty-two years.

In settling his kingdom Escandón virtually exterminated the Pima Indians. His promises of a land of small freeholders mostly fizzled, as military leaders had the political influence to become large landowners. But at least some of his followers did establish modest private ranches, and the surnames of those followers—Anzaldúa, Longoria, and Treviño, for example—remain common today in what has become the long, coast-hugging state of Tamaulipas.

Bourbon expansion into northern New Spain achieved only mixed success and left a troubled legacy for the later Mexican nation. While the late-breaking initiatives of the 1770s onward greatly expanded imperial territory, they did little in the way of establishing firm political control or sustained settler colonies. If anything, Spanish-speaking colonists resented Mexico City's distant control even more than they did encroachment by rival empires. Settlers complained constantly of New Spain's inability to defend them from Apache, Navajo, and Comanche groups that, increasingly squeezed between Mexico and the United States, found little alternative to raiding Mexican settlements as a way of surviving. The great northward push thus added a new set of concerns quite different from those of the entrenched colonial order of the Mesoamerican heartland.

Reasons for these shortcomings varied. Certainly, a daunting geography and tenacious indigenous resistance combined to limit colonization. But above all, the policy foundered for a lack of settlers. The viceroyalty's insistence on Spanish Catholics ruled out the sort of immigrant waves that defined the nineteenth century. Indigenous peasants, meanwhile, stayed rooted in their southern villages, partly from the weight of ancient custom, partly from the very policies that New Spain had implemented. The community land grants and legal protections may have ensured inequality and relative poverty, but they also guaranteed subsistence and survival, and few families willingly traded these guarantees for some imaginary wealth in the vast wastelands beyond Querétaro and Guanajuato.

The problem became obvious enough even before independence. After 1790 the office of Spain's chief minister had fallen into the hands of a favorite, one Manuel de Godoy (1767–1851), who led the country through a series of failed attempts at restoring national power. In his eagerness to reassert European clout, Godoy sacrificed sprawling chunks of northern New Spain. Madrid had already begun to retreat from the Pacific northwest (roughly, southern Alaska and the coasts of Washington and Oregon) in 1790; five years later Godoy added to the dissolution by ceding to the United States the Alabama-Mississippi territory, a land that later became the scene of the great cotton boom and an essential motor of the world textiles economy. For all intents and purposes, then, the northern frontier remained a weak flank, exposed to both indigenous resistance and a predatory Anglo expansion, and those problems would fall squarely onto the laps of Mexican statesmen after 1821.

Napoleon Convulses the Empire

For there to be Mexican statesmen there had to be a Mexico, and as yet no such nation existed. Throughout history poor people—like the campesinos of Bourbon times—have suffered, but their protests and up-risings have seldom succeeded without some calamitous division within the ruling classes. That fact applied to Mexico as well. Creoles occupied the key slots in late colonial society, and, rhetoric notwithstanding, few of them envisioned some sort of egalitarian, multiethnic republic. And while they might resent snubs from a haughty Spaniard, they found it hard to sever the bonds of heart and mind that tied them to the monarchy. Perhaps it was force of habit; perhaps creoles needed a hierarchy that assured their superiority to indigenous Americans. Spanish-speaking colonials knew that it was the king of Spain, and not the papacy, who presided over their Catholic world order. He promulgated the laws they obeyed; his right of patronato real made him the overseer of the colonial church; and the conquests of his ancestors invested him as the symbol of their right to rule over subject peoples of the Americas.

In the early 1800s these grand securities crumbled, and they did so with a speed that amazed everyone. Destabilization began in Europe it-self. Spain had opposed the radical forces of the French Revolution of 1789 onward, going so far as to side with its ancient enemy, Britain. But the great Terror of Robespierre ended in 1795, and seven years later Napoleon, now firmly in control of France, imposed a peace treaty that bound Spain and France together in mutual defense. It was under these conditions that Carlos IV, partly at the urgings of Godoy, returned the

Louisiana Territory to France in October 1802, on the condition that it not be sold. Napoleon betrayed that promise six months later, thus handing the nascent United States the key to continental hegemony. The cumulative losses of colonial territory, together with the chief minister's continuing influence over the royal family, turned the country into a hive of pro- and anti-Godoy intrigues.

Still, the French-Spanish alliance continued, and its cost led the Spanish Crown to impose a provocative solution. Much of the loan capital active in Mexico, particularly the smaller loans that kept the country functioning on a daily basis, was in the hands of the clergy. Small-scale provincial entrepreneurs in particular depended on capellanía loans to keep them operating. Under an 1804 decree known as the Consolidación de Vales, the king of Spain demanded that all such loans be recalled and that the money be handed over to the Crown. Viceroy José de Iturrigaray applied the law with unflinching rigor, and within four years the Consolidación squeezed more than ten million pesos out of New Spain. In exchange the loan-holders were to receive long-term bonds that would supposedly allow them to recoup their lost capital, but those who knew anything about the Spanish Crown's many debt defaults realized that they would never see their money again.

Worse news soon followed. The prospect of life without monarchy suddenly became reality when Napoleon invaded the Iberian Peninsula in 1808. Fed up with the intrigues of the Spanish court, he deposed the decrepit Carlos IV, arrested his son Fernando, and placed his own brother Joseph at the head of a pro-French Spanish state. Thus began a brutal six-year civil war that was to transform both the European and American worlds. Spaniards rallied in defense of their monarch, now Fernando VII, *el deseado*, and their guerrilla struggles and the consequent French counterinsurgency inspired the horrific scenes of Goya's canvases. Under these circumstances Spanish and American liberals came together at Cádiz, a free Spanish territory located at the tip of a peninsula and protected from French attacks by the dual presence of the Spanish and British navies, to compose a constitution for the society that they hoped would emerge following the eventual expulsion of the French.

The question of who held sovereignty placed Viceroy Iturrigaray in a delicate situation. The Junta de Sevilla had emerged as the leading force in Spanish resistance, and it demanded loyalty from the colonies; Iturrigaray was no separatist, but he maintained close relationships with the Mexico City ayuntamiento, a collection of wealthy creoles who saw themselves as colonial leaders. After all, Mexico had always dominated American affairs, and the viceroy was uncertain whether he could trust representatives of Sevilla. Money lay at the heart of the matter, since Iturrigaray sat on the millions collected during the Consolidación de Vales, waiting to direct the money to its proper destination. A coup organized by more conservative members of the New Spain establishment settled the matter; Iturrigaray fell, the aging if reliably pro-Spanish Marshal Pedro Garibay took his place, and the ten million pesos sailed on to Sevilla. But the coup deeply angered Mexican creoles, and resentment over rough treatment by peninsulars led in direct fashion to later armed uprisings in favor of Mexican independence.

A Radical Priest Calls the People to Arms

These twists and turns naturally affected Mexico's stability. Would-be separatists had existed for some time now, but they amounted to little more than a fringe element, coffeehouse radicals who lacked the support of either the indigenous masses or the creole upper crust. Psychological restraints kept extremism in check, for most creoles balked at the idea of life without a Spanish monarch. But equally powerful was the fear of bloodshed: once the lower classes had risen up, might they not kill creoles and peninsulars alike? After all, precedent stood against them. The separation of Britain's North American colonies from their monarch had for the most part avoided social upheaval in England, but the subsequent French Revolution had brought about the execution of the king and thousands of the French aristocracy. Worse still, the Haitian Revolution of 1791–1804 had spiraled from a quest for greater creole privileges to the death or exile of every single white colonist. This consideration kept would-be Mexican nationalists in their parlors and well away from the Indian and mestizo masses.

When revolutionary leadership did come, it took a familiar form: someone whose birth and education positioned him as part of the ruling classes, but who for some reason became disaffected and turned his abilities against the very order that nurtured him. In the case of Mexico, the individual whom fortune chose to break the colonial impasse was both a man of his time and yet a perpetual misfit, a visionary soul in search of some better way that even he did not fully comprehend. Miguel Hidalgo y Costilla was born in 1756, the son of a hacienda manager in the province of Guanajuato. Of European ancestry, he grew up speaking not only Spanish but also the indigenous languages of the men his father supervised. Hidalgo attended the Royal and Pontifical University in Mexico City, and in 1778, at the age of twenty-two, became a priest. Between 1779 and 1792 he taught at the Colegio de San Nicolás Obispo (essentially a high school) in Valladolid, eventually rising to the position of rector.

Miguel Hidalgo was intellectually brilliant, gifted in languages, charismatic, and in most regards the very picture of the Bourbon creole establishment. But the man had a dark side. Though now a priest, Hidalgo was rebellious by temperament and greatly enjoyed gambling, dancing, and the company of attractive women. His knowledge of French brought him into contact with the French *philosophes*, leading him to doubt many of the dogmas of his own religious institution. A Mexican in a Spaniard's world, he inevitably collided with the authorities around him, while his intellectual gifts and often reckless behavior, together with his position as a man poised midway between the highs and the lows of society, uniquely qualified him as the leader of a rebellion that no one else dared to ignite. Eventually Hidalgo's penchant for randy living and his haphazard administrative style caught up with him. Church authorities removed him to a series of remote rural parishes where, they erroneously assumed, he could do no harm. In 1804 he settled in as the cura of tiny Dolores, Hidalgo, a town very much part of the Bajío's complex of mines and haciendas.

Unwittingly, the bishops had tossed the bothersome Hidalgo into a briar's patch. By the time the new cura said his first mass, the great boom of the previous century had gone flat. Bourbon-era mining initially took advantage of cheap labor and low prices, but over time prices rose, causing profits to decrease. Maintenance of the shafts and adits remained expensive, while inputs like the mercury used to smelt the silver grew more expensive. Desperate to salvage their investments, mine owners tried abolishing the *partido*, the share of mineral ore that miners had traditionally enjoyed as part of their pay, but this provoked only discontent. In 1776 one of the Conde de Regla's mines experienced the first-ever

Miguel Hidalgo y Costilla, the man who launched the Mexican war for independence on September 16, 1810. A born rebel, Hidalgo tapped into a vast undercurrent of discontent, but he proved a poor political strategist and a hapless military commander. His remains now lie with those of other leaders in a mausoleum beneath the Angel of Independence monument, commonly called "El Ángel," in Mexico City. Courtesy of the New York Public Library.

strike by Mexican mine workers; an inspector sent from Mexico City concluded in favor of the strikers, the first-ever victory by Mexican organized labor. Winning back silver nuggets must have felt good, but this minor victory did nothing to arrest the overall decline, and by the beginning of the nineteenth century the Bajío was in full-on recession. At its height it had drawn men from all over the colony, coaxing them out of their subsistence villages and into the vicissitudes of global price changes. For the first time Mexicans tasted the bitter drink called unemployment.

The crisis quickly bled into other sectors of the Bajío. Property owners had drawn workers to handle the traditional corn-and-cattle agriculture, but as New Spain's economy expanded, estate owners increasingly shifted to wheat and other products for urban markets. Fundamentals like corn and beans became increasingly expensive, and troops often transported what was available to feed the cities. Meanwhile, the Consolidación in 1804 had hammered smaller businessmen who depended on loans from village priests, while a severe drought in the years 1808–09 worsened the situation. Area food costs rose to four times their earlier value. Finally, the once-prosperous textile industry also staggered as Catalan, and later British, producers began to inundate the Mexican market. Anyone casting his eyes around the once-splendid region now saw only a world of hurt.

In other times and places, the self-reliant peasantry might have shrugged off these misfortunes. Years of stagnant tradition had enveloped the rural communities like amber around flies, immobilizing them in a never-ending colonial yesteryear; when hard times came, people retreated to the security of the backstrap loom and the cornfield. But the boom changed all that, leaving the Bajío's transplanted population unprepared for bust. The province of Guanajuato, one of the most densely populated in all of New Spain owing to its dazzling mining industry, now faced hard times. Angry people gathered in small groups to curse the day, and in the wealthy Spaniards—with their stately homes, stylish Rococo carriages, and impeccably groomed manners—those same people believed that they had discovered the human face of their misfortunes.

Shocked by the conditions at hand, Hidalgo experimented with a variety of bootstrap remedies. But to his consternation, authorities vetoed such local development projects as silkworms, beekeeping, and brickmaking as running counter to mercantile policy. However abortive, these initiatives yielded considerable purchase in terms of Hidalgo's relationship to his parishioners. They saw him as the people's pastor, an intelligent and socially committed leader whose decisions merited their support and obedience.

As if in an opera by Giuseppe Verdi, Hidalgo found himself drawn in to a secret plot for independence. A group of Guanajuato gentry had concocted the idea of suborning the local military garrison and pronouncing against Spain. The group included military officers Miguel Allende and Juan Aldama and the highly competent mining engineer José Mariano Jiménez: affluent creoles all. Once involved, the impetuous and brilliant Hidalgo quickly assumed a position of leadership. Their original plan called for action in December 1811, but someone betrayed them, and the group learned that a squadron of soldiers was coming from Mexico City to arrest them. Desperate, Hidalgo rang the church bells of tiny Dolores on the morning of September 16, 1810—the date ever after revered as the beginning of Mexican independence—and summoned the people of his parish to arms.

Events veered off script almost immediately. In his call to the people of the Bajío, Hidalgo said nothing about Mexican independence, which after all was a construction straight from gentlemen's parlor talk and mostly incomprehensible to the ethnic masses. Rather, he denounced bad government and called on his people to rise up to defend the sadly sequestered Fernando VII as the rightful King of Spain. But whatever his exact words, they struck a note among the poor folk of hard-hit Guanajuato province. Within a short time Hidalgo found himself heading the largest armed movement seen in this land since the days of the Mexica. Peasants, destitute sharecroppers, and laid-off miners all howled for revenge against a late Bourbon upper crust that had profited at their expense. Allende and the others urged caution, but Hidalgo insisted that mass uprising was the only way, and with the crowd behind him, assumed the title of *generalísimo*.

Allende's concerns proved all too prophetic. The mob tore through the Bajío, destroying lives and property. Among other jacqueries, they destroyed pumping equipment; Mexico's great silver mines flooded and collapsed, not to be revived until the latter decades of the century. Things reached a peak on September 28, when his forces overwhelmed the Spanish loyalists holed up in Guanajuato's Alhóndiga, the fortress-like public granary. In addition to killing all the defendants, the insurgents sacked and burned the building—which Hidalgo in earlier years had actually helped to construct.

Even his fellow insurgent leaders found Hidalgo's personal behavior alarming. At first he maintained a degree of discipline, but eventually success went to his head. Far from containing the rampages, Hidalgo at times seemed to revel in the violence, and he countered all protests with an argument that many revolutionaries have adopted: lead the parade or it marches over you. To that effect, Hidalgo took to wearing an enormous sword and somewhat incongruously adopted the additional title Su Serenísima Alteza (his most serene highness), a sobriquet later adopted by Antonio López de Santa Anna and often mentioned with a tone of ridicule, but that was in fact a creation of the village priest turned liberator. (Incidentally, we have no portrait of Hidalgo drawn from life. All likenesses follow artistic convention by depicting him as a tall man in his fifties, eyes soulful in expression, with white tufts of side-hair on a bald head.)

The insurgent wave looked unstoppable, but as Hidalgo moved southward and out of the unique conditions of the Bajío, his army lost momentum. The self-sufficient Indian villages that dotted the Valley of Mexico were isolated from the sort of international economic downturns that had flogged the Bajío, and those same villages failed to rally to the insurgent cause; in fact, those same communities more commonly supported the royalist cause. Nor did support materialize in other quarters. Hidalgo's banner images of the Virgin of Guadalupe failed to reassure the city's wealthy and privileged creoles, who closed ranks in defense of the colonial order, exactly the opposite reaction for which Hidalgo and others had hoped. For the next fifty years Hidalgo and his rebels became for conservative Mexicans what France's Committee for Public Safety was to the European ruling classes of the early nineteenth century: a taste of the bloodshed they could expect from social levelers and populist rabble-rousers. Finally, Hidalgo held back from attacking Mexico City itself. Perhaps he nursed reservations about unleashing destruction on the epicenter of a colonial culture of which he himself was a part. Or perhaps he feared the victory would be too costly. Although he possessed overwhelming numerical superiority, his forces lacked weapons, training, and discipline, and even if victorious, they were likely to be mauled in the process.

Whatever the reason, Hidalgo ultimately decamped from the city's outskirts. The decision provided the Spanish government with the break it needed. General Félix Calleja readied a trained and disciplined force of some six thousand men outside of Guadalajara, one of the viceroyalty's principal cities. There he defeated Hidalgo's troops at Puente de Calderón, outside of Guadalajara, on January 11, 1811, in part owing to great discipline and military professionalism on the part of royalist forces, in part owing to a stray shell that hit and exploded the insurgents' munitions carriage. Hidalgo's great rebellion had lasted a mere four months. He and the other leaders fled north toward San Antonio, Texas, where they hoped to find support and protection, but they were captured near Chihuahua City and inevitably condemned to death. The hapless Hidalgo was defrocked and forced to recant his actions. He was condemned to death along with all his co-conspirators. The cell where he spent his final night is still preserved beneath the city's central post office. Hidalgo suffered a singularly messy execution. The first volley missed altogether and the second succeeded only in inflicting painful wounds; at last the frustrated commander had to position his soldiers' rifles at point-blank range, aiming them directly at Hidalgo's heart. Once the four insurgent leaders were finally dead, their heads were packed in bags of salt and taken to Guanajuato, the soldiers stopping at all points in between so that locals could behold the price of rebellion. The heads were at last displayed in iron cages hung outside the very Alhóndiga the insurgents had so dramatically stormed. There the macabre trophies dangled for the next ten years.

In death as in life Miguel Hidalgo y Costilla has stirred controversy. Proclaimed the father of Mexican independence after the final break with Spain in 1821, his image today graces money, murals, and textbooks, and his tempestuous career continues to inspire both scholarly research and popular biography. To those who see mass action as central to Mexico's social evolution, Hidalgo towers as an inspiration. Those inclined to a more conservative vision, as well as many skeptical historians, point to the incoherence and weakness of his movement and to his glaring personal defects and simple inadequacy as a leader. They second the words of Mexican conservative statesman Lucas Alemán, himself a survivor of the sack of Guanajuato, who was eager to discredit the insurgents: "Hidalgo accomplished nothing." Both of these views stake out an extreme position. The radical priest's strategy of mass insurrection failed, and quite possibly the Mexico that emerged after 1821—to say nothing of the later dictatorship—bore little resemblance to the dreams of his enraged followers. But it is hard to ignore the fact that Hidalgo's chaotic assault on colonial hierarchies unleashed a series of events that inspired others, gave subsequent leaders the chance to attempt more successful approaches, placed grand issues on the table, and above all led many people to consider for the first time what had once been unthinkable: a Mexico for Mexicans alone.

After the Executions

As this tragedy played out, prominent citizens of Spain struggled to craft a new form of government: neither the hidebound conservatism of the Hapsburgs nor the radicalism of France, but something that lay midway between the two. The resulting constitution of 1812 mapped out a plan for what would have been one of the most forward-looking political charters of its time. It abolished the Inquisition and stripped the Catholic Church of its right to tax the peasantry. The constitution also authorized freedom of the press, separation of powers, political representation for the colonies, and universal suffrage for all male citizens except blacks— slavery at that time still motored the export economies of many of Spain's American colonies.

The constitution's authors inadvertently set in motion another chain of events that was to bedevil rural Mexico for the next hundred years. As part of their vision of legal uniformity, the Spanish liberals abolished the repúblicas de indios that had governed rural villages for centuries and instead granted the right of ayuntamiento to any town of a thousand or more residents, with office-holding theoretically open to all. Non-Indians hailed the move as a democratic advance. At last, it seemed, they could control their own destinies. But indigenous peasants discovered a quirk of physics: namely, that on a supposedly level playing field, water rolled downward onto them. Although equals in theory, with the old Hapsburg safeguards removed Indians simply could not compete with aggressive creoles and mestizos. They lacked they financial resources, political connections, and command of Spanish language and law necessary to succeed in public affairs. It was exactly the same problem that bedeviled liberal reformers a half century later, when the Mexican constitution of 1857 hypothetically guaranteed legal and political equality for all but instead birthed a powerful new class of hacendados, village merchants, and the political operatives who worked on their behalf.

For better or worse, the constitution of 1812 had little chance to sink roots. No sooner had the reforms made their way into urban and rural life in 1813 and 1814 than Spaniards finally expelled the French who occupied Spain. Fernando returned and immediately revoked the document, asserting royal absolutism and a return to the earlier Bourbon order. Mexican liberals saw the revocation as a heinous betrayal; conservatives remembered the brief constitutional months as a distasteful experiment in democratic misrule. The great political divide that was to torment Mexico for the next seventy years had begun.

Meanwhile, and contrary to what the colonial aristocracy had hoped, the rebellion did not die with Hidalgo. Leadership passed to one of his lieutenants, José María Morelos y Pavón (1765–1815), another parish priest dissatisfied with Spanish rule and its enforced injustices. In many regards he embodied the polar opposite of his late predecessor. Morelos was man of humble origins and scant academic brilliance; he worked for a time as a rancher and muleteer, and his iconography always portrays him clad in the head bandana of that latter profession. But the young man had higher ambitions. Through dint of individual study he managed to enter the Colegio de San Nicolás, there to train for the priesthood. As fate would have it, he came under the instruction of his distant relative Miguel Hidalgo and ultimately followed Hidalgo down the road of revolution.

Though less intellectually accomplished than Hidalgo, Morelos demonstrated a far keener understanding of people and conditions. He realized that it was better to have the campesinos remain in their villages, where they were able to furnish his troops with information and material support. He also recognized the value of guerrilla strategies, in which his ragtag forces waged a hit-and-run campaign against a superior royalist military. Morelos dominated western Mexico from 1811–15, operating mainly in what are today the states of Guerrero and Michoacán, but he also managed to take the distant cities of Orizaba and Oaxaca.

Breaking from the turbulence of Hidalgo, he made efforts to build a political framework for his movement. Morelos managed to draw in urban support, in part by practicing personal integrity and in part by curtailing the undisciplined massacres that have so marred his predecessor's reputation. In September 1813 Morelos convened the Congress of

Chilpanzingo; this body, intended as a forerunner of a national government, issued an extremely forward-looking document that proclaimed an independent Mexico free of slavery, torture, and tribute, a logical step beyond the 1812 Cádiz document. Stealing a page from George Washington, he consistently refused grand titles and instead presented himself as nothing more than a servant of the new nation of Mexico.

A series of unfortunate military setbacks soon followed, effectively halting any chance for the congressional declarations to become law. No longer distracted by the war against France, Spain responded with a campaign of counterinsurgency that was as brutal as it was thorough. Morelos struggled on until November 1815, at which point he was defeated and captured at the Battle of Tezmalaca, in Puebla province. Like Hidalgo, he was excommunicated and executed and soon entered the pantheon of national heroes. Unlike his volatile predecessor, Morelos won recognition even in his lifetime for honor, solid leadership, and unquestionable humanitarianism and patriotic sentiments, and his enormous reputation has endured to the present day.

By 1820 an observer might reasonably have concluded that the decade of separatist wars had ended and that something resembling the old order was about to return. Hidalgo, Allende, and Morelos had all perished, the great patriot armies had shriveled to mere bands, and surviving leaders remained hidden in remote redoubts, incapable of threatening the great centers of power. However, politics soon played an unexpected card. In 1820 Spain found itself caught in the same bind that would later hamstring its attempt to halt Cuban independence in 1898. Having alienated much of the colonial population through merciless counterinsurgency, the mother country succumbed to internal political currents. Spanish army officers discontented with Fernando's decision to revoke the constitution of 1812 revolted and forced the king to reverse himself: Spanish liberalism had returned, it seemed, and along with it the threats to monarchical absolutism, aristocratic privilege, and established religion.

The man who took advantage of this momentary reversal was another Mexican creole, albeit far different from the firebrand Hidalgo. Agustín de Iturbide y Arámburu (1783–1824) had carved out a reasonably successful career in the Bourbon military. He bore a well-earned reputation for cruelty and at various moments had stood accused of corrupt handling of government funds; neither of these charges were particularly unique for officers of the time, and in fact Iturbide had spent much of his professional life suppressing the insurgency. In later years conservative Mexicans came to look back on Iturbide as a glorious savior, rather in the way that conservative Chileans of today celebrate Augusto Pinochet. In fact, in his lifetime no one had anything particularly nice to say about him, and except for one brief moment he came up short on political skills.

Disagreeable fellow though he may have been, by 1820 Iturbide realized Spain's growing unpopularity. Like so many creoles, he shared a distaste for peninsular liberals and their insistence on constitutional power. Sent to ferret out Vicente Guerrero and other insurgent leaders, Iturbide instead opened secret dialogues with them, negotiations in which he promised the long-sought independence. The fruit of Iturbide's negotiations with insurgents and well-placed creoles was the Plan of Iguala, one that promised retooled Bourbonism in the form of three guarantees: independence (for Mexico), religion (via an established church), and monarchy (details to be arranged). The plan appealed to everyone. For the well-heeled set in Mexico City and other urban islands, it headed off radical upheavals. For the insurgents, it held out the possibility of a Mexican nation for which they had so desperately fought and allowed them to come in with dignity from the cold, hard life of the guerrilla warrior. In all this time the Great Facilitator fought no battles. His advance toward Mexico City became a procession, with one community after another fêting Iturbide and embracing his cause. He entered the capital on September 29, 1821, and proclaimed the beginning of a new nation.

As with Miguel Hidalgo, controversy has swirled around Iturbide long after the latter's untimely demise. More conservative Mexican interpreters see him as a transitional figure who worked to assure social stability and favored negotiation over violence, a founder whom the nation willfully neglected in favor of violent demagogues. Others dismiss Iturbide as a witless opportunist mostly acting at the prompting of others, a man who failed to perceive that the Bourbon era had really ended and whose political incompetence emerged clearly enough in his later—and conspicuously brief—career as national leader. Nevertheless, the event that he had so greatly helped set in motion, the independence of Mexico, had indeed come to pass.

4

Time of Triumph, Time of Troubles
The Early Mexican Nation, 1821–1876

Some nations, it seems, are born under a bad sign. Independence struggles often give way to conflicts concerning the rules and overall course of the new nation, but Mexico's case proved particularly traumatic. Within ten years the dreams that had motivated people to war against Spain turned into angry squabbles over taxes, representation, and military service. The country was to endure bitter civil wars, two massive foreign invasions, and the loss of nearly half of its national territory. What had gone wrong? And to this question we must add another, less commonly asked but equally important: What had gone right?

The new nation of Mexico, a political entity that strode confidently onto the world stage in 1821, glimmered with ideals and possibilities. The country burst with resources like minerals, forests, and farmlands. Its extensive coastlines gave access to fisheries and foreign trade. Above all, Mexico entailed a vast territory, including what is today California, Arizona, New Mexico, and Texas, and for a while stretched southward all the way to Costa Rica. Had the nation's original boundaries endured, the history of the entire Western Hemisphere might have taken a radically different course.

Beneath this bounty, however, the new republic faced problems so numerous and deep-rooted that they would have defied the wisest of statesmen. The land had ideally suited the peasant communities of ages past, but such organization ill prepared Mexicans for the brutal competition of the nineteenth century. Colonial settlements had taken root atop pre-existing Indian communities that depended on rain-fed agriculture, not river irrigation; as a consequence, the cities and towns of the new nation were not linked by navigable river systems that manmade canals could augment. Mule teams, plodding if sure-footed, offered the sole means for carting heavy freight over the mountains. Only primitive, bandit-infested roads connected one city with another. And while silver mining had an ancient vintage here, Mexico lacked the iron and coal deposits so essential for the dawning industrial age.

Worse, the wars for independence had devastated much of the existing infrastructure. The great silver mines of the Bajío, once a motor of the global economy and the recipient of millions of investment pesos, had flooded and collapsed. Haciendas were raided or in many cases simply abandoned. The rich sugar properties of the southwest lowlands had suffered extensively under waves of insurgency and royalist repression. In the hardest-hit areas agriculture simply reverted to subsistence farming—in the short run better for the common people, if prejudicial for long-term development.

Intimately connected to all of these problems was the social structure bequeathed by New Spain. In 1821 the population amounted to somewhere between 6.5 and 8 million people. About 18 percent were creoles. They had prospered under Spanish rule but were consistently denied the upper positions of church and state. Under the new order they resolved to correct that injustice. After 1821 creoles managed to claim their place in the sun, but time was not on their side: over the next two centuries intermarriage, together with changing social attitudes, remade the population of Mexico.

Some 22 percent of the population was mixed—both biologically and culturally—and was identified variously as casta or mestizo. The minutely graded caste system of the colonial period, the result of the Spanish obsession with *limpieza de sangre* (literally, "cleanliness of blood"), was falling into disuse; archaic terms like pardo took on a loose application, one often based on dead reckonings of wealth and phenotype, while *coyotes*, *tentes en el aire* (literally, "suspended in air," because one moved neither backward nor forward in social terms), and other exotic monikers had decamped altogether. Mestizos originally met with scorn in both Indian villages and polite Iberian society, but the passage of centuries changed the situation. Children of mixed unions assumed many of the creoles' aspirations, probably spoke Castilian as a first language, and bristled at the

Outside Mexico City and the provincial capitals, most citizens of the early republic lived in extremely humble dwellings. Thatched huts like the one seen here were a common sight in the hot lowlands of the two coasts. Nature provided the basic construction materials and quickly reclaimed the structures after they were abandoned. Courtesy of the New York Public Library.

thought of being considered indios. They might have lacked the expected social imprimatur, but the new republic needed individuals of talent, a need that allowed mestizos to attain positions in the army, in government, and, ever so slowly, in the Catholic Church itself. Finally, some six thousand blacks were still enslaved—not quite 1 percent of the total population—and most of them labored on sugar plantations in the hot country. They and their predecessors added their DNA to the Mexican population through unions with Spaniards, Indians, and mestizos. By 1821 people of mixed race no longer found that every man's hand was against them, but they were slated to fulfill at least one other biblical prophecy: the mestizos would inherit the earth.

The remaining 60 percent of Mexico's population was indigenous. Although the term "indio" was common, it lacked clarity and could serve a number of ends. Indigenous peoples varied significantly in both language and culture, from remote mountain dwellers to yeoman farmers living just beyond city limits. Their highest concentrations lay in the south, where even today such languages as Maya, Nahuatl, Zapotec, and Mixtec retain vitality. Commonly accepted markers of the indio included use of

For almost the entirety of the human habitation of Mexico, it was the fate of the women to spend most of their productive lives grinding corn and patting out tortillas. Only the coming of electric mills in the twentieth century liberated them from this task. Courtesy of the New York Public Library.

an indigenous tongue; clothing like *huarache* sandals, short pants, and embroidered, hand-woven fabric; residence in a rural village, with its ceremonial year based on public piety and a rough-cut equality; and, above all, profound poverty. In its most fundamental sense, the term "indio" had begun its journey toward current usage: namely, to refer to anyone whom the speaker considers to be inferior.

Beyond its physical limitations and its idiosyncrasies of folkways, Mexico also suffered from inexperience with its adopted form of democratic government. True, for years creoles had worked as lawyers, scribes, secretaries, educators, and ayuntamiento members and had acquired a crash course in parliamentary procedure via the constitution of 1812 and the independence debates. But actual democratic process was a novelty here—as it was elsewhere—and often conflicted with colonial Mexico's tradition of top-down governance, to say nothing of the millennium of rule by a pre-Columbian nobility advertising itself as divinity incarnate. Rule by popular vote can be challenging under the best of circumstances, but it proved especially elusive in the poor, illiterate, and tenuously connected young nation.

If anything, the electoral process simply reinforced existing inequalities. The newly created town governments, products of the constitution, remained the preserves of prosperous landholding and merchant families. Many creoles dreamed of somehow wresting land away from the peasants, who, they assumed, were holding everyone back. But at least for the first four decades of the Mexican republic, these plans gained little traction. Instead, the proud fathers of the ayuntamientos dedicated themselves to granting concessions for services, collecting rents and fines, and hosting genteel gatherings known as *tertulias* for their friends and families.

This same social division plagued one of Mexico's few national institutions, the army. Iturbide's merger of insurgent and royalist forces failed to do away with the hatreds, and officers from both camps attempted to use their power to eliminate rivals and to advance opposing views rooted in the independence struggle: one side populist, ethnically diverse, and socially liberal; and the other side steeped in Bourbon elitism, blood purity, and authoritarian politics. The key difference between 1808 and 1828 was that both sides could now operate more or less in the open, and both could plausibly claim political legitimacy.

Despite the glorious rhetoric of a nation for all Mexicans, then, the society remained deeply divided along class and ethnic lines. The more optimistic creoles believed that someday, perhaps in the course of a hundred years or so, Indians might perhaps evolve into viable citizens; the less-generous-minded assumed that "biological inferiority" made that evolution impossible. One way or another, just about everyone from the upper strata of society assumed that for the foreseeable future, real power would have to remain in their own hands and that any form of democratic government would require stage management in order to keep it from falling into the hands of the ignorant masses. These problems were by no means unique to Mexico, but here the long colonial past rendered them deeper and more intractable.

Finally, larger geopolitical issues intruded, as Mexico now began to feel the effects of the rapid and incomplete Bourbon expansion into the sprawling northern territories. The successful war for independence in the United States had swept away British restrictions on homesteading beyond the Appalachians; the optimism of the new republic, its prosperity, its burgeoning markets and growing population, had sent people spilling westward, bringing them into contact with a region in which the Mexican state had only a light presence and tenuous political control. To the contrary, Mexico's densely inhabited south generated little pressure for a northward push. The original colonial land grants, together with high infant mortality, an almost innate social conservatism, and strong linkages to place, kept indigenous peasants where they were. Mexico's vast northern desert, together with resistance from western and plains Indians, made northward population shifts difficult, while the United States' entry into Texas was simply one more step in a westward migration across a temperate zone, a migration that required few adaptations in farming, housing, or animal husbandry.

Pain, Passions, and Politics

The first fork in Mexico's path came in the dispute between federalists and centralists. The early federalists proposed a greater concentration of power at the provincial level, and they packed some strong arguments. Mexico's poor infrastructure made it impossible for someone in the capital to exercise quick and efficient governance. Moreover, conditions and needs varied radically from one place to the next, and that fact militated against rigidly uniform national policies. Finally, the federalists asked, what was the purpose of breaking with Spain only to recreate that same relationship with Mexico City?

Though by no means radicals, and certainly not social levelers or redistributors of wealth, the early federalists did lean toward a more liberal outlook. None of them considered indigenous peasants the equals of urban creoles, but they nursed an innocent faith that constitutional rule and expanded education would gradually improve the public and elevate political life. They also demanded personal liberties—in reading matter and public expression, for example—long denied under Spanish rule. Not surprisingly, federalists imbibed the late Bourbon resentment against the Catholic Church. While embracing religion as a source of public virtue, they feared both a Roman-controlled clergy and a return of inquisitional values, and they bequeathed those attitudes to the next political generation.

Centralists proposed the opposite arrangement. This viewpoint drew its consequence from a hard kernel of metropolitan merchants, but it also found favor among men whose home institutions operated along centralist lines: chiefly the church and the army. Rather like John Jay and his *Federalist Papers*, they argued than a fledgling republic required a strong guiding hand. They nursed grave doubts about the Indians as voters and looked to British-style property requirements as a way of disenfranchising those deemed unsuitable for public life.

Far more than did their federalist rivals, centralists celebrated religion as a common experience, the glue that held everything together. And on that point they did not err. Whether in the city or in the countryside, there was no faith but Roman Catholicism. At its upper levels the church constituted one of the few national organizations with a trained intelligentsia, and that fact made it a voice for social conservatism. The village priest, meanwhile, retained a leading voice in town affairs, while the physical church loomed as the largest and most imposing of urban constructions. The liturgical cycle dominated the calendar as always, and a culture of boisterous public piety still flourished, whether in the rituals of Holy Week or Corpus Christi, or in the more folkloric *finados*, the Day of the Dead celebrations, when loved ones returned to garner their respects from the living. People still preferred processions—the louder and gaudier, the more power the spiritual impact—featuring participants dressed as an odd assortment of figures ranging from pre-Columbian beings to Catholic saints to characters from Greek mythology. Throw all this out, conservatism warned, and Mexico would slide backward to the days of Tlaloc and loin cloths—or worse, turn Protestant.

Agustín de Iturbide was the first man to navigate these conflicting currents, and his time at the helm was destined to be brief. He assumed the presidency in 1821 and became "constitutional emperor" the following year. Taking advantage of sympathizers in Guatemala, he even succeeded in briefly annexing Central America. But in presenting an independent Mexico as a copy of late Bourbon Spain, with all its social conservatism safely intact, the hero of Iguala failed to control the popular democratic tendencies awakened over the preceding decade. A profederalist military coup deposed him in 1823 under the Plan of Casa Mata, allowing the liberator to pass into European exile. As Iturbide went, so too went his empire, and Central America withdrew from Mexican governance. Unable to resist hopes for a restoration, he returned the following year; he landed on the coast of Tamaulipas but was quickly arrested and shot.

Casa Mata may have ended the Iturbide's career, but it made a national name for one of its key supporters, a colonel named Antonio López de Santa Anna. Born in Xalapa, Veracruz, in 1794 to a Bourbon officer, he joined the military at a young age and served in a bloody counterinsurgency campaign in Texas during the time of Hidalgo. Santa Anna was most comfortable in Veracruz and resided there as much as possible, far from the *políticos*. Detractors paint him as epitomizing the creole caudillo: vain, ambitious, self-serving, attracted to cock-fighting and younger women, and not terribly competent in matters of state. Recent reappraisals deal more generously, arguing that he actually possessed charisma, tremendous energy, and strong organizational skills, and he was simply trying to forge a national direction under near-impossible circumstances. Regardless of the interpretation, though, there can be no denying that Antonio López de Santa Anna dominated Mexican politics for the next thirty years.

The short-lived empire and the ensuing litany of military coups, uprisings, and pronouncements that followed 1823 have drawn reams of ridicule, most of it centered on a creole machismo and egocentrism that placed personal ambitions above the national good. In reality Mexico's military officers had several reasons to claim national (if praetorian) leadership. They were virtually the only individuals in their society with experience in large-scale administration of resources and human beings. Given the many brushfires of the late Bourbon and early national period, they had acquired a more national perspective than that held by regional elites (to say nothing of the peasantry). They could look back on a tradition of service—sometimes, like Iturbide himself, on both sides of the conflict—in the wars of independence. Finally, they had the requisite skills of literacy, mathematics, and communication, making them the only serious rivals of the church. Just as the political order of the modern United States draws heavily on lawyers, so too, the circumstances of Mexico's early republic selected for men of arms.

The constitution of 1824—Mexico's first—broke sharply with the past. Unlike the rigidly centralized mechanisms of yore, the new order guaranteed extensive rights and autonomy to the provinces. It allowed states to govern themselves, and that practice appealed to the merchants, landed interests, and moneyed families who dominated most local and regional affairs. Early federalist state governments walked a balancing act: on one side lay the new promise of democracy and participatory government; on the other the inescapable facts of racial divides, language barriers, and the trinity of *latifundismo* (the system by which land was held in a few hands), unequal wealth, and concentrated power. Keeping faith with the 1812 document, state charters typically allowed for ayuntamiento elections for towns too small to have them before.

But beyond that, certain safeguards kept the old order in place. While all adult males could vote, presidential elections were indirect, meaning that voters-at-large elected patrician congressmen, who in casting their collective vote (each state had one) were almost certain to prefer individuals of their own class. Of equal importance, governors controlled potentially rowdy elections and city councils by means of an appointed administrator known as the *jefe político*, a late colonial holdover useful in managing Mexico's often unpredictable rural affairs. Jefes possessed broad powers, but most critically they functioned as the governor's eyes and ears. Below them, stationed away in remote villages, were the jefe's assistants, the so-called *alcaldes mayores*, another Hapsburg leftover. They performed the blunt-ended work of keeping indigenous peasants in line while administering from-the-hip justice in the small matters of local life. In the long course of the nineteenth century, the power of the jefe político only increased and in fact became a lynchpin of the later dictatorship of Porfirio Díaz.

States also controlled their own militias. The so-called Active Battalions, essentially armed civilians under the leadership of some prominent local, supposedly guaranteed against the return to monarchy, colonial or otherwise. During the Casa Mata revolt Santa Anna had insisted on them: to round out Mexico's leaky defense network, to offer sinecures to the local oligarchs who were to lead them, and to counterbalance the national army itself. The federal government's only fulcrum over the provinces lay in the form of the *comandancia militar*, a presidentially appointed officer drawn from the more dependably centralist forces.

Problems arose from the very beginning. For one thing, national tax collection proved difficult under the federalist arrangement. The constitution's indirect democracy also malfunctioned, since the electors whom popular votes selected invariably came from the more established and conservative sector, and their decisions more likely than not discounted the very voters who had placed them in power. Rather than electing the more popular liberation leader, General Vicente Guerrero (1782–1831), in 1828, state congresses opted for the conservative and elitist Manuel Gómez Pedraza, who had fought against the Hidalgo-Morelos revolutionaries only a decade earlier. The reverse put Guerrero in a ticklish situation: the vote had proceeded constitutionally, but as he and his supporters perceived, it had aborted popular will. Guerrero thus denounced the Gómez Pedraza government as fraudulent and crypto-Spanish, and with the aid of Santa Anna he overturned the results and assumed the presidency under the Plan of Perote. It was the first time since the death of Moctezuma that someone of indigenous blood had governed this land.

This coup ushered in a period of profound instability that was to persist for an incredible forty-eight years. Guerrero tried to deal generously with the defeated centralists, but kindness proved his undoing. The Plan of Perote allowed conservative stalwart General Anastasio Bustamante (1780–1853) the vice presidency, thus positioning him to lead a coup. Like his fellow centralists, Bustamante disdained Guerrero for his swarthy skin and garbled Spanish and hated as well the rabble who supported him.

But for the moment Guerrero, counseled by liberal Yucatecan ideologue Lorenzo de Zavala (1788–1836), had the argument, and for the next year or so attempted to move Mexico toward populist federalist governance.

The event that destabilized this already wobbly arrangement came from an ill-conceived scheme that had no chance of success and posed little danger. A certain Padre Joaquín Arenas, a fanatically pro-Spanish Franciscan, had attempted unsuccessfully to interest anyone who would listen in a scheme to reinstate colonial rule. When he approached a Mexican general about the possibility of leading a revolt, Arenas found himself betrayed and imprisoned. In the minds of his now-paranoid captors, isolated voices of pro-Spanish unrest magnified into a sweeping conspiracy, and Arenas, while failing in his dream of revolt, at least enjoyed the martyrdom he thought he deserved. But the damage was done. Immediately the Guerrero government decreed the removal of all Spaniards from Mexican territory. Fitfully applied, the campaign nevertheless reduced the approximately 6,600 peninsulars by two-thirds.

The hysteria failed to achieve national unity, but it did arouse the wrath of Spain, which now saw its citizens subjected to mindless persecutions. In response the Crown sent a protective detachment under General Isidro Barradas Valdés. Motives were mixed, because hard-liners held out hopes for a popular uprising that might restore the empire. In July 1829 the soldiers landed in remote Tampico, whose citizens conspicuously failed to rally to their support. Quite the opposite: when Santa Anna received the condition to dislodge them, he instantly recognized the publicity value of his mission and threw himself into it with full-on energy. Barradas found himself outnumbered and with no groundswell of support; the Spanish general was forced to sign a peace agreement on September 11. This victory made Santa Anna a hero, but, sensing that the time was not right for national power (if indeed that really was his goal), he retired with his accolades to his beloved hacienda Manga de Clavo, in Veracruz, thereby avoiding the crossfire of coming events.

As Santa Anna doubtless perceived, time was running out for the Guerrero government, whose anti-Spanish campaign had antagonized the wealthy creole sector. The president created a secondary army base wherein to prepare soldiers to assist against possible invasion; Vice President Bustamente headed it, but rather than gear up for another war with Spain, he instead used the situation to organize a coup against Guerrero

Antonio López de Santa Anna symbolizes nearly four decades of Mexican history. The Xalapa-born general tried to defend national sovereignty and stabilize an unruly early republic, but conditions consistently got the better of him—and of everyone else who tried to govern. He died in Mexico City in 1876, a forgotten pariah who has ever after taken the blame for circumstances beyond any single human's control. Courtesy of the New York Public Library.

himself. His plan succeeded, and in December 1829 Guerrero was forced to resign and retreat to his rural property in Michoacán.

For the next two years Mexico became the laboratory of conservative centralists. Lucas Alamán (1792–1853), a mining engineer as reactionary as he was talented, replaced Zavala as the state's ideological architect, while a host of lesser-known but equally elite individuals tried to roll back what they perceived as the disruptive effects of democracy. Defeated and isolated, meanwhile, former president Guerrero was lured into negotiations, betrayed, and executed shortly thereafter. But it quickly became apparent that Bustamante's own attempts to bring stability amounted to a police state. In 1832 the resulting instability led Santa Anna, by now Mexico's most popular and experienced general, to pronounce against the government. His revolt succeeded easily. Santa Anna, who detested Mexico City's cold, damp air and its superheated politics, conceptualized a majestic presidency headed by a kingly figure who would entrust actual governance to a carefully selected and more hands-on prime minister. For all these reasons he relinquished the reins of government in order to return once more to Manga de Clavo. Power thus devolved to physician and liberal ideologue Valentín Gómez Farías (1781–1858).

To its everlasting misfortune, the new government inherited another Iturbide project, a scheme to homestead the Texas area with settlers from the United States. This was no isolated experiment; rather, the Texas colony formed part of a larger Latin American initiative to populate and develop outlying provinces with settlers from either the United States or Europe. Iturbide's version of the project had begun when Connecticut entrepreneur Moses Austin, working through a shady intermediary who adopted the false name and title of Baron de Bastrop (in reality one Philip Hendrik Nering Bögel, a Dutch tax collector who had fled Europe to avoid charges of embezzlement), made contact with the Mexican emperor. Working through Bastrop, the elder Austin procured a concession to settle much of east-central Texas. However, Austin's death in 1823 handed the project to his more capable son, Stephen F. Austin (1793–1836). From Mexico's point of view, at least, the plan was to bring in settlers on favorable terms and convert them into Mexican citizens—as opposed to losing the territory by force or through uncontrolled immigration. The *empresarios*, concessionaires like the Austins, were to recruit settlers and award individual land titles. Settlers were to learn Spanish, convert to Catholicism, and take oaths of Mexican citizenship. Thus was born the settlement of the "Old Three Hundred" grants.

Trouble dogged the Texas scheme from its inception. Austin himself intended to keep the bargain, but his colonizers had different ideas. Few spoke Spanish, and while frontier piety lagged, the predominantly Scotch-Irish newcomers had inherited England's long-standing disdain for Catholicism. Mexicans were also alarmed by the way in which the plan exceeded expectations. With Texas land costing less than a quarter of its equivalent in the United States, settlers came in droves. By 1833 only

7,800 old-stock *tejanos* lived in Texas, mostly in San Antonio, but the so-called Texians now numbered around 30,000.

More ominous still, slaves comprised a third of that latter group's number, and this issue put the Texians in an international crosshairs. In some ways, at least, slavery was a dying institution. Following the epochal Haitian Revolution of 1791–1804, Great Britain closed down most of its trade in 1807, and complete abolition followed in 1834. Mexico itself had slowly let go of African slavery as the indigenous population rebounded from the late seventeenth century onward. José María Morelos made final abolition a key goal of his campaigns. It was thus logical and fairly painless for Vicente Guerrero to outlaw the practice altogether in 1829. But slavery remained vital to the remaining Spanish empire, as Cuban planters, eager to pick up the sugar profits that Haiti lost, had begun to import vast numbers of Africans. Brazil also entered the nineteenth century very much as a slave-based society. So, too, in the United States: the invention of the cotton gin in 1794 gave the "peculiar institution" new life, and the American South now embraced slavery—self-destructively, as events would show—as the key to export-driven wealth. It was precisely this southern mentality that the Texians brought with them.

Federalist Wars

Meanwhile, back in the altiplano, the Gómez Farías years offered a sobering lesson of what happens when a visionary politician gets out in front of public opinion. Most of the fracas centered around abolishing corporate privileges left over from colonial times, especially those privileges of the church, which the vice president disdained. Goméz Farías ended the obligatory payment of tithes and reduced, however temporarily, the size of the armed forces. His larger objective was to strip both the church and military of an ancient privilege known as the fuero, an arrangement that kept members of both institutions exempt from civil courts. Men of the old order saw abolition of the fuero as an assault on all that was just and proper, and their opposition to Gómez Farías boiled over.

By mid-1833 Santa Anna's views on federalism had begun to curdle; he perceived the country spinning into chaos, and he laid much of the blame at the feet Gómez Farías's premature anticlerical reforms. For that reason the general returned from the Veracruz hot country, put aside his vice president, and assumed direct control. In 1835 he revoked the federalist constitution and began measures that he hoped would safeguard national stability and territorial integrity. In so doing, Santa Anna inadvertently set off a series of civil and separatist wars that would nearly tear Mexico apart.

Conflicts broke out in numerous provinces, all of which lay far from Mexico City: Sonora, Zacatecas, Coahuila-Texas, Yucatán, and Tabasco, to name only the most sensational. The central seat of government lacked adequate control over these regions. Communication and travel were snail-like, while the paucity of funds and training kept the civil bureaucracy and military forces in the outer regions limited in presence. Moreover, the peripheries had matured differently from the center; for example, the southeast had not shared in the popular mobilizations against Spain. No people's army shouldered muskets against the hated *gauchapines* (European-born whites) here, and military service provided no shared experience that could bind different strata into a single identity. Strong concentrations of indigenous language–speakers also limited the diffusion of national news, debates, and the overblown rhetoric of nation-building.

In the far northwestern province of Sonora, the Yaqui people found opportunity in this moment of early state weakness. Originally, they were a seminomadic culture that had always returned to the seasonal rivers of melting snow and rain runoff to farm the rich lands of the Yaqui River basin, one of the finest agricultural zones in all of Mexico. The Jesuits had settled the Yaquis in mission towns and in the process had instilled in their culture a coherence and organization that that it had previously lacked. The Yaquis themselves—tall, powerfully built people with superb powers of endurance and a tight connection to the land—had no use for the *yoris*, or outsiders, save for those who might assist them in their ongoing quest for autonomy. In 1825, led by one Juan Banderas and armed with little more than bows and arrows, the Yaquis managed to expel the Mexican state from their territory, but their lack of firearms eventually caught up with them, and they were defeated by a superior force in 1833.

But the most dramatic conflict came in the province of Coahuila-Texas. There, a significant faction of the Texians, led by Sam Houston and James Bowie, clamored for independence from Mexico (and the right to own slaves) under whatever pretext available, while a more restrained faction, under Stephen F. Austin, remained Mexican loyalists almost to the end. The more extreme of the settlers found the outrage they were looking for when Santa Anna abolished the state legislature in 1834 and assumed dictatorial power the following year.

Santa Anna might conceivably have quashed the revolt; after all, late Bourbon authority had put down these sorts of insurrectionists before. The rambunctious Texians itched for gunfire, and Santa Anna, now personally leading the Mexican army of pacification, discovered that it was all too easy to trap them in indefensible positions like San Antonio's Alamo mission (which headstrong separatists had actually been sent to destroy, not defend). But dynamics had changed significantly since the revolution of 1810; Texians now constituted a strong majority, and they were able to obtain supplies and reinforcements from New Orleans. Santa Anna's initial success lured him into letting down his guard and dividing his forces, and he was defeated on April 16, 1836, when Sam Houston caught the general's troops napping by the banks of the San Jacinto River and captured the general himself. Once in Houston's hands, Santa Anna agreed to sign away Texas. Upon returning to Mexico he argued, with some plausibility, that any treaty made with the rebels would involve congressional approval, and since he knew that the Mexican congress would never consent, he had in fact given away nothing.

But the loss of Texas hit Mexico hard, and despite the cogency of his argument, the catastrophe kept Santa Anna out of power for another four years. It also placed Mexican statesmen and generals in a bind. However prudent it might have been to cut their losses, no politician could back down on the vow to reconquer Texas. Any operation of this sort would require massive treasure and manpower, and both of these resources could only be obtained by canvassing a group of provinces already furious over the rollback of federalist privilege.

More than anything, massive military conscription in the campaign to reverse the San Jacinto loss succeeded in destabilizing southeast Mexico. Centralist recruiters leaned heavily on the densely populated southeast, and in the process united the interests of Maya peasants and their hacendado patróns, who had no intention of sacrificing their workforce in order to correct someone else's mistake. In 1836, with San Jacinto still fresh in everyone's minds, a landowner in northeast Yucatán, Santiago Imán y Villafaña, organized his Maya workers and nearby villagers for a revolt against heavy-handed recruiting tactics. Betrayed and jailed, Imán escaped two years later, and this time, with virtually the whole Yucatán Peninsula indignant over renewed centralist control, he headed a successful campaign that ended in Yucatán separating itself from the rest of the nation. Following Yucatán's example, neighboring Tabasco launched a copycat movement, but in this instance things got out of hand. An ambitious Cuban soldier of fortune, one Francisco de Sentmanat, overthrew his federalist employers and took control of Tabasco for himself; for two years the province was his private fiefdom.

Continued instability allowed Santa Anna to return to power in 1841. This, his second presidency, gave a respite to the weary nation. He restored a measure of fiscal solvency, and his army eventually removed Sentmanat. That same army failed to reclaim Yucatán, but what it lost on the battlefield diplomats won at the negotiating table, and the perpetually wayward peninsula returned to Mexico voluntarily in 1843. But the end of his tenure came from a familiar source, when army officers, disgruntled over pay issues, overthrew Santa Anna the following year. His supporters had little time to complain, because from that moment on, national attention redirected itself northward, to what seemed an unavoidable war with the United States.

The Great Invasion

It began, as U.S.-Mexico problems so often begin, with borders. The 1836 loss set off another international problem: What *was* Texas, and had its campaign for independence simply disguised the real issue of U.S. expansion? The impresario grants had always recognized the Nueces River (roughly, San Antonio to Corpus Christi) as the southern boundary. But the early leaders of the Texas Republic claimed rights all the way to the Rio Grande, believing that this river would give them control of a potentially vast trade network coming out of the southern Rocky Mountains, a new system resembling the Mississippi trade. The infuriated Mexican government made clear that any attempt to annex Texas to the United States, or to occupy the disputed territory, would be cause for war.

Concerns about further U.S. expansion proved accurate enough when, in January 1846, just as he was leaving office, President John Tyler annexed Texas. Washington immediately accepted Texian claims of territory up to the Rio Grande. Both sides positioned their armies for a showdown. When Mexican forces shot a U.S. scout on April 25, 1846, the event furnished the justification for a full-blown declaration of war.

On the surface, at least, the conflict seemed weighted in Mexico's favor. The southern republic enjoyed a far larger army (60,000 men to the United States' 32,000) and a superb cavalry, and their army had the advantage of fighting on a home territory that Mexicans knew intimately. But much of the Mexican infantry consisted of poorly trained and equipped conscripts drawn from peasant villages, men who longed for nothing more than to escape the conflict. Mexico had no arms factories but instead armed its soldiers with old "Brown Bess" muskets left over from Europe's Napoleonic wars: smooth-bored and muzzle-loading, they had less range and accuracy than the newer U.S. weapons. Mexico also had a far smaller navy (most of the ships having departed along with the Spanish) and at times contracted British merchants to carry soldiers from one port to another. The United States, to the contrary, fought with a volunteer army, had factories to mass-produce firearms and superior artillery, possessed more and better-armed vessels, and had a highly competent corps of engineers. And while the U.S. generals suffered their share of rivalries and hatreds, they came nowhere close to the deep political rifts of Mexican leaders, who were still bitterly divided among federalists and centralists as well as between republicans and supporters of a flat-out return to monarchy.

The war began with a series of U.S. victories that took General Zachary Taylor all the way to Monterrey, in Nuevo León. Fearing that Taylor was becoming a political rival, President James K. Polk sent General Winfield Scott to neutralize the ports, occupy Veracruz, and lead a march to the Mexican capital. Battles largely favored the aggressor, but in fact Mexico put up a better resistance than is commonly recognized. U.S. forces suffered several defeats in their march to final victory. For example, Commodore Matthew Perry's armada was turned back when it attempted to occupy the city of San Juan Bautista de Villahermosa in Tabasco. Perry returned in November, this time armed for a full-scale assault and occupation. He succeeded in taking the city, but Tabascan defenders retreated to the countryside and allowed tropical disease to exact its toll on the invaders.

General Zachary Taylor defeated Santa Anna at the Battle of Buena Vista on February 23, 1847, thus guaranteeing U.S. control of northeast Mexico during the course of the Mexican-American War. In reality, the battle was closely fought. Moreover, Taylor's own success caused a jealous President James K. Polk to sideline Taylor in favor of General Winfield Scott. Courtesy of the Library of Congress.

Scott's forces took Mexico City's Chapultepec Castle on September 13, 1847, and the fighting largely came to an end. It was at this point that the United States learned a lesson that has flummoxed powerful forces from time beyond memory: the real challenge comes not with the invasion but with the occupation. While the larger army had surrendered, armed Mexicans simply dispersed to safe positions. Occupation was expensive, and soldiers recruited from places like New England began to perish in numbers from tropical diseases to which they had no immunity, a reversal of the dynamics of sixteenth-century conquest. Finally, treaty negotiations suffered from the slow communications between Washington and Mexico City, so that Polk's representative, Nicholas Trist, had to make key decisions on his own. Under these pressures Trist opted for terms that, while favorable to the victor, hardly satisfied the grandiose expectations of the more ardent expansionists. Mexican leaders, meanwhile, feared losing control to the diverse irregular forces that had formed throughout the country; thus they had their own reason to negotiate as swift a conclusion as possible.

Signed on February 2, 1848, the Treaty of Guadalupe Hidalgo remains the two nations' most important joint diplomatic agreement, and for all its haste, its creakiness, and its nagging ambiguities, it continues to serve as the foundational document of U.S.-Mexico relations. Mexico ceded approximately 40 percent of its national territory, including the flashpoint provinces of Texas and California. The latter carried particular importance, because sensational gold strikes made that same year made it a magnet for settlers. Henceforth, the West's immense wealth of minerals, agriculture, and grazing land would accrue to the aggressive northern republic.

Simultaneously, the treaty awarded Mexico $18 million for damages and loss of land, roughly a year's federal budget. Mexican residents in the ceded areas had one year to choose citizenship, after which time they automatically became U.S. nationals. Some seventy-five to one hundred thousand Mexicans remained where they were, thereby internalizing the northern nation's first appreciable Spanish-speaking minority. Pre-1848 Mexican property rights in the transferred territories remain a controversial theme to the present day. In still another article of the treaty, the United States committed itself to patrolling the border against Indian attacks. The growing presence of settlers, entrepreneurs, and state power in the sprawling border region increasingly squeezed groups like the

Comanches and Apaches and made cattle theft and violent raids their last means of survival. But in fact neither government would be able to do much about the matter for almost forty years. The coming civil wars distracted them, while final subjugation of the Apaches had to await the fierce trinity of railroads, telegraphs, and repeating rifles.

As another of its many far-reaching consequences, Guadalupe Hidalgo also established, at least on paper, the new border between the two countries. The Rio Grande now definitively separated Mexico from Texas, but determining the exact placement of *la gran línea* westward from El Paso was no simple task. U.S. and Mexican teams worked in tandem, dividing the stretch from the river to the California coast into fifty-four units, each mapped using a combination of astronomical and geographical surveys. In reality the U.S. team tended to lose its way in the desert, so most of the work took place under one of Mexico's most highly trained engineers, José Salazar Ilarregui. Even the Rio Grande itself refused to cooperate; like the Mississippi and other great waterways, it tended to shift course rather frequently in those days. In the process of one of these shifts, chunks of national territory could change hands, and one particularly controversial case, a strip of land known as Chamizal, was only resolved in 1963 when President John Kennedy, feeling pressure for improved inter-American relations, resolved the matter in Mexico's favor. (Kennedy's assassination postponed the actual transfer until the presidency of Lyndon Johnson.)

Treaties supposedly resolve conflicts, but in an unforeseen twist, the accord set both nations on the road to civil war. For the United States the treaty facilitated westward expansion, but in so doing it reawakened the explosive issue of slavery versus free soil; and while North and South papered over the controversy with the Compromise of 1850, both sides came away feeling cheated and angry. In Mexico, meanwhile, the terrible loss, coupled with other setbacks that were soon to follow, brought to power a new generation determined to transform their nation at any cost. As with the United States, Mexico's political reckoning spawned by Guadalupe Hidalgo took less than fifteen years to mature.

But those conflicts lay in the future. For the moment Mexico had to deal with the Caste War of Yucatán, an event as confusing as it was prolonged and violent. Yucatán's Maya peasants had long lived in a state of legal subordination. In the doldrums of a lethargic colonial economy,

Maya life had reconstituted itself in communities centered around milpa farming; the Catholic ritual year; a splendid, hybrid complex of folk knowledge; and governance by prominent men of the village. The indigenous past proved so resilient that mestizos and even Spanish-descended creoles often used the Maya language as the basis of daily communication. (Even today Maya accents and loan words strongly inform peninsular Spanish.) After independence much of Yucatán's status quo began to disintegrate. Non-Maya presence had been filtering into the villages since the late colonial period, generating land pressure. The new state imposed head taxes that, coming on top of the long-standing church taxes known as obventions, antagonized a broad stretch of the population. Moreover, Yucatecan society had never really restabilized after the Imán revolt. From at least as early as 1832, centralists and federalists had both relied on Maya recruits for their campaigns; caudillos used promises of tax relief and protection from national military conscription to attract followers. But creole leaders could neither settle their own differences nor deliver on promises. Maya followers felt cheated, while their engagement with creole factional politics exposed them to a political violence unknown since the days of the Conquest. These factors eventually pushed a string of eastern villages, however divided and uncertain in their aims, to take up arms.

Within six months of Guadalupe Hidalgo, the peninsula was lost in a madness all its own. The Caste War, which erupted on July 30, 1847, was the largest rural rebellion in all of nineteenth-century Mexico. Insurgents prospered from state weakness as well as from access to arms and supplies from neighboring British Honduras (for borders often favor rebels). The Yucatecan army eventually bottled the insurgents into the extreme southeast; the latter rallied there under the dictates of a Speaking Cross oracle, to hold their own as Yucatecans closer to Mérida spent the next three decades fighting each other.

A World Reformed

The U.S. invasion provoked massive soul-searching among the Mexican political set. But whereas earlier quarrels had revolved around either personalities or the old federalism tussle, the humiliation of Guadalupe

Hidalgo divided the country into two ideological camps, each with its own formula for revitalizing the nation.

The late 1840s saw the rise of a new political generation. Its members had come of age after 1821 and lacked emotional investment in the glories of Spain. Most came from the provinces and had worked overwhelmingly in the legal profession; some, at least, had suffered slights from the Catholic Church owing to their mixed-race ancestry. Though in many ways the heirs of the federalists, they no longer accepted gradualist approaches such as inadequately funded public schools. Rather, men of this new generation proposed to seize power and to impose wrenching changes to Mexico's deeply entrenched systems of wealth and privilege. These men came together in what they called the Liberal Party.

Made indignant by the spectacle of national disintegration, the Liberals identified colonial institutions as the problem. They blamed the inefficient system of latifundia for holding back economic development. They lashed out against the military for devouring budgets and fostering privileges, such as the fuero, that weakened the rule of law. Some of these new firebrands proposed returning to the old system of a national guard, but all of them agreed on the elimination of the fuero. Liberals also scorned the Indian village, with its illiteracy, its refusal to learn Spanish, its corporately held land, and a mentality that discouraged innovation and personal initiative. They bitterly resented the ascendency of caudillos, men who used chains of personal loyalty to circumvent legal process.

But most of all they blamed the Catholic Church. To their eyes it was the bulwark of an outdated mentality; it fostered community over the individual and hence worked against dynamic capitalism. Its special courts, together with its control of education, placed it outside of national laws and made it a bastion for petrified beliefs and leftover Spanish racism. And, they believed, it was too rich for its own good, the result of century upon century of deathbed donations. Nearly fifty years after the Consolidación de Vales, capellanías continued to be the only real financing system in the country—and not a very efficient one at that.

Liberal solutions were equally uncompromising. Members advocated ending colonial monopolies, liberalizing foreign trade, creating juridical equality for all citizens, converting corporate to private property, and disestablishing Mexico's Catholic Church and removing it from both educational and financial affairs. They proposed to achieve all of these goals via a constitutional republic with an electoral process, a political order in which clearly defined statutes and institutions displaced clientalist ties. All in all, their philosophy proposed to "liberate" the power and initiative of the individual.

It all sounded logical enough, particularly for those weaned on thinkers like Adam Smith and Thomas Jefferson. But Mexican liberalism concealed within itself a contradiction that only grew with time. Champions of individual initiative and limited government, Liberals nevertheless required the services of a powerful central state to wipe away the past. This latter necessity became more and more evident as the new order's plans for restructuring met with resistance at all levels. Concealed within liberalism, then, lurked the tendency toward a modernizing dictatorship.

Naturally enough, the Liberals' new philosophy inspired a foil. Mexico had always nursed a conservative streak, but that streak emerged in clearer relief now that the colonial corporate state came under assault. Conservatives had their own arguments. As they saw it, Mexico's immense regional and cultural fragmentation meant that religion still remained the glue holding society together; to disestablish the church meant splitting the national atom. Pointing to both theory and experience, conservatives believed that electoral politics simply got the population worked up and were best avoided in favor of top-down decrees and appointments. They perceived that Mexican industries, such as the production of hand-loomed textiles, were too weak to stand against Britain's free-trade juggernaut. Mexico City–based merchants and producers still prized the old guild monopolies. Finally, conservatives argued that Indians lacked the experience, the language skills, and probably the intelligence to participate on equal footing with men of European descent, and they believed that the old system of the two republics needed to be upheld.

Essentially, it was Spain without the Spaniards, a postcolonial retooling surrounded by tall walls built of tariffs. And while these arguments bore some substance, the overall vision's weakness lay in its static nature. Perhaps the old Bourbon arrangement could go on for ten more years. But for twenty? Or fifty? The traumatic losses of 1848 showed that deserts and oceans were no longer the barriers of old and that protectionism had bred neither military nor industrial efficiency. In retrospect, it is also clear that conservative thinkers like Lucas Alamán overestimated the unity of the elite corporate groups upon which they hoped to found their state. Landowners had suffered too much devastation and were far too separated by geography and local conditions to act as a unified body. Military officers also had differing opinions about national direction; one of the few privileged sectors not educated by the church, many shared the Liberals' anticlericalism.

For four years the nation teetered in a precarious balance. But in 1852 Santa Anna returned to power one final time. By now he had given up on the idea of democracy and simply hoped to establish some sort of order in the face of national disarray and dismemberment. The men who promoted Santa Anna saw him as a stopgap who would allow them time to comb for a European monarch to assume control of Mexico. Santa Anna himself proposed a massive build-up of the armed forces as a way of imposing central power; as a result, the army more than quadrupled in size, from ten thousand to forty-six thousand soldiers. Desperate for funding, he agreed to sell 29,670 square miles, mostly in what is now southern Arizona and part of southwest New Mexico, in exchange for some $10 million. Railroad developers had coveted the area because of its level topography, and in fact thirty years later it became the route of the Southern Pacific line. Representatives from the two countries (including U.S. ambassador James Gadsden, from whom the sale took its name) signed the treaty on December 30, 1853, and it was ratified by the U.S. Congress the following June.

At the same time, Santa Anna elected to go after an old rival, Juan Álvarez (1790–1867), who operated a private fiefdom in the area around Acapulco. Alarmed by news that the president was planning a highway to connect this wayward province with the capital and recognizing the Gadsden Purchase as a wedge issue, Álvarez galvanized anti-Santannista sentiment in his Revolt of Ayutla, launched on March 1, 1854. Thus began nineteenth months of war and counterinsurgency, fought mostly in the southwest. On August 12, 1855, Santa Anna, perceiving that he had lost the contest, abdicated his presidency.

His power had finally ended; what awaited was a long, bitter exile in the Caribbean and Colombia. Santa Anna spent the remaining twenty-one years of his life alternately snubbing politicians and dreaming of one last chance. As he sat and waited, vengeful enemies confiscated his estates. The man who had struggled so long to guide Mexico's affairs, and who in achieving so little had brought ruin upon his own house, became the whipping boy for all the failures and frustrations of the early national period, problems that for the most part lay outside his control and against which no other leader achieved much success. Antonio López de Santa Anna eventually returned to Mexico City in 1874, a one-legged, half-blind, and forgotten old man, and he died in obscurity in the capital two years later.

Juan Álvarez had triumphed, but he had no intention of governing. Uncomfortable in the chilly capital, he retreated to his feud in the hot country, happily turning over the reins of power to younger men with the temperament and legal training necessary for governance. Ignacio Comonfort (1812–63), a Puebla-born politician of French ancestry, assumed the presidency. More important for Mexico's future, leadership of the supreme court went to Oaxacan-born Benito Juárez (1806–72), a Zapotec Indian who had served in a wealthy Oaxacan household where he received a decent education; the young man studied to law, entered politics, and rose high in the Liberal ranks. This time the change of power would be different. Young Liberals now controlled all branches of government, and they set out to restructure virtually every aspect of Mexican life. In 1855 the Juárez Law stripped the church of legal privileges such as the fueros. The following year the more explosive Lerdo Law decreed the breakup and sale of corporately held properties: ostensibly those owned by the church, but applicable by extension to the communal Indian village grants made in the sixteenth century. Both documents were ultimately enshrined in a new national constitution, ratified on February 5, 1857.

The Liberals' rosy developmental scenario hit snags almost from the beginning. Their belief that vast amounts of property held by the church lay in rural areas turned out to be unfounded. Most of the institution's material wealth took the form of urban townhouses; the nascent middle classes gobbled these up immediately and became rock-ribbed Liberals ever after. True, on paper the church held a fortune in mortgages, but once again, things looked different in practice. Because of the sluggish economy, priests who held the rights to collect on these mortgages almost always preferred to roll over the debt for a few more years rather than to foreclose. Both debtor and lender thus limped on in a perpetuity of token payments and droopy productivity. Under the reform capellanía mortgages often were simply erased, and occupant-ownership became formalized. In places where the state actually did sell of church-owned

Benito Juárez now stands as one of the commanding figures of Mexican history, but during his lifetime he generated as much hatred as he did respect. Conservative Mexicans considered him the devil incarnate. Juárez finally succeeded in ousting the French interventionists (1861–67), but out of sheer necessity he ended up constructing many of the features of the later dictatorship. Courtesy of the Library of Congress.

properties, it seldom earned the dreamed-of bonanza. Sales typically strengthened the holdings of large property owners, a class of colonial holdovers whom the Liberals had hoped to weaken but who were in actuality the only ones with enough liquidity to compete in the bidding. More disastrous still, the state's low returns vanished in the civil wars of 1857 onward. Rather than providing some sort of economic stimulus, then, the Liberal state came away empty-handed while antagonizing an enormous cross-section of Mexico's population.

The War of Reform (1857–60) was the first full-scale civil war since independence; it was a conflict that transcended mere regional issues and split Mexican society into ideological camps. It began in December 1857, when General Félix Zuloaga, acting in the name of the newly formed Conservative Party, pronounced in Tacubaya against the Liberal order. Never a strident ideologue, Comonfort resigned from the presidency and went into exile, leaving supreme court head Benito Juárez as the constitutional head of state; for the next fourteen years Juárez would govern under near-impossible circumstances and without the benefit of having a popular vote to underpin his legitimacy.

Outside the capital the war split the country vertically, and not by simple class divisions. Clergy naturally favored the Conservative cause, but landowners and urban gentry split their allegiances between the two sides. Even Indian villagers took different sides: while older generations defended the hereditary colonial ways, the Liberal package appealed to younger (and more often landless) peasants. Others liked the party's rhetoric of progress and its campaign to abolish church taxes. Still others were drawn into the Juárez camp by ties of patronage.

In the end the Liberals prevailed. Their occupation of the Port of Veracruz choked off the Conservative government's access to customs revenues. The United States provided critical naval support to the Liberal cause, while the complex network of allies proved sufficient to carry the day. The last Conservative forces surrendered in December 1860. On January 1, 1861, Juárez reentered Mexico City, but he now presided over a nation bankrupted and embittered by warfare. Having little alternative, he declared a two-year moratorium on the payment of Mexico's foreign debt, then attempted to get on with the work of rebuilding.

An Empire, of Sorts

The next major episode of national history, the tragicomic interlude of the French Empire, was in essence a second act to the War of Reform itself. Stung by their loss, defeated Conservatives cast about for allies in the reactionary landscape of post-1848 Europe. The search posed greater challenges than they had imagined. At that moment British investors held some 80 percent of all Mexican bonds, but the Foreign Office begged off Latin American quagmires: not only was the United States on the brink of civil war, but Britain's diplomats were busy converting the Asian subcontinent from an East India Company project to a formal colony. Nor did Spain, continually wracked with wars involving liberals, nobility, and ambitious generals, show much interest in reclaiming its lost colony.

Not so France. Louis Napoleon, ambitious nephew of the first Napoleon, had ridden his uncle's name to power in 1850 and laid claim to a vague populist mandate as the president, and later monarch, of France. He dreamed of rivaling Britain as a colonial and industrial powerhouse. Checking the expansion of the Protestant United States via a successful intervention in Mexico might establish his credentials as a world leader, he reasoned, while access to the Bajío's long-dormant silver mines could hardly hurt. The project also picked up support from his fervently Catholic, Spanish-born wife, Eugénie, whose presence inspired a long-standing French fascination with all things Iberian (a trend best remembered today through Georges Bizet's opera *Carmen*). For these reasons Mexican exiles received a warm hearing at the French royal palace of Tuileries.

The French invasion actually began disguised as a mission of debt collection. Louis Napoleon persuaded the governments of both Britain and Spain to participate in this limited engagement, and their collective troops arrived in Veracruz in December 1861. Mexican forces kept them bottled up until they agreed to a debt payment arrangement, whereupon Napoleon's allies returned to Europe. But with their bluff called, the French expeditionary forces began their march toward Mexico City.

In their first serious battle the interventionists suffered an embarrassing defeat. Fortified at a hilltop outside Puebla, General Ignacio Zaragoza, aided by a spirited cavalry under the command of one Porfirio Díaz, dealt the French a surprise thrashing on May 5, 1862. The Battle of Cinco de Mayo entered national mythology, but it failed to avert the invaders from their larger project, and the following year they returned, carefully marched around the fort's vicinity, and took Mexico City almost unopposed.

Now governing without benefit of elections, Benito Juárez took care to avoid the defeatist stigma of a government-in-exile. Rather than fleeing to the United States, he operated a peripatetic administration that always managed to stay one step ahead of French troops. The furthest point of his wanderings today bears his name: Ciudad Juárez, just across the border from El Paso.

Astute enough to realize that he needed a front man to govern, Napoleon recruited Maximilian (1832–67), unemployed nobleman and younger brother of Franz Joseph, Emperor of the Austro-Hungarian Empire. After some dallying Maximilian agreed, and on May 29, 1864, he and his Belgian wife, Charlotte, soon to be rechristened "Carlota," disembarked at the Port of Veracruz. The hotel where they spent the first night in their new empire still operates on the southwest corner of the city's main plaza. Once in Mexico City, Maximilian adopted a conciliatory and often eclectic strategy. In some ways his own thinking was more in line with that of the Liberal Party, and he left in place much of the legislation limiting clerical power. He redesigned a considerable portion of Mexico City, creating what today is known as the Paseo de la Reforma. He also gave Mexico a faint, early taste of twentieth-century revolutionary policy by establishing tribunals and ombudsmen to protect indigenous peasants, especially in matters of land rights. Still, Maximilian discovered that he needed army support above all things, and at the insistence of his generals he signed the so-called Black Decree, which allowed the French Army to execute captured Mexican combatants without due process.

Underneath Maximilian's Hapsburg regalia, most of the old dynamics of Mexican life still applied. The provinces, where most people lived, remained in the hands of Conservatives, who struggled to reconcile private agendas with the often-contradictory decrees of the new emperor. Yucatán offers an example. Convulsed by Liberal-Conservative struggles before 1864, it received as a new administrator an imperial appointee, José Salazar Ilarregui (1823–92). Now famed as a border surveyor, Salazar was brought by favorable marriage into Conservative circles. He tried a conciliatory tack but found himself flummoxed by lukewarm imperial support for the church; by a renewed Caste War (as usual, insurgent communities of the deep forest sensed political weakness in Mérida); and by land laws not necessarily applicable to the peninsula. At no time did Salazar receive much in the way of armed French support.

Meanwhile, neighboring Tabasco formed one of the great exceptions to an empire of parts. Imperialists briefly succeeded in occupying the capital, Villahermosa, under the leadership of a Spanish adventurer named Eduardo González Arévalo. But control of Tabasco's capital city never guaranteed the submission of the countryside, and by early 1864 Tabascan republicans were back in control and actively supplying the rest of southeast Mexico with a base of support for continue resistance.

By 1866 the international circumstances that had facilitated Napoleon's misadventure were rapidly changing. The Union had decisively triumphed in the U.S. Civil War, and almost immediately Washington began to transfer arms and money to the Juárez forces. Closer to home, France now found itself threatened by a pugnacious Prussian state bent on defeating continental rivals as a means of unifying Germany. Napoleon had no choice but to withdraw his troops. Carlota returned to Europe to plead for help, but none came. Maximilian, meanwhile, chose to fight it out with his last remaining troops. He remained a romantic visionary to the end, putting the finishing touches on his manual of court etiquette even as the republican forces closed in. Eventually he was captured, along with loyal generals Miguel Miramón and Tomás Mejía, the latter of whom was an Indian born in a mountain village near Querétaro, a man who had found both social mobility and meaning in service of Conservative causes.

Telegrams poured in from the nations of Europe, begging for clemency for the defeated Maximilian. But the deposed emperor had signed the Black Decree, and Benito Juárez understood that to free his opponent might well be signing his own death warrant; for all its *opera buffa* overtones, the intervention had claimed the lives of some thirty thousand Mexicans, and any sort of pardon would carry a stiff political price. Moreover, Juárez and his advisors believed that the old European powers needed a lesson about poaching in Mexico. For those reasons, on June 19, 1867, Maximilian was executed at the Hill of the Bells, named for the resonant sound of its mineral-rich rocks, outside the city of Querétaro. His remains were embalmed, photographed, and eventually returned to the family crypt in Vienna. Maximilian's widow Charlotte lived on in a precarious mental state for another half century, eventually dying in 1926 at the age of eighty-six. Her sad fate in no way put the family off imperial schemes, since her older brother, King Leopold of Belgium, imposed upon the African Congo a colonial regime that made Louis Napoleon's ersatz Mexican adventure seem benign by comparison.

The French left some unusual baggage in the cloakroom of the Mexican psyche. Imperialists founded the nation's first music conservatory, which continued its rehearsals long after Maximilian's coffin finally made it home. Mexico City's grand Paseo de la Reforma, Maximilian's pet project of imperial grandeur, still ushers pedestrians and motorists from the city center to the lush parks of Chapultepec. Light-colored eyes allow some people to claim, however dubiously, to have descended from French soldiers or their German mercenaries. And even today, any sort of bread vaguely resembling a baguette bears the name *pan francés*, or more simply, *francés*, as though Spaniards and Mexicans had never quite cracked the secret recipe.

Beyond these details, what had emerged from the ten-year civil war? More than dispirited Liberals might have expected, things turned out in their favor. No one could any longer defend a Conservative Party that had so blatantly betrayed national sovereignty. Conversely, the Liberal Party's steadfast struggle against the intervention set the seal on their image as defenders of the nation. The name of Benito Juárez ceased to invoke atheist tyranny and instead began a slow ascent to sainthood. Men and women who could not and would never read the constitution of 1857, the very document enshrining legal mechanisms for the breakup of village lands, came to believe that it was a wise, august document that guaranteed all things right and just—so much so that many of the peasants who took up arms in the 1910 revolution actually claimed its support. Modest benefits from the initial land sales and subsequent confiscations did ultimately filter downward, and Mexico saw the rise of something resembling a class of private rancheros, hardy as mules and patriotic to a fault.

In other regards the reform's effect on indigenous communities took some irregular turns. Part of the complication lay in regional differences in landholding patterns. So, too, distance from the political center typically weakened the reform's power. In the southeast, for example, politicians dreaded a reignition of the still-smoldering Caste War and purposely did nothing. The governor of Veracruz softened the blow by allowing a period of jointly held properties by way of an institution known as *condueñazgo*; the approach generated no end of conflict, but it allowed the state's small-scale vanilla growers to extend the alienation process over whole decades. Similar practices also turned up in such places as the Mixtec Alta of Oaxaca. But communities closer to Mexico City were not so lucky. In particular the reform broke up the two enormous indigenous *parcialidades*, or corporate land reserves, located just outside the urban nucleus. These twin bodies resembled counties more than villages and were so vast that they included settlement nuclei built around different churches. Prior to 1870 the capital had scarcely grown and still resembled the exquisite landscapes that José María Velasco painted from the vantage point of hilltops outside the city. But with the two parcialidades dissolved, and especially with the economic explosion of the century's final three decades, *la capital* began its expansion into the monstrous urban sprawl of today. On the whole, however, the Lerdo Law failed to eradicate village commons prior to 1876; sweeping land alienation lay further in the future.

The reform period left several other major issues unresolved. What would become of the church now that its armed champions had suffered twin defeats but while most Mexicans remained believers at one level or another? Although devout Conservatives did not recognize it at the time, the reform ultimately gave the church a path forward. Anyone who has perused the haphazard and inconsistent demographic records that parish priests maintained prior to 1876 will recognize that no modern state could rely indefinitely on such methods. More importantly, the reform removed the church from a world of modern finance in which it was ill-equipped to function and instead forced it to concentrate on its spiritual mission. With accusations of Babylonian riches now neutralized, the institution's appeal as a moral authority grew all the greater, particularly when seen in contrast to the vast polarization of wealth and the notorious insensitivity of the late nineteenth century's upper crust.

If the church enjoyed extensive but fundamentally "soft" power, the issue of what to do about foreign investment posed sterner realities. Efforts aside, Mexicans simply lacked the capital and technical expertise to create a modern infrastructure of mines, railroads, telegraphs, and electrical power. The dearth of that infrastructure loomed all the greater when seen against the dramatic changes that were reshaping life in the North Atlantic world. But memory of territorial losses to the United States remained bitter. For this reason Liberal statesman Sebastián Lerdo de Tejada's apocryphal riposte to the suggestion of foreign-financed railroads linking north and south: "Between strength and weakness, a desert."

The reform also redefined the way the state exercised its power. The fourteen years of violence and civil unrest since 1857 had also forced Juárez to impose methods of top-down control. To deal with the waves of banditry that followed French imperial collapse, the president coopted highwaymen by deputizing them into newly created and later notorious *guardias rurales,* or, as they came to be known, the Rurales. With their distinctive charro costumes of elegant, tight-fitting pants, embroidered jackets, and the broad sombreros favored by western horsemen, they became the local enforcers whose reputation rested more on bluff and legend than actual competence.

Juárez also changed the fundamental structure of Mexican politics. Faced with the possibility of former Conservatives assuming electoral power by means of provincial voting bases and fearing a return to the violence and anarchy of the last two decades, he built state political machines that guaranteed his supporters would occupy governors' offices and seats of congress. Elections took place, but voting shriveled to a paper formality, while actual results came down from above. The Rurales and the political machines were probably unavoidable, but over the long run both became fundamental components of a dictatorship.

Any final evaluation of Mexico's first half century of nationhood must weigh loss and achievement with great care. On one side, the end of Spanish colonialism ushered in an age of public violence, national fragmentation, and instability at all levels. The country failed to achieve a system that allowed for orderly transition of power. The fact that political actors had to resort to pronouncements and revolts to achieve their aims tells us much. Similarly, no one can ignore the loss of the enormous, resource-laden territory to the north.

But we must temper these facts with other considerations. To begin with, the blemishes of early Mexican society were hardly unique. In almost no place dominated by European powers did the upper classes evince much respect for indigenous cultures. Marginalization of native peoples defined the United States, Canada, Australia, southeast Asia, and South Africa, to name only a few. National fragmentation and mayhem frequently follow secession movements, and the United States itself only achieved national unity at the cost of a civil war whose casualties exceeded anything that happened in early Mexico and whose effects on the defeated South continue to reverberate today.

We also tend to ignore what the first two generations of Mexicans achieved. To begin with, the densely inhabited southern part of the country did cohere, together with much of the northern provinces that did *not* fall into foreign hands. The core of what had been New Spain thus emerged largely intact, while Iturbide's absorption of Central America had never amounted to anything but an ephemeral experiment. At its heart, Mexico remained Mexico.

Citizens of the new nation could point to other solid accomplishments as well. With the Mexico-Veracruz line they had taken their first step toward railroad construction. Arts and sciences continued in spite of the chaos, and the various works of pre-1876 literature, if less commonly recognized than the twentieth-century counterparts, still repay reading. The country had retained and expanded the means of reproducing its intelligentsia; Mexican jurists doggedly continued to administer justice and craft legislation. The 1829 abolition of slavery, issued at a time when unfree labor had acquired new life in Cuba and North America, shines as a brilliant achievement. And at the grassroots levels, a diverse Mexican people persisted in spite of politics and pronouncements. They fed their families, bolstered their communities, and retained a sense of moral decency and a respect for time-honored tales and customs, while at the same time placing one toe into that great expanse known as the outside world. Little did they suspect that the outside world would soon come to them and in ways that many would have preferred to avoid.

5

The Strongman of the Americas
The Age of Porfirio Díaz, 1876–1910

O ut of the turbulence of the restored republic came a new political order. It built directly on earlier models and often wrapped itself in their mantle as a means of purchasing legitimacy. But in other ways this new order departed from anything that had come before. Its spectacular economic boom reached into the most isolated corners of Mexico, transforming them for both good and ill. Above all, the last third of the century was dominated by a personality cult built around one man, a president-dictator whose words championed limited government and popular sovereignty but whose actions spoke otherwise.

The Porfiriato, or the period of Porfirio Díaz, ran from 1876 to 1911, and it divides historians today just as it divided the Mexican citizens who lived under it. A triumph of national sovereignty? A thoroughly constitutional order? A span of visionary state building? Or a ruthless dictatorship that fostered exploitation, pseudo-scientific racism, special privileges for foreigners, and a government that if in some ways was *for* the people, was not for *all* of them, was certainly not *by* them? The fact that one can answer "yes" to all of these questions gives some measure of the complexity of Díaz's reign, as well as of the explosive forces the dictator struggled to contain, which eventually escaped his grasp.

Rise to Power

Porfirio Díaz Mori was born in rural Oaxaca in 1830, the son of a mestizo saddler. He enrolled in seminary classes as a youth, but the 1846 invasion of Mexico by the United States led him to abandon his studies and sign up with a local militia; from that moment on, the military remained his home. He rose quickly in the ranks, and in 1855, at the age of twenty-four, he became the military governor of Tehuantepec. Díaz remained a key Liberal general during the French intervention. He led the successful cavalry charge at the Battle of Puebla in 1862, was captured in 1863, and later escaped from French troops. He went on to score key victories for Benito Juárez, returning to liberate Puebla on April 2, 1867. Díaz's early years taught him lessons that he brought to bear in later life. The Oaxaca of his youth was not a land of powerful hacendados; indigenous communities retained both their land base and their vitality, and those creoles and mestizos who prospered did so by commerce and negotiation. Hence, early on Díaz understood the value of compromise.

His military record and administrative success, combined with personal ambition, convinced Díaz that he was the man for the presidency. When Benito Juárez engineered his own election in 1871, Díaz launched his Revolt of La Noria, named for his property in Oaxaca. But poor planning got in the way, and La Noria's leader ended up fleeing to foreign exile. Two years later Díaz received a second chance when Juárez himself died of a massive heart attack while reading a newspaper in his office in the National Palace. The presidency passed to the dead president's closest associate, Sebastián Lerdo de Tejada, pitting him in direct competition with Díaz.

The split between these two ambitious statesmen traced a basic fissure of the Liberal Party. Lerdo's support drew heavily from the more elite side: better educated, and more urban, men who had only contempt for colonial institutions but who nevertheless saw themselves as the receptacles of Spanish culture. They often hailed from the legal profession, had worked in and benefited from Juárez's state-level political machines, and held strong nationalist ideas concerning the methods and overall path of development.

Díaz supporters, to the contrary, enjoyed more populist roots. Quite often these men came from the military, where midlevel officers had direct contact with regional and community leaders. Excluded from the machines, they gravitated toward a doctrine of states' rights that promised to keep federal interference from opposing their ambitions. And at least some of them were *ferrocarrilistas*, proponents of expanding Mexico's

General, patriot, sagacious president, cunning dictator: the figure of Porfirio Díaz Mori towers over much of Mexican history. The Oaxacan mestizo rose from humble origins to preside over one of the most transformative periods in all of Mexican history, but he fell to the epochal revolution of 1910. This photograph reveals a younger Díaz, before age had whitened his hair and facial powder had lightened his skin. Courtesy of the Library of Congress.

nascent railroad system via foreign investment. Because of their insistence on strict constitutional procedure and popular sovereignty, these latter adherents to the Liberal movement were known as the Puros, the "pure ones." Claim and reality often diverge, though, and once in power the Puros, starting with their leader, put aside their earlier ideological rigidity in favor of a pragmatism that led them to abandon a number of their earlier positions.

Congress dutifully chose Lerdo to complete Juárez's term. Díaz took advantage of an amnesty and returned to Mexico, but when Lerdo used the political machine to orchestrate his own reelection in 1875, Díaz went to the United States to round up support for yet another rebellion. Flush with funding and a robust assortment of foreign mercenaries, he proclaimed his latest revolution from the wooden verandas of Brownsville, Texas, while supporters safeguarded his nationalist credentials by issuing the Plan of Tuxtepec from deep in northern Oaxaca. Díaz naturally inveighed against machine politics and reelection, but just as important to his cause were Lerdo's doctrinaire applications of the laws of secularization and land alienation, his steadfast resistance to foreign investment, and his failure to suppress border violence. Moreover, Lerdo lacked the gravitas and determination of Juárez and thus posed an easier mark. This time the revolt succeeded, and by November 1876, Porfirio Díaz entered Mexico City in triumph.

The Porfirian Solution

The victors of Tuxtepec feared above all a return to the chaos and civil wars of earlier decades. They had championed popular sovereignty and limited government, but they ultimately chose stability over these more-lofty goals. The solution was to hold elections, but always with careful stage management to minimize conflict and avoid surprises. It was not so much that voting itself was rigged: rather, control came from above via selection of candidates. Díaz himself stepped down in 1880, and under his strong recommendation he was succeeded by a trusted general, Manuel González (1833–93), whose four-year administration actually instituted many of the key legislative changes. By 1884 twelve years of continuous peace and growth had cleansed the idea of reelection of its old taboo. Porfirio Díaz now became the indispensable man; he was returned to office continually, and without serious opposition, until the fateful events of 1910.

Much the same process transpired in the states. Elections had a tendency to bring out the worst unrest, and gubernatorial contests in particular had always been dangerous tinderboxes. Under the new order elections took place in faithful compliance with the constitution of 1857, invariably producing individuals loyal to Díaz himself. It was not that Díaz cronies hid or falsified results or roughed up would-be challengers; rather, the "strong candidate," the man guaranteed to keep peace and promote development, was chosen in advance, the approval of the president being the clinching factor. Fearing exclusion, people learned to line up behind the chosen individual. Some states were more tractable than others, and Díaz gauged his appointments depending on how firm a hand he felt the situation required. Difficult situations required strongmen selected from his coterie of generals, rather in the style of the Roman proconsul, whereas relatively peaceful states permitted the president to draw from a pool of local talent.

But Díaz understood that electoral reforms alone could not solve Mexico's problems. The nation also required economic development, and while the president and his associates actually nursed deep suspicions of foreigners, and above all of the United States, they understood that only foreign funds and technology could bring about the necessary changes. But in order to function, international capitalism requires friendly regimes abroad. Governments in host countries such as Mexico had to rewrite laws in favor of foreign investment, to make resources and labor available for purchase, to honor debts and protect foreign-owned infrastructure, and to guarantee stability and safe operating conditions.

The first step was to normalize Mexico's ancient and often bewildering patchwork of land tenure systems. The changes that optimistic (or perhaps opportunistic) reformers had attempted to bring about since as early as the 1820s had made only limited headway: either the state was too weak to enforce its plans over peasant resistance or else initiatives bogged down in such objective difficulties as political dogfights, lack of competent surveyors, or unique regional conditions. During the Revolt of Tuxtepec Díaz had campaigned with promises to undo the Lerdo Law, but he had no intention of doing so, instead believing that Mexico required massive privatization of resources in order to escape from its economic penury. The first change came with the railroads. Lacking funds to actually pay surveying companies (*deslindadores*), in 1883 the federal government adopted the practice of gifting the companies with one-third of the land they surveyed, while the state kept the rest in hopes of generating revenues for itself. A second national land reform in 1894 further clarified and expanded these practices. Some fifty companies, almost all of them U.S.-based, conducted most of the surveying, in the process acquiring rights to 10 percent of Mexican territory. Ambitious nationals were also quick to take advantage of the legislation; acting at the state level in such places as Chihuahua and Morelos, they carried out legally sanctioned land grabs that continued into the first decade of the twentieth century. By 1910 approximately 2 percent of the population controlled 98 percent of the land.

The key to a revived mining industry—and to just about all aspects of nineteenth-century growth—was the railroad. U.S. railroad expansion had exploded after 1850; even as the Civil War raged, construction on the first transcontinental line had continued. Mexico managed to create only one line during the early national years, Antonio de Escandón's four-hundred-mile connection from Veracruz to Mexico City, begun in 1857 and completed in 1873. But under González and Díaz, three major railways reached southward from the U.S. border. A central line ran from El Paso to Mexico City, while further to the east lines descended from Piedras Negras, Laredo, and Brownsville, reaching Mexico City via Monterrey. Finally, between 1880 and 1882 the Southern Pacific laid tracks connecting Nogales, at the Arizona border, with Mazatlán.

The grand prize for would-be investors remained the vast mineral wealth in the rugged territories north of the Valley of Mexico. To reach that prize required a complex strategy, the first step of which was to change the legal structures demarcating state and private property. The silver mines had provided Spain with its most reliable source of colonial revenue, and for that reason subsurface mineral rights had always belonged to the Crown. This arrangement may have sufficed in 1550, but to tempt the enormous capital necessary to revive the industry in the late nineteenth century, investors required stronger incentives. To facilitate this the Díaz administration began to revise the relevant laws. Following a series of piecemeal reforms, in 1884 a national mining code replaced all

The railroad system generated much of the growth that marked Porfirian Mexico. But only foreign (and mostly U.S.) entrepreneurs possessed the capital and the technical expertise necessary to surmount Mexico's often forbidding terrain. Courtesy of the Library of Congress.

state legislation; it gave full control of mineral wealth to investors and in the process guaranteed that those wishing to conduct mining operations knew exactly by what terms they would operate and what sort of profit margin they might expect. These changes worked. In 1876 Mexico had a mere forty mining concessions; by 1910 the number had exploded to thirteen thousand, the majority of which belonged to foreigners, who possessed greater capital and were willing to take far greater risks. Now, as oil baron J. Paul Getty later put it, the poor still might inherit the earth but surely not the subsurface mineral rights.

The mining industry, reborn at last from its late Bourbon heyday, diversified with the rise of industrial technology. Silver once predominated, but the new entrepreneurs now dug for lead and zinc. Moreover, nature had generously endowed Mexico with copper, the nerve fiber of the new electrical age. American Smelting and Refining, an operation of the Guggenheim family, became Mexico's largest company, capitalized at 200 million pesos. Following that was Standard Oil's Anaconda

Mining in Porfirian Mexico was no idyllic stroll through a garden of gold and gems. The extraction of silver, lead, copper, and zinc demanded grueling, hazardous labor by men who were often in the employ of foreigners. Miners are seen here with many of the tools of their trade. Courtesy of the Library of Congress.

Copper, then Phelps-Dodge, in part a creation of Cleveland Dodge, the man who later underwrote much of Woodrow Wilson's presidential campaign in 1912.

As the new entrepreneurs worked their way into Mexican territory, the nature of mining itself changed. While deep-shaft mining continued, open-pit and strip mining became common methods, and the mine workers themselves lost much of the elite skill set that had made them princes of labor in colonial times. The mines' new managers, men raised in a different and far more puritanical culture, imposed new discipline against such ancient practices as drinking pulque in the mines or carrying off part of the ore as bonus pay. Mining towns themselves were squalid and unsanitary. The University of Texas medical school sent its students to intern in these horrendous places, reasoning that after a year of service they would have seen every malady known to man. Still, the mines grew and the people came.

The evolving political package also involved co-opting Mexico's wealthy extended families. These networks of blood and business had always dominated matters entrepreneurial, and having them on one's side mattered to politicians who wished to stay in power. Prior to 1876 many affluent clans had opposed Díaz; he could love them or hate them, but he could not simply ignore them. The new president co-opted the families he could, assuring them the positions and investment opportunities they craved, but he harshly excluded those who had opposed him, such as Luis Terrazas Fuentes (1829–1923), head of Chihuahua's most powerful clan. Over time most of the anti-Díaz elements came around, and once restored to the strongman's good graces, these dynasties could resume their old practices of ruling their provinces like feudal barons.

To carry out the grandest of the infrastructure projects, Díaz found his man in Weetman Pearson, a dapper and talented British engineer who turned down teaching appointments in Oxford and Cambridge in order to work in the field. Pearson had already made a name for himself by constructing railroad tunnels in the United States. In Mexico City he accomplished what had eluded the Spanish for centuries by draining Mexico City and hence limiting the often-disastrous flooding of the historic capital. Pearson constructed the harbor of Veracruz, soon to prove essential in the growing export economy. He also built the trans-isthmus railroad that connected Oaxaca's Pacific and Caribbean coasts, a dream that had frustrated engineers and entrepreneurs for decades. Pearson understood that Díaz craved recognition from foreign interests, and he kept the dictator supplied with European statues and other validating art objects. Ever enamored of accomplished and well-educated foreigners, Díaz also found the perpetually successful Pearson a good counterweight to the aggressive U.S. investment community.

Regions: The Porfiriato by Parts

For all the talk of nation, Mexico still lived and breathed by province. Under the new order these became nuclei of economic growth, although with some necessarily advancing over others.

Of all of Mexico's different regions, the north experienced the most comprehensive changes. The area had never attracted more than a minimal population. Those who came here were mostly mestizos, and northern provincial leadership drew heavily from the caste of military officers (whether of the federal army or of patrician-led state militias) and from well-healed families playing their accustomed roles of bankers, merchants, and land developers. Under their patronage a hardy class of small ranchers and cowmen plied their trades, always hugging the seasonal rivers that keep this arid territory alive. The north had frequently chafed against Mexico City's dominance, particularly in those days when the federal government demanded taxes and allegiance but was incapable of controlling Apache raiders. But as the web of railroads linked mines to foreign markets, property values rose, and commercial agriculture suddenly found its footing. Haciendas became cities, arid stretches transformed into farming and grazing land, mining ore flowed out in boxcars, and the well-to-do adopted an ever more sophisticated way of life.

Chihuahua was a typical northern boom state. For many years its mines had lain dormant, victims of the political upheavals of the previous half century. The state itself was the fiefdom of the Terrazas family, but the family patriarch, the aforementioned Don Luis, had sided with Lerdo in the conflicts of the 1870s, thus putting himself on Diaz's bad side. The intervention of Terrazas's son-in-law, Enrique Creel, at last restored good relations, and the Terrazas family empire resumed its growth apace with the mining and ranching industry. He and Creel practiced rural monopoly capital as an art form. In politics they took turns in the governorship, seeing to it that the laws favored their own investments. As the owner of more than seven million acres of land and half a million head of cattle, Don Luis liked to say, "I'm not from Chihuahua; I own Chihuahua" (No soy de Chihuahua; Chihuahua es de mi). The quip did not stray far from the truth, and Terrazas would pay dearly for this avarice in later years, when Pancho Villa made it his personal mission to destroy the family and its empire.

The north's sudden growth produced a society different from that of the south, characterized by its Indian languages and deeply rooted village life. The mines and railroads drew men from all over the country, men who surrendered tradition and family in search of economic opportunity. This was a mestizo culture, overwhelmingly Spanish-speaking and not overly devout in religious views; they prized self-reliance, horsemanship, and quickness with a gun. They did wage-work where they could find it or else settled temporarily into positions as sharecroppers and field hands. The more fortunate managed to carve out small private properties, with title if possible, but more importantly, with crops in the soil, an animal or two in the corral, and some access, however limited, to irrigation water.

The north also had its share of ethnic variety. Indigenous groups such as the Yaquis, Mayos, and Tarahumaras held on by combining wage and subsistence work or by retreating into remote mountain areas thus far unclaimed by the advancing mestizo state. Gringos settled here aplenty, drawn to places like Chihuahua and Baja California by generous land policies and a high demand for English-speaking managers and engineers.

The situation of western Mexico's Huichol Indians (or Wixáritari, as they call themselves) offers a classic example of commercial values intruding upon altogether different relationships between human beings and the land. From time beyond memory the Huichols had endured in their fields and forests in the area of what is today Jalisco and Nayarit, venturing out only to the Wirikuta, a mountainous region of San Luis Potosí where ceremonial ingestion of peyote connected them with the spiritual forces that governed their lives. The Huichols had guarded their land base tenaciously, emerging relatively intact into the early 1850s and siding with mestizo Manuel Lozada (1828–73) in his resistance to the intrusions of the Juárez government from 1869 to 1873. Armed conflict lost its appeal with the capture and execution of Lozada. Díaz's land reforms soon increased pressure from hacendados intent on seizing western lands for their market potential. Disagreements among villages on aims and responses limited the effectiveness of indigenous resistance; fortunately for the Huichols, the sheer remoteness and rugged terrain kept their homelands from becoming a second Chihuahua.

In the 1890s, meanwhile, a new group of immigrants began to make its appearance in the north: Asians, mostly Chinese and Japanese. The pressure of dense populations, coupled with the economic decrepitude of the late Qing (Manchu) Dynasty, had been pushing them eastward across the Pacific since the California gold rush of the mid-1800s. Their greatest concentration was in the western United States, where they farmed, ran small businesses, and provided the manual labor for the transcontinental railroad. But as the gold strikes played out and competition for jobs increased among the western regions' working class, nativist sentiment eventually caught up with the Chinese immigrants; in 1882 the United

States passed its first anti-immigration law, exclusively targeting Asians. Chinese immigration thus settled on northwest Mexico. Here the new-comers either made a new home for themselves or else bided their time until they were able to move northward. In places such as Sonora, Chi-nese immigrants' success provoked a reaction similar to that of California. Indeed, one of the more deplorable features of the Mexican Revolution (1910–20) was its profound anti-Asian sentiment, an air of nativist hostil-ity in which the killing of Chinese nationals did not necessarily violate the Ten Commandments.

Another northern region that experienced rapid change was the state of Coahuila. Commercial agriculture in this arid northern state had cen-tered around the Laguna region, but the volume of river water varied tremendously from year to year, while the region itself lay far from profit-able markets. These facts slowly changed, first when dam projects began in the 1850s, and second when a railroad line came through in 1884. The Laguna quickly began to produce bumper crops of cotton, which grew alongside the indigenous guayule plant, whose resins could be used to waterproof tarp.

Many small farmers and sharecroppers worked the wetlands here, but two major forces contested for domination. The Madero family had come here from Spain in the 1780s and had gradually extended its reach into every area of the regional economy. No foes of positivist progress, the Madero clan engaged in mining, retailing, and banking, but above all it reaped a fortune from its Laguna plantations. Somewhat against their will, however, they found themselves at odds with President Díaz, who showered concessions and favors on the British-based Tlahuililo Com-pany. In their struggle to defend their own water rights, the Madero fam-ily inadvertently became the champions of the many sharecroppers and small freeholders who shared their nationalist perspective as well as their urgent need for irrigation. For all their Porfirian cut, then, the Maderos ever so slowly came to epitomize northern commercial resentment of the old regime.

Unquestionably, the most unique experiment in northern develop-ment came in the state of Nuevo León—in particular in its shining city, Monterrey. Díaz remembered the province as a troublemaker; it had been the personal fiefdom of Santiago Vidaurri (1809–67), the man who had done all possible to resist federal control, who had sided opportunistically with the French, and whom Díaz had executed as ignominiously as possible, making him kneel in a pigsty as he faced the firing squad. To prevent further troubles, in 1885 Díaz sent his most trusted general, Bernardo Reyes (1850–1913), to develop the area while simultaneously assuring peace and regional subordination to national interests.

Reyes carried out this charge to a degree that surprised even the dictator. The United States' Sherman Silver Purchase Act (1890) had committed the federal government to buy silver but had simultaneously forbidden the importation of foreign ore—a boon aimed to help western mine owners. But the law made no prohibitions against importing foreign *bullion*: that is, silver ore that had already been processed into pure metal bars. Taking advantage of this loophole, in 1890 Reyes oversaw the creation of a smelting and refining complex, the Fundidora, based in the city of Monterrey. It was the first of its kind in Mexico, and it succeeded brilliantly. While the Fundidora's owners, the newly wealthy Garza-Sada family, liked to celebrate the spirit of free enterprise, the truth was that it had all happened by means of direct government intervention, rather like the state-conglomerate partnerships that developed the Asian Tigers after 1963.

To assure a large urban workforce, Reyes took the unprecedented step of outlawing debt peonage in the state of Nuevo León. Without this legal mechanism, haciendas were unable to function, and the workers fled in droves to seek higher wages in the big city. Reyes was no friend of labor: he used force to break up strikes and had no tolerance for any sort of worker organization not under his own control. But his policies did transform Monterrey into Mexico's industrial giant. After the Fundidora, Monterrey also opened a glass refining plant and Mexico's first commercial brewery, the Cuauhtémoc, which produced such standards as Carta Blanca and Tecate. Living standards rose, Monterrey emerged from its cow-town cocoon as a metropolitan butterfly, and Reyes himself seemed poised to succeed Díaz as Mexico's chief executive. No one was more aware of this than Bernardo Reyes himself; though unflinchingly loyal to the dictator, he saw himself as inheriting the presidency after Díaz's departure and built up a large political clientele that included the influential Madero family.

The south, meanwhile, was undergoing its own transformation, mainly in the form of conversion to commercial agriculture. Coffee, vanilla, sugar, and henequen now displaced the production of basic foodstuffs. Perhaps no region experienced so profound a transformation as the Yucatán Peninsula. Alternately home to a drowsy economy of corn-and-cattle plantations and the scene of political mayhem, Yucatán also offered an undreamed-of source of wealth when the newly mechanized wheat industry of the United States demanded vast amounts of cheap, strong binder twine. Yucatán's henequen fiber provided the solution, and the resourceful peninsulars even invented their own mechanical defibrator to accelerate production. The change took time, but by century's end king henequen ruled. With only a few exceptions in the peninsula's center and deep south, villages gradually lost their surrounding common lands, peonage became the norm, and a new wealth swept the land, concentrated almost exclusively in the hands of the henequen barons, the commercial houses, and the urban property owners and entrepreneurs. When their wars with Spain knocked Cuba and the Philippines out of the competition altogether in the 1890s, Yucatán held a virtual monopoly on a product now essential to the processing of a basic grain in the western world. Even today tales of *henequenero* decadence abound: the palatial homes and swimming pools, the unending parties, the shirts sent to European laundries for just the right amount of starch. Porfirio Díaz needed these revenues, but he feared Yucatecans as presumptuous troublemakers. As one way of keeping them in line, he promoted henequen baron Olegario Molina to the position of minister of development (*fomento*), thus keeping a potential enemy close at hand and far from his own base of power.

Further to the west the Soconusco region of Chiapas became the platform for a coffee boom. With a tentative Mexico-Guatemala border agreement inked off, the Díaz government encouraged German families to settle in the region. Between 1895 and 1900 the Germans built on their successful economic colonization of Guatemala by buying into the Soconusco coffee industry, making the area one of Mexico's premier agro-export zones. The ancient highland communities of Tzeltal, Tzotzil, and Tojolabal did not disappear, but they increasingly served as holding tanks for a migrant labor force that descended from the highlands each year into the southern lowlands to plant and tend the crops, only to return when the harvest was over.

Neither the Maya campesinos of Yucatán nor the fragmented Indian groups of Chiapas and Oaxaca could do much about their plight, at least for the moment. Linguistic barriers kept them isolated from the larger society and one another. Not so, however, the inhabitants of the state of Morelos, just to the south of Mexico City. This had been a land of ranchers and yeoman farmers, men and women who in many instances had fought with the Liberals in the great midcentury wars and who saw themselves as solid citizens of Mexico. Haciendas had always existed here, beginning with the great estate of Hernán Cortés, and had always produce a certain amount of sugar for urban markets, but they had existed in a certain balance with small properties. Two factors changed all of that. First, the railroads came through, giving Morelos entrepreneurs access to faraway markets; the city of Cuautla became a southern rail hub. Second, the brutal Cuban war for independence (1895–98), combined with the island's difficult postwar recovery, temporarily knocked the world's foremost sugar producer out of competition and handed Morelos sugar planters the opportunity of a lifetime. Almost overnight the old balance gave way to a plantocracy in which commercial estates gobbled up whole villages.

These stories were echoed throughout the republic. Encouraged by a favorable investment climate and the rapid introduction of railroads, telegraphs, and harbors, entrepreneurs built empires out of commonhold or once-marginal lands, converting them into export plantations, some under the domain of old hacendado families, others the prizes of aggressive foreigners. Taking advantage of the low cost of Mexican labor, French investors established an important role in textile industries. Germans carved out a lucrative trade in commodities. British and U.S. nationals turned up everywhere. In almost all cases, profits from these undertakings typically accrued to a privileged minority, while a majority experienced economic changes in the form of high prices, soaring property values, a corresponding loss of land, and the decline of peasant autonomy. Indeed, landless workers became Mexico's fastest growing class.

Finally, at the beginning of the twentieth century, an entirely new enterprise entered the Porfirian economy: oil. The hydrocarbon age had begun in northwestern Pennsylvania in 1859, when developers undertook the first systematic and successful drilling for petroleum. In those days the objective was not gasoline but rather heating oil used to light lamps and power steam engines in addition to providing fuel for furnaces. Then, as now, no one knew how much petroleum really existed, and anxiety set off an ongoing quest to find and exploit new sources.

Mexico offered one possibility. Native peoples had known of the seepage of what they called *chapopote* since pre-Columbian times. They used the black, gummy substance to create torches and waterproof walkways, pre-Hispanic miniatures of our own two-lane blacktops. But for years no amount of exploration had yet resulted in a profitable oil well. That fact changed in 1901, when legendary American oilman Edward Doheny, working through his company El Ebano, struck it big near Tampico. The gusher was the first of many, and within a few years Mexico rose to become one of the world's foremost producers, second only to the United States and surpassing such major fields as New Guinea and Russia's Baku region.

The oil business differed substantially from mining. The old Mexican families had no experience in this new endeavor, and the extraction and refining of crude passed completely into the hands of Standard Oil and Texaco. Even the normally accommodating Díaz found the U.S. firms pushy and difficult, and to establish some counterbalance he showered concessions on his favorite, British engineer Weetman Pearson, whose Aguila Mexicana, capitalized at some 60 million pesos, became the country's largest oil concern and the second-largest company in all of Mexico. Within a decade of Doheny's discovery, the oil business accounted for some 10 percent of the national economy. Pearson and the others worked mainly in the so-called Faro de Oro, the "golden lane" that ran along northern Veracruz. They also become aware that large deposits lay along the southern Gulf Coast, but decades of political violence and the nationalization of the industry would postpone the development of Tabascan and Campeche oilfields until the 1970s.

Dealing with Dissent

Change hurts. Díaz and his supporters understood perfectly well that their reforms would disrupt the lives of a broad stretch of Mexican society. Moreover, they feared a repeat of the instability and political violence that had so marred the early national years. To answer such fears, they developed methods of administration and policing to contain unrest.

Having risen to power through the military, the new president remembered only too well the institution's capacity to cause trouble. To close that avenue, he pulled up the ladder after him. Díaz slashed the size of federal troops; this alone bought him deep popularity, not only among the former soldiers but also among their wives and mothers, many of whom doubtless never dreamed of seeing their drafted husbands or sons again. He also slashed the bloated officers corps. Those who remained grew old and alcoholic in the job. By 1900 the army existed almost entirely as an instrument of internal repression, an attack dog that Díaz kept safely leashed within the cities, from which point railroads could whisk its now-reduced numbers to necessary points. Rurales often handled control at the state and local levels, while the army itself became a floating prison for criminals and troublemakers; a word from a local property owner sufficed to have a man hauled off for service, a bitter reality in the world of future revolutionaries like Emiliano Zapata. Finally, Díaz maintained a presidential guard that, despite its spit-and-polish reputation, suffered the same incompetence and dry rot that permeated the Rurales and other contemporary institutions.

As we have seen, Díaz made his peace with machine politics. While elections for governorships and national legislators continued, these amounted to little more than storefront exercises, empty formalities simulating inclusion and democratic principles. So it went in towns and villages. The dream of self-government through ayuntamientos had fueled political discourse since the days of the constitution of 1812. But in practice these new bodies had often failed to meet expectations. Small cliques of merchants and landowners typically took power and refused to budge, and many times voting brought on attacks, whether political or physical—not revolutions but partisan skin rashes that could, under the wrong circumstances, bring about even greater problems.

Under Díaz the treasured ayuntamientos continued, but real power increasingly gravitated into the hands of the governor's hand-picked administrators, the jefes políticos. Jefes formed the system's eyes and ears. Stationed at the district level, they kept tabs on populations, productivity, public schools, and troublemakers. By 1910 the jefe wielded vast powers over his appointed district; below him, assigned at the level of the subordinate villages, stood his own henchmen, the alcaldes, who had even less accountability. Indeed, the further one went from the city and the governor's office, the more brass-knuckled and arbitrary became the method of governance.

But the system had its weak joints. First, the federal government often operated in a fog of misinformation. Both governors and jefes had all the reason in the world to hide bad news from their superiors: above all else, the system favored stability, and reports of bad news thus became prima facie arguments for dismissal. Reading reports from the jefes can be a maddening experience: one forms the impression that rural districts contained no women, no indigenous people, no angry voices, no Catholics secretly carrying out such prohibited activities as religiously based schooling or unauthorized processions—in sum, nothing that might cause the jefe's superior to sit up in his chair.

Once in power, a new governor faced the challenge of rivals who, anxious for power but unwilling to confront Díaz directly, did everything possible to destabilize the administration in control. The idea was to create the impression that the governor was unable to maintain peace—the Porfiriato's cardinal sin—and would have to be removed, hopefully to be replaced by someone of the rival camp. This strategy remained normal procedure well into the late twentieth century.

State and local executives naturally tried to bury the mischief made by troublemakers in bland and antiseptic reports, a public pretense that everyone involved understood to be eyewash. Yet in the face of real problems, the under-armed jefe had to tack in the opposite direction, sending telegrams of the most alarming nature in hopes of obtaining federal or state troops to shore him up in a tight moment. The president or governor would have to decide whether the call for support was real or simply an incompetent appointee trying to rescue his own privileges. Such was the vast tissue of performance and disinformation that enveloped the whole of Porfirian Mexico.

Beyond the matter of electoral politics, Díaz also understood that growth would generate working-class unrest, and he took measures to control the problem. In short order the president eliminated the handful of radical groups, both foreign and homegrown, that had been agitating since the wide-open days of the French occupation. For example, the Greek anarchist Plotino Rhodakanaty found himself deported to Europe, his dream of a classless, stateless society not one day closer for all his years of proselytizing; Mexican followers who tried to apply his ideas to their rural worlds enjoyed no such gentle treatment and were more likely to be shot without trial.

Booting out bearded anarchists cost Díaz nothing, but confronting the Catholic Church posed a far more daunting mark. Deeply rooted and widely supported, its many rituals and community activities helped carry believers through the hard times in life; indeed, for many poor individuals a prayer to the santo was the only insurance policy available. At least until midcentury the Catholic Church had surpassed the secular state as a producer of trained intellectuals. Liberals disdained clerical privilege, and Díaz, himself a former seminary student and a mild believer of sorts, was also a lifetime Liberal militant who had no intention of turning over his hard-won power to some star chamber of bishops. But he realized the need for accommodation. In a Solomon-like strategy, the president left the old Liberal anticlerical legislation on the books, but in most instances the state declined to apply those laws. Rather, he employed sanctions only in those extreme cases where priests became troublemakers. Everyone knew that at local levels the supposedly outlawed Catholic schools continued to operate. Matters of public piety, such as processions and outdoor masses, could indeed take place, providing sufficient deference to and notification of secular authorities. While Díaz and the Liberal Party remained anathema for the more reactionary clergy, most priests and bishops understood that the new regime was extending them an olive branch, and they quietly accepted it.

Díaz also signaled a spirit of compromise on multiple fronts through his personal life. Following the death of his first wife, Delfina Ortega (his blood niece, who was fifteen years his junior), the president married the even younger Carmen Romero. Daughter of Matías Romero, a staunchly pro-Juárez diplomat from Oaxaca, she had a reputation for religious piety, and her influence helped push Díaz in the direction of compromise. As he once put it, "I go to church because my wife makes me, and because the life of the aristocracy has always been thus."

The Liberal revolt may have weakened the Catholic Church both economically and politically, but events soon showed how deeply rooted and how adaptable the institution really was. During its darkest years parishes had survived by switching to programs of volunteerism—urging believers to commit themselves to financial support, rather in the way of modern fund-raising. All the while the clergy received messages from Rome urging them to resist concessions to the modern age and to fight the growing forces of secularism and individual rights at all costs. However, in 1891

Pope Leo XIII issued a bull entitled *Rerum Novarum* (of new things), in which he urged Catholics to understand and attempt to rectify the many problems caused by the industrial revolution and growing urbanization. One of the most important redefinitions of the Catholic faith in modern times, *Rerum Novarum* fell on fertile ground in Mexico. Sympathetic bishops now promoted such projects as working-class education, youth clubs, and public health. During the Díaz years, at least, such projects remained carefully apolitical, but the return of visible Catholic activities gave both laymen and clergy a growing sense that the faithful had some say in national events, and they increasingly felt that their voice deserved to be heard. Yet the tragic upshot of this renewed public fervor still lay two decades in the future.

Despite these many precautions, Porfirian development did not go uncontested. One of the strongest challenges came from the province of San Luis Potosí. There, between 1879 and 1884 a radical priest named Mauricio Zavala rallied area peasants under the promise of a return to an idealized Catholic communitarian order, one that respected indigenous culture and enforced a rough equality of both riches and manners. Zavala's forces struck a surprise attack at Ciudad de Maiz, but the revolt eventually succumbed to the usual weaknesses of peasant insurgency as the federal army rushed to contain it. Zavala himself was taken prisoner and deported to Yucatán, where he spent the remainder of his life serving safely depoliticized coastal towns and writing dubious guides to the Maya language, guides that for some reason or another are still retailed in local pharmacies.

In the 1880s at least two regions of Mexico remained under the control of indigenous groups that in one way or another rejected state authority. In the Sonoran region the Yaqui peoples managed to fend off the intrusions of those whom they called yoris, or non-Yaquis. Meanwhile, in the faraway subtropical forests of southeast Yucatán, the various splinter groups of the Caste War still clung to a rough independence. These groups never formed a unified whole; some descended from the original rebel-settlers of Chan Santa Cruz, now fragmented into a number of isolated hamlets like Tusik and Señor. They pledged war to the death, and they would maintain that pledge long after it ceased to be anything more than performative, a kind of ceremonial exercise carried out to hold themselves together internally or else conducted for the benefit of curious outsiders. Others, the so-called *pacíficos*, signed peace treaties with the Yucatecan government, treaties that allowed them complete autonomy in exchange for not allying with their more warlike neighbors. Most of these pacífico communities lay in the deep south, and only rarely did they ever have contact with outsiders anyway.

Different as they were in just about all things, the Yaqui and Maya groups shared one important advantage: poorly controlled borders gave them access to the tools their struggles required. Yaquis were able to cross over into Arizona, where they picked up valuable wages working in the mines and fields. Autonomous Maya communities traded with merchants from British Honduras, using revenues obtained from leasing out logging rights in order to purchase arms and their most treasured commodity, gunpowder, utterly unreproducible under the geological limitations of the peninsula. Beyond that, the Maya insurgents benefited from the fact that Yucatecans had thrown themselves heart and soul into the great henequen boom and had lost interest in their long-standing dream of reconquest.

As Díaz consolidated his control over Mexico, he launched campaigns to reclaim both of these wayward territories. In 1886 the president sent the federal army to subdue the last remaining Yaquis. Now aided by railroads, telegraphs, and repeating rifles, the army successfully occupied the Yaqui River valley; it deported about seven thousand Yaquis to the henequen fields of Yucatán, where they earned a reputation as surly agitators. The best farmland in northern Mexico was now open for commercial development.

The campaign against Maya insurgents had to wait another fifteen years. Díaz held a low opinion of Yucatecans, whom he considered treacherous Florentines. Fully aware of the wealth being generated by the henequen boom, the president stepped back from any approach that might increase peninsular power. At last, in 1909, Díaz launched a sizable federal division under General Miguel Bravo, a man too old to benefit politically from any success. Within two years Bravo entered Chan Santa Cruz and drove its people into smaller, more remote encampments dotted throughout the forest. To keep control over these recently reclaimed areas, he established the federal territory of Quintana Roo, named for a Yucatecan turned Mexico City statesman of the independence wars of the 1810s. The coastal city of Chetumal, located just north of the border with British Honduras, became its capital. For the next half century all sorts of entrepreneurs, explorers, and simple adventurers crisscrossed this territory, working it for chicle and archaeological treasures. Rebel Mayas continued to hold out in the south and east, and although no longer a serious military threat, they certainly possessed the power to make commercial life difficult. Quintana Roo only gained statehood at the comparatively late date of 1974.

In brief, those who chose to confront the dictatorship faced challenges that, at least for the moment, remained insurmountable. Export-driven growth and liberal privatizations yielded too many benefits for Mexico's middle and upper classes to complain; against that support discontented workers and peasants stood little chance of fomenting a national movement of unified leadership. Díaz did not have to extinguish a national conflagration, only the occasional brushfire. And because his troops increasingly enjoyed the benefit of railroads, telegraphs, and industrially produced weapons, even the downsized federal military forces and their often-incompetent commanders sufficed to keep discontents in line.

Foreign Affairs

Mexico's growing stability and enticing investment opportunities naturally placed it in greater contact with the world of foreign affairs. First and foremost, that meant addressing the question of how to coexist with the often-predatory United States, which had already taken two-fifths of national territory and whose business community by 1876 was clamoring for access to Mexican markets and a greater control over border violence. To judge from private correspondence, Díaz himself shared this mistrust, but he and his fellow Puros accepted the idea that Mexico's development could only come from foreign investment. Indeed, the Tuxtepec revolt in 1876 had received extensive financing from investors in the United States, and especially Texas, and with Díaz's victory came expectations that the new order would deliver what its foreign underwriters had requested.

Not much happened in Díaz's first term (1876–80). His political hold remained tenuous, challenged by Lerdista revolts that broke out as late as 1879. At one point border relations hit such a rough patch that armies mobilized on both sides. But Díaz managed to score three major accomplishments in the way of enforcing border security and restoring peace. He arrested Juan Cortina, the caudillo of Tamaulipas, who had made an issue of championing Mexican squatters' rights along the Rio Grande. Second, in 1880 the Mexican army cornered Apache leader Victorio in the hills of Chihuahua; Victorio perished in the final encounter, either committing suicide or else picked off by a rifleman. Apache border raids declined markedly thereafter. Finally, Díaz made the first payment of Mexico's U.S.-held foreign debt, and under his successor Manuel González relations improved considerably. Whether by the agency of González or by Díaz, the presidential period of 1880–84 witnessed the first legal and administrative changes that opened Mexico to foreign investment.

Díaz may have given the U.S. investment community a loose leash, but he did make some efforts to distance himself from the United States on matters of foreign affairs. As an answer to the Monroe Doctrine's pretension to defend all of the hemisphere against European aggression, Díaz proposed his own approach, which was to pose Latin American unity against interventions. Unfortunately, the strategy fell on its face. Most Latin American peer nations were too deeply involved in their own wrenching transformations to bother about Spanish-speaking unity. In the 1890s, as the U.S. became distinctly more aggressive in Central America and the Caribbean, Díaz found his independent position increasingly difficult to sustain, and that fact stoked accusations that Porfirian Mexico was a lapdog for Uncle Sam.

On October 16, 1909, Mexico boasted yet another first: President William Howard Taft visited the country, meeting his counterpart Díaz in Ciudad Juárez. Each man had his agenda: by this time the Porfirian regime was struggling, and Taft wanted to verify the security of the astronomical amounts of U.S capital invested south of the Rio Grande. Díaz, meanwhile, hoped to signal to the world, and more specifically to his own people, that he enjoyed Washington's rock-solid support. Together they posed for photos: Taft portly and tall, Díaz decked out in his military uniform and medals. It was an exercise that would not be repeated until Franklin Roosevelt's brief trip to Monterrey in 1943 and, of far greater impact on bilateral relations, Harry Truman's much-remembered visit to Mexico City in 1947.

Then, as now, Mexico has a second and less commonly recognized border—its southern boundary with Central America. Relations with Guatemala have never been sunny. First came Iturbide's brief annexation of the region in the early 1820s, followed by a long-standing dispute over rights to part of Chiapas, especially the lucrative planter zone of Soconusco. The ongoing matter of Guatemalan migrant workers continued to be an irritant, and in more recent times, the spillover from the three-decade Guatemalan civil war. In his first administration Díaz made headway by extending support for the new liberal government of Justo Rufino Barrios, coming as it did after the long and archconservative rule of Rafael Carrera, who made Guatemala a home for anti-Liberal Mexicans. In exchange Barrios recognized Mexico's claim to Chiapas's Soconusco province, thus ending the decades-long territorial dispute. The man who eventually led surveying teams to map out the Mexico-Guatemalan border was none other than the same individual who had surveyed the Gran Línea: José Salazar Ilarregui. He had served the French as interventionist governor of Yucatán (an appointment that was its own punishment), had fled to New York in 1867, then returned under Díaz's policy of reconciliation. To this day Guatemala has never entirely recognized the sovereign existence of Belize, and perhaps for that reason Mexico has always shown considerable tolerance for and protection of this, the only English-speaking Central American nation. Yet Díaz also had to contend with Barrios's megalomaniac campaign to unite Central America by force. Fortunately for Don Porfirio, Barrios himself perished in the attempt in 1885, thus defusing a potential crisis of precisely the sort of unrest that Díaz dreaded.

In the Porfirian Style: Society and Culture

Porfirian Mexico exhibited changes at many different levels of society; the most evident took place among the urban middle and upper classes. Economic growth and expanded connections with the outside world naturally put it in line with global changes in lifestyles and mores. Doubtless these trends would have taken root even without the dictator—Mexico had absorbed foreign styles and ideas for years—but the conditions of the late nineteenth century, such as expanded foreign links and open investment policies, turned what had been a trickle of outside influences into a torrent.

In the world of ideas, Mexican thinkers thrilled to the writings of French philosopher Auguste Comte (1798–1857). Comte held that all

societies progressed from a religious age dominated by priests and su-
perstitions to a metaphysical age of idealistic doctrines to a scientific age
founded on observation and reason. In this last stage democratic dema-
gogy yielded to scientific management that, if discounting the voices of
the masses, at least brought peace and plenty. In this telling, quantitative
advances such as miles of railroad line plotted a nation's progress along
the three-stage path. Called Positivism, this doctrine appealed because it
justified the retreat from earlier Liberal ideals of constitutional process
and because it restricted decision-making to a tiny circle of informed elite
who called themselves *científicos*, the apostles of scientific management.

Under Díaz the upper crust certainly had more money than before, a
key Positivist marker, and with that money came an even rarer treasurer:
leisure time. They embraced such foreign fascinations as bicycles, baseball, and mountain climbing and learned to disdain blood sports such
as boxing and bullfighting. They spoke English for business, French for
culture, and indigenous tongues never at all. Italian baroque architecture
became the rage for urban makeovers. Porfirians adored those pursuits
that spoke of order and refinement and excoriated anything suggesting
the mud and manure of rural life.

The lives of women varied as much as any other aspect of Mexican
society at this time. In rural villages the ancient onus of bearing children and grinding corn persisted in all of its monotony, and if peasant
women felt changes, it was through sharing the misery that heaped upon
rural people as the available land base contracted. The cities, however,
told a somewhat different story. Those mothers, wives, and daughters
who came with their families to find work in the booming cities had to
carve out new means of existence: as cooks, vendors, washers, servants,
and the dozens of other low-paying female occupations that allowed the
great urban machine to function. Meanwhile, women of affluent Porfirian families fared immensely better. Their lives included piano and
French lessons, foreign vacations, and favorable marriages. Liberal civil
codes abolished mandatory partible inheritance (which had protected
young women's rights to inherit), yet these same laws freed unmarried
adults, females included, from parental control, allowing them to marry
as they wished. On the whole, most of the paternal attitudes toward
female sexuality and personal rights remained in place until the twentieth century.

One obsession of Mexican state-builders was the fostering of national holidays. Prior to the reform era of the mid-nineteenth century, Mexican holidays had always hinged on the annual religious cycle, the most important dates being Semana Santa (Holy Week, the week before Easter Sunday), the Feast of Corpus Cristi (celebrated in May or June), Día de Muertos (Day of the Dead, November 2), el Día de Reyes (Day of the Three Kings [Epiphany], January 6), and the various feast days of the village saints. But as part of their consolidation of the secular state, Liberals promoted a new set of holidays based on the emergence of Mexico as a sovereign political body. The first of these was the Dieciséis de Septiembre (September 16) fiesta patria, built around Miguel Hidalgo's fateful call to arms to the people of the Bajío. A set of rituals attached themselves to this event: an assembly of public officials in the town square, patriotic discourse, improvised orchestras and noisy brass bands, fireworks, and the evening tertulias. It so happened that the dictator's own birthday fell on September 15, and to collapse the two events, Díaz and all subsequent Mexican presidents began to inaugurate Dieciséis with the *grito*, or cry of Hidalgo, in the closing hours of that day. Donning the presidential sash, the leader steps out onto balcony of the National Palace and rings the very bell that Hidalgo once used, crying, "¡Viva la independencia! ¡Viva México!" Of all the grand ceremonies that the Liberal movement summoned up, this one alone took root, perhaps because the war with Spain had touched so many people in so many provinces.

Porfirians had less success with two secondary holidays: Cinco de Mayo and April 2. The former commemorated the surprise defeat of the French expeditionary force at the fortress outside Puebla. It gained some popularity in its place of origin but made only limited headway in the outlying provinces. Cinco de Mayo's real apotheosis came, ironically, in the United States, where the beer and restaurant industries used it as a marketing strategy to target growing Latino populations in the twentieth century. The April 2 festival observed Porfirio Díaz's 1867 victory over the last French defenders of Puebla. The political machinery went to surprising lengths to position the event on par with the great national holidays, but to no avail; April 2 today is largely forgotten. Indeed, almost all of today's major Mexican holidays have roots in the liturgical year.

Meanwhile, technology was changing faster than calendars, and it effected Mexico along with the rest of the world. Telegraphy, which Samuel

Morse had unveiled in 1837, was already connecting diverse points by the time of the Tuxtepec revolt. In 1881 an underwater telegraph line connected Galveston with Tampico and Veracruz; connections via land lines soon made it possible to send messages from Mexico City to Washington, New York, and the European capitals. Telephones made their entry in the last decade of the Porfiriato, and even though telegrams remained a part of national life until well after 1950, humans could now speak with each other over long distances, directly and without the use of complicated codes and their readers. In the villages the first telephones were typically set up in the office of the jefe político and connected him with offices in the state capital. The practice of owning private telephones lay further into the future.

People could not only send voices across wires: they could record them. When Thomas Alva Edison invented the gramophone, with its wax cylinders and immense lily-like tubes, he cannily sent models to heads of state throughout the world. The first exposition of this new technology took place before an astonished audience, who struggled in vain to find the man they assumed was hidden beneath the gramophone's table. Among the oldest known recorded voices of Mexico is, not surprisingly, that of Porfirio Díaz himself, who in August 1909 sent an appropriately Positivist message thanking Edison for the "happiness, well-being, and wealth" that his many inventions had generated for mankind.

Equally surprising was the introduction of the motion picture. Invented by the Lumière brothers in France in 1895, this technology quickly reached into the far corners of the world, including Mexico. Here the new invention quickly conquered popular imagination; its early use also reflected the personalistic and authoritarian nature of the Porfiriato. One of the oldest known films made in Mexico shows Díaz himself riding his horse in Chapultepec Park. Motion-picture cameras also captured Díaz's historic meeting with Taft in Ciudad Juárez, snippets of which footage still survive. However, the man who did the most to promote Mexican filmmaking was unquestionably Salvador Toscano Barragán, a Guadalajaran who had originally trained as an engineer and who began to produce short films in 1896. He opened his first movie theatre in 1897 in Mexico City; the following year he produced Mexico's first feature-length film, a version of Spanish poet José Zorrillo's *Don Juan Tenorio*. Toscano mainly inclined toward documentaries, and he covered such uniquely national topics as popular celebrations, the newly formed (and, to most citizens, exotic) Territory of Quintana Roo, and the centennial celebrations of 1910. Beyond these firsts, though, Toscano will forever be remembered for taking up the camera in time to capture large swatches of the Mexican Revolution, including the presidential campaign of Francisco Madero in 1910. Toscano's work survives only as unedited rushes that have been edited in a variety of forms, including a fictional narrative scripted by his daughter Carmen and released in 1950 as *Memorias de un mexicano.*

The pursuit of humanistic arts continued alongside Mexico's technological revolution. Suddenly peace reigned, and young men who earlier might have had to take up arms in one cause or another now enjoyed the time to develop their talents. Funding for academies curved upward; wealthy and even middle-class Mexicans discovered the means and the inclination to collect *objets d'art*. But did the results live up to hopes? Sadly, Porfirian-era art has acquired a spotty reputation. Modern-day critics, especially those enamored of revolutionary ideologies and the bold public murals they inspired, often find pre-1920 creations ponderous, mawkishly sentimental, and above all inferior derivatives of European trends—cloying artifacts of the unlovable nineteenth century. The accusation lacks merit. While it is true that Porfirian artists were no modernists (neither were most of their European contemporaries), the age did call forth some significant talents who produced works of lasting power. A comprehensive examination would far exceed the pages of this volume, and here we must limit ourselves to a few of the more outstanding individuals.

Topping any list of gilded-era Mexican artists is José Luis Velasco y Gómez (1840–1912). Born in the unlikely metropolis of San Miguel Temascalcingo, just outside of Toluca, Velasco rose through a combination of application, luck, and a remarkable innate talent. His long, extremely varied corpus of work includes portraits, illustrations of flora and fauna, pen-and-ink sketches, and first-rate draftsmanship. Velasco traveled to, and meticulously rendered, the majestic ruins of Teotihuacán prior to their Porfirian restorations. Above all, he set himself the task of capturing on canvas the breathtaking landscapes of an Anáhuac valley that had yet to be transformed by urban sprawl. He arguably stands not only as Mexico's finest painter (all apologies to Diego Rivera and his contemporaries) but also as one of the most accomplished visual artists the Western Hemisphere has ever produced.

Visual art of a different sort emerged in the work of José Guadalupe Posada (1852–1913). Born in Aguascalientes, he learned his craft in the popular newspaper and broadsheet trade, for which he provided engravings and lithographic images. Posada's profession naturally thrust him into the role of crusading visual journalist who uses his art to denounce abuses, chastise the powerful, and identify causes. Above all he is remembered for his *calaveras*, whimsical skeleton figures that he used to satirize the Mexican people in all aspects of their lives and foibles. Posada died a complete pauper, but the coming generation of revolutionary painters revered him as an artist who did not shrink from political controversies and who embraced the dynamic vernacular of popular art. Adaptations of his iconic work can be found throughout the length and breadth of the country today.

In terms of music, the Porfirian era also called up luminaries, the most famous of whom is certainly Juventino Rosas (1868–94). A native of Guanajuato state, Rosas achieved his fame the hard way. He received some training at the National Conservatory, but his family's poverty forced him to withdraw, and he earned a living as a street musician and in various short-lived musical acts. He composed an impressive corpus but is best remembered today for "Sobre las olas" ("Over the Waves"), a much-loved waltz that many listeners erroneously attribute to the Viennese master Johann Strauss and the rights to which Rosas sold for the grand sum of forty-five pesos. Rosas garnered attention in the last years of his life but died at age twenty-six of spinal myelitis. His works continue to be performed today; he also became the subject of a biographical film, *Sobre las olas* (1950), starring matinee idol Pedro Infante as the composer. Beyond Juventino Rosas, Porfirian Mexico also produced an enormous songbook. Its much-loved melodies drew from a variety of venues, including the popular Spanish-derived music hall productions known as *zarzuelas*, as well as songs composed specifically for performance at the *salóns* that were a feature of life for the upper class.

Porfirian literature enjoys a limited readership today: in part because sustained reading has suffered with the rise of digitalized information, but also because that literature's preoccupations and perspectives often strike us as dated, detached, and hopelessly elitist. The idea of making a living in Mexico as a professional novelist or poet was out of the question, given the extremely low literacy rates and skewed distribution of wealth.

Writers therefore tended to come up through the world of journalism or else maintained full-time careers while plying their literary talents on the side. Some scrambled to survive; others hailed from the monied set and enjoyed the privilege of writing history, literature, or essays at their leisure, as a kind of self-entertainment.

Here too there were standouts. Manuel Payno (1810–94) had actually militated on the side of Conservatives, going so far as to embrace the interventionist government of Maximilian. He made peace with Benito Juárez after 1867 and while carrying out diplomatic work in Spain produced his sprawling masterpiece, *Los bandidos de Río Frío* (1889–91), a classic nineteenth-century work complete with complex, intertwined plotlines, thick naturalist descriptions, and more characters than the average reader can keep straight. At least one of the more prolific writers produced something of a political allegory against the Díaz regime. Ignacio Manuel Altamirano (1834–93), a man of Nahua origins from the state of Guerrero, rose to become both a man of letters and a militant Liberal, fighting in all of the midcentury reform struggles. However, by the end of his years he had become concerned with the nation's political drift under the dictator and produced a novel entitled *El zarco* (1901), which concerned the rise and demise of a bandit who, at least when examined in a certain light, might be taken as a symbol of Díaz's betrayal of Liberal ideals. Possibly fearing repercussions, Altamirano withheld publication of the manuscript, which in fact did not appear in print until eight years after the author's death.

Advances in all of these arts stemmed from a common root. While hard on peasant freeholders and Indian communities, the Porfiriato did bring the peace, stability, and urban markets (together with the requisite patronage) necessary for widespread artistic training and production. The Porfirian creative set may have turned their backs on an earlier generation's *costumbrismo* (folkways), the celebration of which characterized much of early Latin America's national literature. But the best of them continued to reveal a keen appreciation for Mexican culture and society and mustered the talent and the determination necessary to produce works of enduring quality.

The years of Porfirio Díaz left an indelible print on Mexican society and spawned a never-ending debate on the period's advantages and disadvantages. Advocates point to the enormous material gains, the stability, and the advancement of urban culture. Porfirian Mexico is a quantifier's dream, and at least some of its numbers paint a showpiece of progress. The population nearly doubled, from eight million at the time of Hidalgo to fifteen million in 1910. Instead of the paltry forty miles of railroads, there were now forty thousand. Mining concessions that formerly numbered around forty had grown to thirteen thousand. A hundred years earlier it would have been hard to find one out of a hundred Mexicans who could read and write; now, one out of ten enjoyed basic literacy, with a somewhat higher figure (15 percent) in the north. Though still an overwhelmingly rural nation, Mexico witnessed considerable urban growth: in Monterrey, in Mérida, in Guadalajara, and above all in Mexico City. The capital remained a far cry from the sprawling megapolis known today, but like its counterparts in Peru, Argentina, and Brazil, it had begun to take in the refugees from a collapsing rural world, men and women who came in hopes of higher wages, a better standard of living, and the chance to educate their children. Tellingly, most of the later revolutionaries endorsed these changes, even as they proposed a greater sharing of political power.

Detractors, meanwhile, have no difficulty in pointing fingers at the regime's weaknesses. The conspicuous public violence of Mexico's early years may have declined, but systematic, low-grade repression took its place. Díaz may have succeeded in consolidating control over national territory, but he did so by ceding enormous economic leverage to the foreign investment community. And in terms of metrics, two statistics tower above all the rest: a single-digit minority now controlled over 90 percent of cultivable lands, while the fastest-growing class of people in the country comprised landless workers. The changes that the urban intelligentsia celebrated came at the cost of a dispossessed rural peasantry whose demands for agrarian reform became the background hum of the next half century. Simultaneously, the wave of industrialization produced an urban working class that Friedrich Engels would have recognized instantly: poor, exploited, and cut off from the protective support of the village. Even the vaunted Porfirian efficiency was more sham than reality. Most political institutions, such as the jefes políticos and the Rurales, operated with ramshackle inefficiency. And in every province, Don Porfirio's brand of top-down politics had corrupted public life and led to rule by cliques of ruling families. The detractors' strongest argument remains the fact that Mexico's *belle époque* gave way to the most violent episode in the entire history of Latin America. In this telling, the many scenes detailed above—an august statesman reading into a gramophone, yester-year's general bedizened with medals, the flickering film images of a man on horseback—were not the beginning of something but were rather the final moments of an outworn period and an outmoded mindset that were about to crumble under the blows of revolution.

6

A Confusion of Armies

The Mexican Revolution, 1910–1920

The twentieth century is remarkable for its dramatic social revolutions. In Russia, China, Bolivia, Cuba, Vietnam, Nicaragua, Iran, and elsewhere, radical forces overthrew an aging regime, cast out foreign imperialism, stood the social order on its head, shook the pockets of the rich, and even tried to change the way human beings think and act. Revolutions usually caught their world off guard. They began as some minor rumpus, spread unexpectedly like wildfires, partially transformed their world, and then receded, leaving behind a messy legacy, a traumatic period endlessly debated between defenders and detractors.

It was Mexico's fate to be first, and that fate surprised friends and critics alike. Indeed, in 1910 Porfirio Díaz stood at the pinnacle of his world. In thirty-four years he had achieved the impossible, bringing revolts and separatist wars to an end, curtailing indigenous autonomy in the northwest and southeast, and spreading railroad lines and telegraph wires like so much bunting across the land. As Andrew Carnegie famously remarked after returning from a visit to the great statesman, "The idea of a revolution in Mexico is now impossible." Perhaps, but it was soon to be a fact: the Porfirian order was about to be consumed in the flames of a conflict that stoked passions, baffled outsiders, and above all wrought incredible suffering on large sections of the Mexican people. Those who endured it, together with the generations that came in its wake, were destined to spend endless hours questioning its causes and its consequences, reliving with inescapable fascination this bloody entrée into the modern age.

The Death Struggle of an Old Order

Porfirio Díaz had dominated his world, but following his 1900 reelection he succumbed to a three-part crisis, and like some prehistoric beast caught in a tar pit, his attempts to escape only mired him deeper still. That crisis spun out of land loss, political succession, and economic downturn.

First and foremost, the country suffered from popular discontent stemming mainly, but not exclusively, from the reapportionment of land. Even historians who strongly disagree about such matters as nationalism, labor militancy, and the overall consequences of the revolution concur that demand for agrarian reform served as the fundamental motor of events. Perhaps the conversion to private property and export agriculture was necessary and, in some ways, inevitable, but it had all happened too quickly, too completely, and in a way that was simply too slick for people accustomed to earning their living by tilling the soil. Actual conditions varied greatly among provinces; still, rural Mexicans shared a belief in land rights and were willing to take up arms to defend that right. The demand for restitution of lost lands may seem archaic to twenty-first-century U.S. readers, oriented as we are to society where only 3 percent of the population actively farms. But during the Porfiriato life meant farming and ranching, and Díaz's rule had relegated the majority of Mexicans to the status of landless workers.

The reckoning had been a long time coming. Land pressures had been building since the eighteenth century as the indigenous population rebounded from the plague years. Prior to 1876, politicians, acting in the interests of the landowning class to which they were kin, made uncertain efforts toward breaking up village lands. Díaz's national legislation of 1883 became the real mechanism for acquiring public or communal property. But more than anything, it was a late round of legislation—often at the state level and often as self-serving instruments of enrichment for entrenched local families—that lit the fuse. The two most conspicuous instances were in Morelos and Chihuahua, both soon to become revolutionary epicenters. In the former, rising sugar prices following Spain's destructive war in Cuba led profit-hungry planters to launch a final assault on village properties, provoking an armed insurgency led by one Emiliano Zapata. To the north, in 1904 the Terrazas-Creel oligarchy enacted a law that enabled the family to take possession of millions of untitled acres occupied by small freeholders.

Problems of the countryside soon bled into the city. Dispossessed campesinos could either go to work on the estates, head north to the mining districts, cross the border in search of U.S. mining work or agricultural stoop labor, or else look for better opportunities in places like Mexico City, Puebla, and Veracruz. The actual number of men who labored in mines or factories paled beside the huge rural masses, and in the early decades of the Porfiriato they had posed little threat. But as factory and mining work expanded, their concentrated numbers and their essential role in key industries gradually led them to collective action.

City life was harsh. Lodging was shabby: mostly one-room apartments in tenements carved out of the baronial town homes of yesteryear. Overloaded trams offered the only form of public transportation. Conditions were unsanitary, pulque bars abundant, and family life unstable. For all its shortcomings, though, this world offered an improvement over the hard existence of miners. Their work exposed them to constant danger of accident and disease, on top of which they bore the disdain of foreign technicians and managers.

Said conditions naturally invited labor unrest. In his early years Díaz had come down hard on nascent organizations, and workers had retreated to such nonconfrontational approaches as mutualist societies in which workers pooled scant resources to help one another through tight moments. But serious militancy returned, particularly in the cotton industry. Though hardly the "satanic mills" of 1845 England, Mexico's textile factories had grown steadily throughout the nineteenth century and had wrought the same changes as elsewhere, reducing artisans to proletarianized wage earners. The owners, the majority of whom were Mexican nationals, imported European technology and used the rivers of Mexico and Puebla states as an energy source. The Porfirian government was certainly no friend of organized labor, but unionization efforts persisted throughout the last two decades of the century, and strikes occurred every year or so, mostly as small affairs that scored only minor gains and soon ended.

The opening decade of the twentieth century witnessed a series of large strikes unimaginable only ten years earlier. Working-class activists found inspiration in the writings of radical intellectuals (discussed below). First came El Mayorazgo, a French-owned textile mill located in Puebla. In 1904 workers surprised management with a shutdown, but the company's large inventory, together with poor union provisioning, forced workers to give up.

More politically damaging was the 1906 strike at Cananea, a U.S.-owned copper mine located in Nogales, in northern Sonora. It was the property of a flamboyant independent named "Colonel" William C. Greene, who kept wages low, conditions poor, and prices at the company store as high as possible. Trouble began when the night shift, coming off duty in the early morning hours of June 1, learned of potential layoffs. An angry but largely spontaneous protest escalated into a shoot-out with management, and the state chapter of the Rurales at that moment was far away. These circumstances prompted the governor of Sonora to allow the Arizona Rangers to cross the border, where he deputized them as state police and allowed them to put down the strike by killing twenty-three workers and wounding as many more. The following year the government suppressed a strike of textile workers at the French-owned Río Blanco factory, in Veracruz, at the cost of over fifty lives. For many Mexicans these incidents laid bare the flaws of the Porfirian system: mother to foreigners, stepmother to Mexicans, and above all an obstacle to the well-being of the working class.

The Porfirian order's second problem came in the form of a succession crisis in which political elites realized that the dictator had to concede power—either by his own decision or by that of Mother Nature—and that some strongman would take his place. But no one could agree on who or how. Since the last decades of the nineteenth century, a fissure had emerged within the upper ranks of Porfirian leadership. The men whom the Tuxtepec revolt had originally brought to power comprised an "old guard" who had risen through military service. Their years of campaigning had brought them into contact with Mexicans of all walks of life. No white-gloved pseudo-Europeans, they were perfectly at ease scooping up their food with tortillas and hoisting a glass of pulque, and their knowledge of the culture, together with their networks of friends and allies formed over decades in the field, helped them to make the dictatorship function. Bernardo Reyes (1850–1913) stood at the apex of this bunch; both his seniority and his administrative success in Monterrey positioned him as Díaz's natural heir, even though Reyes was a mere fifteen years younger.

But two forces worked against the populists: they were growing old (after all, Tuxtepec put an end to the warrior life), while the very changes they had helped to bring about demanded the services of an educated technocracy, a level of accomplishment for which these old soldiers hardly qualified. Enter into this setting a rival elite, the so-called *cientí-ficos*. Devotees of Auguste Comte and all things European, they lacked–and in truth disdained–popular roots, but knew their way around foreign currency exchange, railroad contracts, public utilities, and the latest trends in poetry and education. Not necessarily younger than the populists, they nevertheless had risen in government through more privileged paths. The unofficial leader of the group was José Ives Limantour, the son of a French speculator who had made a fortune off the Liberal land reforms. Education czar Justo Sierra Méndez descended from Yucatecan political royalty: his grandfather had served as governor during the early Caste War, while his father, Justo Sierra O'Reilly, almost single-handedly launched southeast Mexico's literary tradition. These and like-minded individuals harbored deep suspicions of rule by popular will, an arrangement that they held responsible for the disasters of the early national period. Instead they proposed to govern through scientific methods that only educated gentlemen could truly understand.

Díaz himself endorsed neither side. The dictator disdained intellectuals and public debate, and in private he manifested no interest in the theories of social critics and philosophers. His own background positioned him more on the side of his old military compatriots. And yet he needed the services of educated men and so allowed the científicos wide latitude: as long as Mexico had to swim in the waters of international finance, there would be a place for individuals such as Limantour. Díaz also realized that the political division was his own gain and watched with a certain sardonic amusement as the various groups jockeyed for position.

Until his later years Díaz had remained capable and lucid, and the various factions remained content to let him go on without a designated successor. But by 1904 the seventy-four-year-old president was slipping. He no longer walked or spoke with the decisiveness of old. Increasingly deaf in that era before cochlear implants, secretaries had to shout into his ears to make themselves heard. Nor could he occupy the position of a Jupiter, a dealer of political thunderbolts thronged by ministers, advisors, and investors, and somehow still hear with equal precision the voices of his people.

These subtle clues did not escape foreign investors and the frock-coated diplomats who served their bidding. U.S. entrepreneurs once doted on Díaz, but the oil companies resented the favors he showered on the Englishman Weetman Pearson and the immensely successful Aguila Mexicana, and they began to ask whether the old man had not lost his touch. Even those who still revered the dictator feared the instability that might come with a power struggle, and they began to lobby for a vice presidency, a position that Mexico had eliminated since the troubled days of Vicente Guerrero and Anastacio Bustamante. After some indecision Díaz at last settled on Sonora's científico governor Ramón Corral, the man who had presided over the Yaquí removal and provincial development. The move enraged Bernardo Reyes, but ultimately his sense of loyalty prevailed over personal ambition, and instead of challenging the decision he accepted an appointment as observer to European militaries—essentially a foreign exile. This step may have removed Reyes as a contender, but inadvertently it left a huge body of discontented Reyistas searching for an alternative leader, and that fact proved instrumental in destabilizing Mexico.

The nation's changing demographics only intensified the political headaches. As long as a significant body of Mexicans could remember the terrible times before 1876, the dictator's version of law and order looked attractive. But by 1910 Mexico had an extremely young population, the fruits of peace. Virtually all the major leaders of the Mexican Revolution were born after 1867; they had no recollection of the bad old days, and their minds were freer to contemplate the idea of a change in the political order.

This situation nurtured opposition in what might be called a middle sector: its members were neither campesinos nor upper oligarchy, but urban and mestizo; they were often provincially based and educated for such professions as law, medicine, and journalism. Their opposition writings plied a jumbled ideology tinted by anarchism, Marxism, nationalism, anticlericalism, progressive reforms, and appeals to the idealized constitution of 1857. And they rose to action over an unlikely issue. In June 1900 the bishop of San Luis Potosí publicly praised the regime for ceasing to apply the anticlerical legislation of the era of Juárez reforms. His remarks infuriated the young progressives. Among those moved to action was Camilo Arriaga, an engineer from that same state and the nephew of one of Benito Juárez's closest allies. In 1901 Arriaga founded what became the Partido Liberal Mexicano (PLM) to protest the president's seeming drift into cronyism and religious conservatism. The movement attracted like-minded individuals throughout the country. Above all, it drew in the Flores Magón brothers of Oaxaca—Ricardo, Jesús, and Enrique—professionals all and passionately committed anarchists.

The PLM and its newspaper mouthpiece, *Regeneración*, had an effect on Mexico that was as ambiguous as it was profound. The movement's anarchist message provided the catalyst that many people required. Its writers excelled at identifying abuses, naming names, and stirring up discontent. Industrial workers appointed those rare creatures, literate factory hands, to read *Regeneración* to them as they labored. It stirred passion and generated hopes for a better future, and it is safe to say that anarchist literature and ideals exerted far more influence here than any work by Karl Marx. In the long run, though, Mexican anarchism was destined to be a bridesmaid, not a bride. As the Flores Magóns learned to their chagrin, working-class movements stopped short of spontaneous uprisings. Their concentration in key industries and locations, the very fact that gave them clout that surpassed their numbers, also left them vulnerable to repression. They could not take to the hills and backlands like rural insurgents, and once soldiers trained their arms on a factory, any strike was over. Partly for this reason, later Mexican labor leaders consistently accepted deals with the revolutionary state in exchange for such benefits as increased pay, reduced hours, or state arbitration of strikes.

Díaz eventually tired of *Regeneración*'s radical harangues and closed the paper in 1905. The Flores Magón brothers fled to the United States; there they lived the sort of miserable underground existence that only true revolutionaries are prepared to tolerate. They continued to publish both English and Spanish versions of their newspaper and skipped from town to town to evade U.S. authorities, who had no more love for anarchist radicals than did the dictator himself.

Amid these problems a third crisis blew in: an economic downturn that the government could neither avert nor ameliorate. Like so many serious recessions, this one had been years in the making. In October 1907 a banking panic gripped the United States, set off by a failed scheme to corner the copper industry. In those days the federal government had practically no control of either money supply or trading practices; only a massive public commitment by J. P. Morgan and other financiers ultimately stopped the crisis from deepening into a full-scale depression. But the panic had dire consequences for the Porfirian order. Money was recalled, new investments failed to materialize, and within months the Díaz government faced the unpalatable prospect of austerity. And as an old Mexican proverb goes, it's the skinny dog that gets the mange: in an eerie replay of the events leading up to the Hidalgo revolt, the years 1907–08 witnessed severe droughts and crop shortages that raised already steep prices for basic commodities like corn, beans, beef, and wheat. Few developments are as likely to stir up discontent as layoffs, price hikes, unpaid salaries, and unfed workers, and within a year Díaz found himself in the most precarious situation since the failure of the La Noria revolt. Mexico had become a land of angry murmurs.

The Impossible Revolution

In his younger days Díaz might have finessed the situation. But now approaching eighty, he committed a rare and, in this case, fatal error in 1908 by speaking too candidly in a lengthy interview with reporter James Creelman. In the interview the president announced that Mexico had advanced to the point of admitting free and fair elections and that in 1910 he himself would not be a candidate. Díaz may have advanced these disingenuous remarks as a way of smoking out rivals, or perhaps he intended to reassure the foreign investment community, since Creelman actually published the interview in the U.S.-based *Pearson's* magazine. But in the politically charged atmosphere following the 1907 economic crisis, the Mexican press printed a translation, and the election of 1910 quickly became the talk of the Porfirian smart set.

No one saw further into this turn of events than a wealthy young hacendado from the state of Coahuila. At first glance Francisco Ignacio Madero González (1873–1913) seemed an unlikely candidate to overthrow Latin America's great strongman. The eldest son of one of northern Mexico's wealthiest families, Madero had studied in France and at the University of California Berkeley, where he acquired an interest in modern agriculture, corporate paternalism, and above all the Spiritualist movement that so intrigued many turn-of-the-century intellectuals. He returned home to manage and modernize the family properties. Standing

Spirit forces speaking through the ouija board informed Francisco Ignacio Madero that he was to become president of Mexico, but they neglected to mention his tragic fate in that role. Madero launched his movement against Díaz in 1910 with the help of his wife Sara Pérez, who campaigned at her husband's side the entire time. The couple is seen here in during their decade of happiness together. Courtesy of the Library of Congress.

a mere five foot two inches, Madero had a high-pitched voice, was a vegetarian, and was passionately dedicated to séances and ouija boards; he did not cut an imposing figure. But he manifested a shrewd political sense, even if that power abandoned him later, when he most needed it. He correctly perceived that Mexico was approaching a crossroads and that the científico clique suffered from what modern analysts would call "high negative ratings." In 1908 he authored a brief and largely innocuous work entitled *La sucesión presidencial en 1910* (the presidential succession of 1910), in which he lathered praise on Díaz's accomplishments but insisted that the time had come for a more open political system.

Much like the Creelman interview, this bland volume would hardly have lifted eyebrows only a few years earlier, but with Mexico in full-blown unrest, *La sucesión presidencial* went into mass circulation. Madero soon announced his own candidacy. Anti-reelection clubs, the equivalent of state and local party chapters, sprang up around the country. Díaz at first doubted the reality of what he was seeing and did nothing; by the time the seriousness of the threat became apparent, it was too late to suffocate the anti-reelection movement by subtle means. In June 1910 Díaz seized on a minor uprising in the city of Valladolid, Yucatán, as an excuse to accuse Madero of fomenting rebellion. He arrested his young rival to office and declared himself the winner, his eighth term in office.

Invoking a rhetoric of democracy, which Madero measured largely as a ban on reelection and an end to the machine politics endemic since the late 1860s, the young hacendado swept up support from the now leaderless Reyistas and from the middle class, who had been kept down in the time of Don Porfirio. For example, he won the backing of progressives such as Modesto Rolland, a concrete-loving, antiradical engineer who survived every president from Porfirio Díaz to Adolfo Ruiz Cortines (in office from 1952–58) and who dedicated his life to infrastructure projects of grand visibility. But Madero's movement also appealed to poor people who read far more into his call for reforms than the Coahuilan had ever intended. This broad support and his own patrician expectations meant that Madero would not go quietly. The unlikely revolutionary eventually escaped his house arrest and fled to San Antonio, Texas; there, from the safety of his hotel room, Madero issued the Plan of San Luis Potosí, conveniently backdated to his time in that latter city. In it he proclaimed the June elections to have been fraudulent and the government illegitimate and called for the Mexican people to rise up on November 20, 1910.

The appointed day for his call to arms met with virtually no response beyond the deaths of the handful of individuals, men such as Aquiles Serdán of Puebla, who made the mistake of taking it all seriously. Only one place managed to mount a serious revolt, and that was the state of

Chihuahua. Rage had smoldered for years over the Terrazas-Creel monopoly, and rancheros and dispossessed smallholders rallied around Pascual Orozco (1882–1915), heir to a successful mule-team operation. The Plan of San Luis Potosí provided the legitimacy that the politically tone-deaf Orozco needed in order to settle score with his enemies. Orozco's profession had given him extensive knowledge of men, arms, logistics, and territory. He recruited his own group of officers, one of whom was an individual boasting an explosive personality and a highly checkered background: a tenant farmer, muleskinner, bandit, and occasionally respectable butcher named Doroteo Arango, but who, owing to run-ins with the Porfirian security forces, took the name Francisco "Pancho" Villa (1873–1923) instead. Orozco and Villa never liked each other, but for the moment they scored success after success. Orozco's fame grew, and Madero therefore realized that to retain leadership of the revolution he had proclaimed, he would have to enter Mexico and take control.

The nascent revolution fared better under the Madero-Orozco alliance. Insurgents discovered that the federal units were incompetent and that the soldiers lacked commitment to the old regime. After a series of surprise victories, Orozco and Villa, acting against orders from the indecisive Madero, attacked the federal forces that had holed up in Ciudad Juárez. The town suffered a hail of bullets; many inhabitants fled across the border to El Paso, where they found relief efforts organized by local Catholic churches. On May 10, 1911, the federal army in Ciudad Juárez surrendered. Two days later the Zapatistas seized the city of Cuauhtla, a key southern railroad hub. Díaz himself, increasingly deaf and suffering a severe toothache, understood that his government had always rested on consent, something that required the perception of hegemonic power; once punctured, even by so small an event as the loss of a single border city, the entire political edifice was doomed. On May 26 he went to Veracruz and boarded a steamship bound for France.

Díaz spent the next four years bitterly mulling over his fate. As he liked to put it, half of the country had risen up against him, and the other half had sat with their arms folded and let it happen. The former dictator toured the Holy Land, rode on camelback to the Great Pyramids of Giza, received well-wishers in his spacious Champs-Élysées apartment, and died on July 2, 1915. As evidence of the controversy that he and his regime continue to inspire, his remains, interred in Paris's Montparnasse

Cemetery near those of such luminaries as Charles Baudelaire and Jean-Paul Sartre, have never been allowed to return to Mexico.

Upon entering Mexico City in June 1911, Madero received a welcome befitting the return of the Quetzalcóatl. Unfortunately, he soon committed a series of blunders, all of which derived from his idealism, his lack of guile, and his limited agenda of political change. Rather than making the most of his mandate by assuming the presidency and forcing through reforms, Madero insisted on an interim presidency while new elections could be held that November. He won these handily, but not until interim president Francisco de la Barra (Díaz's personal physician, no less) did all possible to poison the water, including launching a vicious counterinsurgency in Morelos.

Second, Madero failed to purge the armed forces, an essential step for any revolutionary who hopes to stay in power. He innocently believed that he could simply fold his own soldiers into existing federal units. In his highly orchestrated progress toward Mexico City following the Díaz abdication, a platform was mounted in the front of Madero's train; upon it a revolutionary and a federal soldier shook hands, a way of teaching the Mexican people that he came to reconcile, not to punish. Porfirian officers deeply resented their defeat and, unconvinced by these contrived theatrics, were already searching for ways to roll the calendar back to 1900.

Third, Madero failed to reward the very men who had placed him in power. His neglect of Pancho Villa was perhaps understandable: the two men had spent little time together, and Madero saw Villa as no more than a minor figure, a ruffian brought over to the path of revolution. Villa himself raised no serious protest; rather, to the very end of his meteoric and violent life he revered the diminutive hacendado who had risked everything to end a dictatorship. But neglect of Pascual Orozco carried more serious consequences. Orozco had assumed great responsibilities, including taking Ciudad Juárez against Madero's orders. He had never recognized any obligation to a wealthy first son from Coahuila, and for his own troubles he had expected at least to become secretary of defense. But Madero, with some justification, could not see his way to extending ministerial positions to men whom he considered rough cowboys. Much like his ill-fated Cuban counterpart José Martí, the new president abhorred the idea of rule by military caudillos. Orozco came away with a minor cash stipend and the position of chief of Chihuahua's Rurales. He was the state's most popular figure, and anyone who wished to overthrow Madero now began to court him.

Madero also failed to win over decision makers in the United States. There, business and political forces had revered Díaz, at least until the dictator's declining years made them fret about a successor. Any attempt to counterbalance U.S. business influence with European concessions invariably led the former to wail about discrimination. At least some U.S. entrepreneurs hoped that Madero, whose family had fought off the British-based Tlahuililo Company, would reverse Díaz's policies, and so they inclined to give the new order a chance. President Taft (whose term ended in January 1913), who was never comfortable in the White House and was far happier mulling over constitutional law, had only a hazy understanding of Mexico's problems and refrained from overt interference. Not so his ambassador, Henry Lane Wilson (1857–1932), a longtime Indiana railroad attorney who had grown hysterical about Madero's mild support for labor organizations. Wilson's shrill reports of Mexican bolshevism, together with his constant scoldings, led Madero to forbid him access.

Beyond all this, Madero's greatest mistake was his failure to force revolutionary change. His movement had been political, a campaign to force the Porfirian order to allow in new blood and expand the electoral process. Madero had little feel for, or sympathy with, demands for the breakup of great estates. When he promised to restore lands taken illegally, he omitted to clarify that most of the land alienations of the last half century had taken place entirely in accordance with the constitution of 1857 and subsequent agrarian laws. This wealthy aristocrat-turned-revolutionary thus failed to address the issue most responsible for tearing Mexico apart.

Revolts were not long in coming. Furious about the overthrow of his mentor Díaz, Bernardo Reyes proclaimed against the new government on December 11, 1911, from San Antonio, Texas. But the plan fizzled, and Reyes, ever the dutiful soldier, surrendered to federal forces two weeks later to take up residence in a Mexico City prison. Meanwhile, a far more serious threat emerged in the form of Pascual Orozco. Disgusted with Madero's elitism and timidity, Orozco conspired with the very forces he had done so much to overthrow. Only the Terrazas-Creel oligarchy had the means to fund his revolt, and Orozco made the mistake of accepting their money; his patrons, meanwhile, overlooked Orozco's progressive program, trusting in their own ability to control the caudillo should he succeed in taking power. Acting with the support and encouragement of Chihuahua's enraged hacendados, the former revolutionary general proclaimed against Madero on March 3, 1912.

The revolt posed a serious challenge for the new order. Orozco knew both the people and the territory, had little problem recruiting from among the sharecroppers and the dislocated of Chihuahua, and he defeated the first Mexican general sent against him. But Orozco's weaknesses emerged soon enough. The Taft administration, still in something of a honeymoon with Madero, suddenly rediscovered the neutrality law and cut off Orozco's shipments of arms and munitions. Moreover, the association with Luis Terrazas and Enrique Creel, the two most hated men in northern Mexico, put an indelible stain on Orozco, one that revisionist history has been powerless to erase. Under these circumstances, the next general Madero sent against Orozco, the stridently pro-Porfirian Victoriano Huerta (1850–1916), enjoyed better luck. He took his time to defeat the insurgents and used the slow grind of this counterinsurgency to weaken Madero politically, but for the moment he avoided any sort of openly disloyal comments. Pascual Orozco eventually abandoned the effort in October 1912 and went into self-imposed exile in the United States, there to await a change of fortune. In that same month Félix Díaz, nephew of the deposed dictator, tried to incite a revolt of the Veracruz garrison but met no success. The officers he tried to recruit perceived him as little more than a dandified, ersatz copy of his famous uncle, and he ended up in the same prison as Bernardo Reyes.

Meanwhile, another of Madero's responses to the Orozco rebellion had far-reaching consequences. To fortify his control of the north and contain the revolt, he also mandated the creation of state militias. These units, particularly those of Coahuila and Sonora, became the basis of the later Constitutionalist Army, and the quintessential Chihuahuan, Pancho Villa, eventually assumed control of that state's guard.

Villa may have been happy to see his rival Orozco defeated and driven out of the country, but he had reason to take issue with the Madero government as well. Once Madero became president, Villa had taken his place in the federal army, but Huerta perceived him to be a dangerous man and falsely accused him of desertion. Madero commuted Villa's death sentence at the last minute but left him to linger in prison as the courts reviewed his case. There Villa remained until almost the end of the ill-fated presidency.

Madero's neglect and conservatism also alienated his supporters in Morelos. Emiliano Zapata had come out of his provincial shell long enough to stake his reputation on an alliance with a faraway northern hacendado; he led the only serious, organized revolutionary insurgency outside of Chihuahua and expected immediate redress for the problems affecting his people. Madero instead dithered throughout the entirety of 1912, until Zapata, despite personal meetings with the president, decided that further talk was useless. Under Zapata's instruction, a Morelos schoolteacher named Otilio Magaña drafted a manifesto whose simplicity and brevity gave little hint of the influence it was to exert on twentieth-century Mexico. The Plan of Ayala demanded immediate restitution of lands taken under the Liberal alienation laws, yet it went one step further by promising land to whoever would work it. This homespun document, and not the finely reasoned critiques of Karl Marx or anarchist Pierre-Joseph Proudhon, became the ideological backbone of Mexico's agrarian revolution and came to influence national policy for the next eighty years.

By early 1913 Madero had survived numerous coup attempts. But time was not on his side. Having thoroughly antagonized the right and disappointed the left, he discovered himself in a hostile political world that possessed neither a center nor the conditions and traditions of the democratic principles he had so zealously preached. In the capital parties hostile to the new president clustered around the person of Ambassador Wilson. What emerged was a complex and singularly underhanded plan of overthrow. On February 9, 1913, jailers simultaneously released Bernardo Reyes and Félix Díaz; the former proclaimed against the president and mustered sympathetic federal troops. Meanwhile, Victoriano Huerta pretended to obey Madero's orders to put down the revolt but instead used his artillery to shell Mexico City itself in order to produce the very chaos he would then claim as justification for a coup. This dark-hearted scheme persisted for what Mexicans call *la decena trágica* (the ten tragic days), leaving substantial portions of the central district reduced to rubble and some four hundred people killed in the process. On February 19, 1913, Huerta entered the palace to inform the now-desperate Madero that he was relieving him of office. Madero and José Pino Suárez, his vice

Seen here with his main officers, Emiliano Zapata (seated, center) led the Morelos resistance against a rapacious oligarchy of sugar planters. Zapata perished in the struggle, but his Plan of Ayala, drafted by a local schoolteacher, became the defining document for later revolutionary land reforms. Courtesy of the Library of Congress.

president, were forced to sign letters of resignation, but fearing future trouble from a president in exile, Huerta had the two men driven to the back of a federal prison on the edge of town and shot. Huerta now assumed the presidency, with old-guard General Aureliano Blanquet as his second. Henry Lane Wilson, the U.S. ambassador, proudly presented the men to international diplomats.

For all but the most cynical, Francisco Madero's reputation has not just endured but prospered. A man who failed to bring about his overly idealistic vision, a patrician blinded by his own blessings, a statesman who erred by showing mercy to those who deserved none, he atoned for all these mistakes with his own life. In death Madero took his place beside other flawed heroes like Hidalgo, Morelos, and Juárez in the pantheon of Mexican history. Meanwhile, the revolution he had so cautiously undertaken was only beginning.

A Nation at War . . . with Itself

Huerta now held power, but he had miscalculated. The events of the previous three years had superheated Mexican politics, and the country could not return to 1890, no matter how many people the usurper ordered shot or exiled. Worse, the bald-faced murders of Madero and Pino Suárez elevated both men to the level of martyrs, reuniting agrarian radicals, labor organizers, and urban liberals. For the old order the assassination of Madero became an original sin with no absolution, and those who committed that sin, together with those who supported it, almost invariably came to bad ends.

The first to die was Reyes himself, who took a stray bullet on the opening day of skirmishes—an ignominious fate for one of Mexico's great leaders but one that he himself had courted. Henry Lane Wilson found himself recalled in disgrace within six months. In trying to restore the order of his uncle's rule, Félix Díaz signed his own political death warrant and spent most of the remainder of his life in a dissolute exile. Aureliano Blanquet died while fighting revolutionary forces in 1919. Francisco Cárdenas, the Rurales officer who carried out the assassinations, fled to Guatemala, where, facing arrest for an unrelated murder, he committed suicide in a public plaza. Conservative Catholics, who had inveighed against President

Madero, earned the unending suspicion of the emerging revolutionary family and would experience serious persecution in the 1920s.

The central figure in the assassinations, usurper Victoriano Huerta, became the target of the greatest military mobilization in Mexican history. Like so many presidents before him, he lacked solid control of the north, where sheer distance and access to the U.S. border gave political dissidents an advantage. Resistance here centered around Venustiano Carranza (1859–1920), the governor of Coahuila, a Porfirian-era politician who had thrown his fortunes behind Madero as part of the fallen president's more conservative wing. Carranza knew that Huerta's federal forces were coming after him, so he gathered together his state militia and marched to the friendlier, and more remote, location of Sonora. This union of state militias became the Constitutionalist Army, backed by Carranza's plausible claim to be the true heir of the Madero movement, the one state executive who had refused to buckle to reactionary intimidation. As his chief of staff he acquired the capable services of Álvaro Obregón Salido (1880–1928), a self-made chickpea farmer with a keen tactical mind, a phenomenal memory, and ambitions that reached far beyond the furrows of his hometown, Huatabampo. Their army initially drew heavily from Yaqui and Mayo laborers but over time expanded to recruit nationally.

At the same time a separate but allied force emerged in Chihuahua, Mexico's largest state, where rule by the Terrazas-Creel oligarchy had generated no end of popular grievances. When Huerta forces assassinated Maderista governor Abraham González, they unwittingly handed state leadership to the cruder and more capable Pancho Villa. Thus was born the legendary División del Norte. At its height in 1914 it was the largest military force in Mexican history; it rolled across the land like some enormous folk pilgrimage as whole families accompanied the soldiers, often transported atop railroad cars. Above all it operated according on personal loyalty to the highly charismatic Villa. He thus became one of the rare cases in Latin American history in which a working-class—even outlaw—individual rose to a position of national revolutionary leadership.

Meanwhile, the chaos in Mexico City and the need to direct the full force of the federal army northward had allowed the Zapatistas a brief period in which they controlled Morelos. But success changed the movement. Huerta's persecution of unions and their intellectual allies forced the latter to flee to Zapata's protection. Men such as Antonio Díaz Soto y Gama (1880–1967), many of them with roots in the early PLM congresses of San Luis Potosí, provided a level of technical expertise that the rough-cut country insurgents lacked. But the newcomers' anarchist roots, and their tendency to invoke socialist, antinationalist rhetoric, probably antagonized officers of the Constitutionalist Army who might otherwise have been disposed to ally with this most agrarian of movements. Together, the loosely allied forces of Carranza, Villa, and Zapata fought off the return of the Porfirian order. Their relationship was never easy and quickly dissolved in acrimonious rivalry once the job was done, but at least while it lasted their combined efforts assured that the Mexican Revolution amounted to something more than a failed coup.

In this second phase of the revolution, Villa did most of the fighting. His unstoppable División del Norte consistently defeated its federal antagonists, especially at the Battle of Zacatecas on June 23, 1914, the largest and most critical engagement of the anti-Huerta struggle. Villa may have been unlettered, but like Alexander the Great he possessed a formidable memory for the names of his officers and had a keen understanding of the geography and the folkways of northern Mexico. Around him Villa kept a special group of skilled fighters known as the Dorados; their name has lived on in modern Mexican parlance as a synonym of elite forces. For his most brutal errands Villa also employed a collection of killers, men who performed their work with sociopathic gusto. In fairness, Obregón as well as Villa lived up to Carranza's saying that "the revolution that compromises is lost." Drawing on the hard lesson of Madero's failure, both men understood that the old security forces had to go, and both often carried out summary executions of captured federal officers. There would be no more Huertas.

Among the most perplexing aspects of this period was the posture of the U.S. government. President Taft remained uncertain as to how to handle the Madero government and followed no clear path. Woodrow Wilson took office in March 1913, a mere month after Madero's murder, and brought his own personal ambiguities to the mix. Though he saw himself as a champion of democratic ideals, Wilson also held deeply racist views inherited from his southern background. He preached constitutional procedure for Latin American and Caribbean nations. But he was beholden to oil interests such as Standard; to the political advice of

Colonel Edward M. House, himself a prominent investor in Mexico; and to Cleveland Dodge, his former college friend and campaign supporter who was also president of the Phelps-Dodge, a mining interest (and later holding company) with significant investments in Mexican copper wealth. Faced with the possibility of recognizing an obvious assassin and usurper, the new president at first hesitated. But his democratic backbone strengthened as reports of Huerta favoring British and German interests began to roll in. Wilson therefore decided to destabilize Huerta by withholding recognition, and, lacking a clear choice of preferred caudillo, he moved to force some sort of coalition government, as powerful states often do in times of international turmoil beyond their borders.

Destabilization came easily. On April 21, 1914, the United States Marine Corps, ostensibly responding to the arrest of a handful of U.S. sailors, opened fire on the port city of Veracruz. In the process more than 150 Mexican nationals perished, some of whom were federal soldiers but others mere civilians caught in the fighting. Three days later the Marines invested the city; they remained for seven months, intercepting German vessels bearing (U.S.) arms deliveries for Huerta. The major revolutionary leaders protested, but most were happy to allow the occupation to do its work. On July 15 Huerta accepted the inevitable and resigned; he left for exile on the very steamship that had once taken Porfirio Díaz to France.

Still, a coalition government eluded its proponents. Carranza had beaten Villa to Mexico City, but the Constitutionalists remained weaker than the hitherto invincible División del Norte, and when an enraged Villa at last arrived, he had every intention of dominating the convention. He picked up unexpected support when Zapatista intellectuals arrived and dramatically embraced Villa. Realizing that they were outnumbered, Carranza and Obregón retreated to the Port of Veracruz.

Ostensibly the stage was ready for a Villa-Zapata government and a turn in favor of some kind of agrarian radicalism—almost as if Vicente Guerrero himself had returned to reclaim Mexico for the poor. Villa and Zapata finally met on November 28, 1914, in a Xochimilco public school for a brief and awkward conversation. They paraded their forces through Mexico City and into the National Palace, posed sitting on Porfirio Díaz's kingly throne, and caucused over an elaborate banquet in which the humble Zapatistas radiated discomfort. Essentially, Villa promised to provide material support, while Zapata pledged to move his troops beyond Morelos in an effort to defeat Carranza and save the revolution from another Madero.

Even Washington initially favored the mercurial Villa. He had maintained good relations with the United States, had expressed a naive faith in its political system, and had admirers among U.S. military attachés, men like Generals Hugh Scott and John Pershing. Most importantly, Villa had scrupulously avoided harming U.S. interests in Chihuahua, instead preferring to finance his revolution by selling off the assets of the Terrazas empire. He controlled the majority of the country, occupied the capital, and captivated the world press. Carranza, to the contrary, epitomized bourgeois nationalism and leaned heavily on the foreign companies for war taxes, earning him no end of hatred. Zapata remained alone and isolated in Morelos, by all U.S. lights a primitive communist out on some atavistic rampage.

Unfortunately for Villa, though, the global political ground was shifting under Woodrow Wilson's feet. When the great European war finally erupted in August 1914, U.S. national interest shifted toward wartime readiness. New priorities included secure borders, restriction of arms exports, and guaranteed access to raw materials from abroad. All of these changes privileged Carranza and disfavored Villa.

Moreover, Villa's accomplishments concealed severe weaknesses. Much of the territory he controlled—the west, for example—was economically and strategically marginal. The mighty Terrazas-Creel empire whose assets Villa had ransacked to finance his army was beginning to dry up. And he lacked adequate organization. Villa's army operated on a deeply personal level, fueled by his own charisma and handicapped by the same. He received sound military advice from luminaries such as General Felipe Ángeles, a brilliant and high-minded Porfirian military officer who had sided with Madero and who remained true to the revolutionary cause ever after; but Villa typically elected to follow his own impetuous instincts.

Nor did he demonstrate the specific aims and ideological clarity of Zapata. Villa certainly embraced the idea of land reform but was never in a position to carry it out, since any redistributed land would go by rights to his soldiers, and he could not spare them from the field of battle.

No man better symbolizes the daring, the violence, and the class hatreds of the revolution than Francisco "Pancho" Villa. Perhaps the most famous Mexican of all time, he rose from poverty to lead a massive army that defeated Madero's assassin-usurper. In 1916 Villa led the only armed invasion of the continental United States after 1812. He lost the contest for national power, but he remained an essential force in Mexican affairs until his assassination in 1923. Courtesy of the Library of Congress.

Indeed, at bottom Villa saw Mexico through the prism of Chihuahua, and although he issued various statements and proclamations, he never appreciated or cultivated urbanites or the growing industrial working classes of the cities. In the long run neither Villa nor Zapata could deliver on their 1914 agreement. The Zapatistas moved only tentatively beyond their home territory, while the dawning European war tightened U.S. border security, making it hard for Villa to obtain the arms and money that had once come his way so liberally.

Not so his new challenger. In Mexico City, Carreza lieutenant Álvaro Obregón had taken the opportunity to cultivate the urban working class. The anarcho-syndicalist labor organizers had returned in force during the six months following Huerta's departure. Obregón listened as their organization, the Casa del Obrero Mundial (house of the world worker), presented a long list of demands; in exchange for promises of future favors, they agreed to mobilize under Constitutionalist leadership as the so-called Red Battalions. While his overtures had no motive beyond simple expediency, they offered more than the quintessentially rural caudillos such as Villa and Zapata had proposed. Moreover, Carranza dominated key export sectors such as petroleum, coffee, and henequen, resources the United States held critical for dawning European war. The U.S. occupation of Veracruz worked mostly to Carranza's advantage, for he came away with far greater contact with officers and representatives of the United States. When the Marines withdrew in early 1915, the city, together with its supplies and war materiel, passed into the hands of the Constitutionalists, possibly with an eye to preserving the balance of power that Washington had long sought.

The Constitutionalist Army also benefited from greater willingness to engage with new technology. Using material left by the U.S. forces in Veracruz, Carrancistas were able to adopt the style of warfare that had already halted German advances in Europe: fortified trenches with barbed wire and machine gun posts, lines of defense impregnable to Villa's assaults. Carranza also made unprecedented use of radio communications. Wireless transmissions had first come to the country in 1899; for the next fifteen years Mexicans did little more than experiment as they gained technical knowledge and built electrical grids. The military conducted its own trials and in fact used radio in the occupation of the Quintana Roo Territory. Carranza recognized an advantage when he saw one. He expanded transmission stations from ten in 1910 to twenty-seven in 1920, using radio to maintain communications with his front lines and convey political orders to subordinates throughout the land.

In the spring of 1915 Villa's weaknesses at last caught up with him. Understanding only too well his opponent's reliance on frontal assaults, Obregón cribbed from the emerging military tactics of the great European war: he arranged his troops outside of Celeya, Guanajuato; there, safe behind barbed wire and machine guns, they awaited the Villista cavalry charge certain to come. Villa did not disappoint. Ignoring the advice of Felipe Ángeles, on April 6, 1915, the Chihuahuan threw his troops at the Constitutionalist position in a series of battles, only to have them cut to shreds. After nine days of these futile assaults, the great División del Norte was no more, and Villa, while alive and dangerous, would never again wield national power or control the field of battle.

Order from Chaos

Despite the decisive Battle of Celaya, the second half of 1915 saw little relief from the confusion of the previous six months. The Constitutionalist Army reclaimed Mexico City, easily dissolving the convention government that had never been more than a civilian front, but Villa retained considerable support, especially in Chihuahua. Isolated but tenacious, Zapata still clung to his Morelos base. Leftover Porfirians eyed their chance for a comeback. To deal with the situation, Carranza worked two related strategies: the military defeat of his rivals and a political package that addressed pressing concerns without descending into what he considered an unhealthy radicalism.

On the political front Carranza was able to carry out a number of much-needed reforms between 1915 and 1920. To break up regional power bases, he abolished the office of jefe político, that all-purpose fixer that Porfirian governors had used to control rural affairs. He oversaw a modest land redistribution (which simply whetted the taste for a more comprehensive solution). Debt peonage also ended; however, in the absence of serious land reform, former peons often had nowhere else to go and remained on the estates. Finally, Carranza tried to weaken the Catholic church by secularizing and greatly simplifying divorce proceedings. While the nation's rapidly proliferating legal industry eventually rendered divorce as costly and messy as ever, for a brief period of time the nation drew foreigners in search of an easy legal separation, thus giving birth to the now-archaic term "Mexican divorce."

Industrial workers met mixed success under the new government. Not forgetting the pact with Mexico City's urban labor organizations, Carranza decreed an eight-hour workday and a minimum wage; minuscule by the standards of upper-middle-class income, the *salario mínimo* remains an important institution, and such matters as fines, fees, and overtime pay are today measured in multiples of the same. Still, with their philosophy of direct action and a worker-led, decentralized society, the anarcho-syndicalists could not resist what looked like their chance for victory. Sensing the advantage, in 1916 the Casa del Obrero Mundial launched a series of strikes that convulsed Mexico City and overplayed the union's hand. Carranza took the opportunity to break the Casa and arrest its leaders; the event marked the end of the Flores Magóns' militant vision and signaled labor's turn to more cooperative relations with the state.

The Constitutional government also focused on controlling the troublesome southeast. Revolutionary winds had stirred here as well, but the region's deeply entrenched hacienda systems of Chiapas, Campeche, and Yucatán and those states' geographical isolation combined the barriers posed by indigenous languages had all worked against anything resembling Zapatismo. Latifundia had never taken root in Tabasco, where rivers and wetlands had checked its expansion. But logging companies, mostly built on foreign capital, operated camps high in the Usumacinta and Grijalva watersheds, where the geography kept out dissident ideas and easy firearms. But Carranza needed the revenues that came from exports of coffee, lumber, and, above all, henequen. To subdue the region he therefore sent a series of generals rather like the Roman proconsuls: well armed, sure of purpose, and visibly contemptuous of local custom.

These men did their work only too well. The most successful of the bunch was Salvador Alvarado, a Sinaloan pharmacist-turned-general who took it upon himself to bring Yucatán into the modern world. He drummed the oligarchs out of office, ended debt peonage and jefes políticos, and gave conservative Catholics a dusting that they have never forgotten. Most important to his mission, Alvarado operated Henequeneros, a state purchasing house for henequen that sent generous yields back to Carranza while using part of the revenues to finance various modernization plans. Although it only lasted three years, Alvarado's reign changed Yucatán forever, introducing new ideas and practices and polarizing the peninsula between reformers and conservatives. Similarly, Cándido Aguilar and Manuel Peláez lorded over the Veracruz petroleum region, Francisco Múgica governed Tabasco, and Jesús Agustín Castro made certain that Chiapan coffee revenues tumbled into Constitutional pockets.

Politics also involved managing revolutionary spillover across the U.S. border, and particularly that long stretch along the Río Grande where profit-driven abuses had left a legacy of fear and anger. In the preceding eighty years Anglo settlers, though a numerical minority, had wrested power from the area's Mexican and Mexican American population; the resulting settler mentality informs Texas culture to the present day. Under these conditions it required only the inspiration of revolutionary violence to set off hostilities. On January 6, 1915, a handful of radicals in

Monterrey advanced the Plan of San Diego, so named as to appear that it had emerged from the tiny town of San Diego, just south of San Antonio. It called for the separation from the United States of those territories taken from Mexico under the terms of Guadalupe Hidalgo. As if this were not sufficiently outlandish, the rebels pledged death to all white men sixteen years and older. Beginning in July small groups of men crossed into the United States and committed acts of violence against frontier ranches. Some evidence suggests that they received prompting and support from Carranza officers, who might have been inciting border problems in order to create a bargaining chip. Indeed, when the U.S. extended recognition to Carranza in October of that year, the raids dropped off; they returned momentarily in July 1916, when U.S. soldiers, much to Carranza's discomfiture, entered Mexico in search of Pancho Villa. Whoever instigated the San Diego movement, there is no denying the repression it brought down: somewhere between three and four hundred Mexicans and Mexican Americans met summary execution at the hands of Texas Rangers and lynch mobs in South Texas in less than eighteen months.

Even as this tragedy was playing out, a very different sort of trouble emerged. With the insurgent victors of 1914 in a full-scale war among themselves, imperial Germany now targeted Mexico as a potential resource against the Triple Entente of Europe. Mexico was supplying a quarter of the oil that the British navy now used to fuel its ships, and Germany considered weakening that navy essential to keeping open its own supply of foreign goods and raw materials. The kaiser's military planners also wanted to keep the United States out of the war. Mexico's chaotic situation seemingly offered the distraction necessary to achieve these aims. In February 1915 a plot, possibly financed and promoted by Germany, brought together the unsavory trinity of Enrique Creel, Pascual Orozco, and Victoriano Huerta. But by now the global political climate had changed altogether, and the Mexican conspirators found themselves unwelcome in the United States. Orozco made it across the Texas border with a handful of men, but in August 1915 they were trapped by a local posse, in a canyon not far from the border, and died under circumstances that remain murky. On June 27 of that same year, U.S. federal agents detained Huerta in Newman, New Mexico, and transferred him to house arrest in El Paso. Madero's blood remained on his hands, and Carranza insisted that Huerta be returned for a trial whose outcome none could doubt. But years of hard drinking at last caught up with the general, and in January 1916 he died, possibly of cirrhosis of the liver. The opprobrium of his dark deeds haunts his reputation to the present. Enrique Creel, meanwhile, escaped repercussion; despite catastrophic losses at the hands of Pancho Villa, he made peace with the revolutionary government and died in Mexico City, as wealthy as he was detested, in 1931.

Those who had fought under Madero in 1911 could take some comfort in the deaths of Huerta and Orozco. But for Villa their defeat hardly sufficed. Most dangerous when on the defensive, Villa responded to the setbacks of 1915 with one of his most daring maneuvers. Recent defeats had convinced him of high-level connivance between Carranza and the U.S. government, the latter of which responded increasingly to the pressures of the European war. Wilson's government now began to enforce prohibitions on border arms trafficking, while Carranza's control of key export regions made him the more indispensable ally. Wilson also allowed Constitutionalists to send a trainload of troops across the border in order to surprise Villa with a rear-guard attack. The perpetually wary Villa now smelled what he thought was a U.S.-Carranza conspiracy. Perhaps fearing the kind of land-for-support deal that had brought down Santa Anna six decades earlier, and angry over withheld shipments of guns, Villa decided to raid the border town of Columbus, New Mexico. He knew that his actions would bring down a U.S. reprisal that Carranza, with his nationalist postures, would have to confront: in other words, almost every possible outcome promised to break in Villa's favor.

If the raid came as a surprise to anyone, it was through no lack of warning. Reports that Villa was headed toward Columbus had trickled into army headquarters there for some time, but the sleepy command did nothing and failed to post even the most elementary precautions. The Villistas' early-morning raid in March 1916 went decisively against the attackers: for every one of the eighteen U.S. casualties, nearly ten times that number of Villistas perished, and by this point trained fighters were hard to replace.

The raid had multiple consequences. Unquestionably, it revived Villa's fortunes, recapturing something of the folk-hero status that had attended him in the days of the División del Norte. And it brought the intervention he was looking for. The Unites States launched its famous expeditionary force, led by General John "Black Jack" Pershing, but Villa, despite a serious leg wound, eluded capture. Carranza also survived but had to endure the humiliation of tolerating foreign troops on Mexican soil. Pershing lumbered through Mexico, but he achieved little more than the capture and execution of a handful of Villistas who had not even been present in the Columbus raid.

With Villa momentarily confined to mountain hideouts, the Carranza regime got down to the business of setting up a new government. To that end, the first chief ordered a convention that was to meet in a theater in the city of Querétero, beginning in November 1916. Carranza himself disliked anything that smacked of radicalism, but the men who actually framed the new constitution were younger and had a sharper sense that peace would require far greater concessions to the lower classes. From that perception came the constitution of 1917, ratified on February 5. This document governs Mexico today and is among the oldest functioning charter document in Latin America.

While much of the Querétaro constitution established concepts and structures of government that would be familiar to U.S. observers, the document stands out as the first to establish broad social rights for Mexican citizens. Drawing directly from Zapata's Plan of Ayala, Article 27 guaranteed land to whoever would work it. It also restored subsurface mineral rights to the nation, thus reversing one of the fundamental tenets of the Porfirian order. Article 123 incorporated many of the reforms that the PLM had long championed: an eight-hour workday, an end to child labor, and the right to organize and strike. Other articles kept faith with old Liberal Party sensibilities by secularizing education and limiting the public and political power of the Catholic Church. In brief, the document advanced a secular, nationalist vision, intricate in its attention to detail but expansive in recognizing and addressing the huge social issues that had fed the violence. The flurry of Carrancista documents and decrees, of course, remained statements of principle and provided no clear idea of how such reforms would actually be carried out. How any of this would play out against the pressure of international investors, powerful landowners, and a religiously conservative society was still anyone's guess. But the regime had opened a space for negotiation and activism. The Mexican people would spend the next twenty years attempting to wed ideals to the practical business of daily life.

Meanwhile, the ghosts of 1848 still haunted the border. In March 1917 the British government leaked to Washington a decoded, secret telegram, composed by German official Arthur Zimmermann, in which Imperial Germany promised Mexico the restitution of the lands lost under Guadalupe Hidalgo in exchange for Mexican support in the war effort. Carranza toyed with the offer yet ultimately rejected it as impracticable, but anxiety over U.S.-settled territories continued, and the Zimmermann telegram resulted in the United States' entry into the European conflict the following month, as Wilson recalled Pershing to lead the U.S. expeditionary force into France.

During his many reform efforts and maneuvers, the first chief remained implacably opposed to any sort of rural insurgency that threatened his control. That led him to orchestrate the deaths of some of Mexico's most high-minded and talented leaders. To begin with, Carranza joined the long list of presidents intent on crushing the Morelos movement and the Zapatistas. After 1915 Zapata had grown increasingly isolated; another Carranza general, Pablo González, now launched a counterinsurgency that beat back many of the Zapatista successes. Arms and external support grew scarce, while the intransigence and radical rhetoric of urban intellectuals made difficult any alliance between the rural poor and Constitutionalist officers. Beset on all sides, Emiliano Zapata himself became sullen and resentful, often taking to the bottle. In a rage, he even executed Otilio Magaña, author of the Plan of Ayala, under false accusations of being a traitor. Still, the insurgency persisted.

Frustrated with military tactics, González instead resorted to trickery. He directed one of his officers, Jesús Gallardo, to lure the caudillo into a parley at the hacienda San Juan Chinameca, supposedly for the purpose of allying against Carranza. Zapata arrived on the morning of April 19, 1919, surrounded by a small guard, but as he rode into the estate he was met with a hail of bullets and died before hitting the ground. Emiliano Zapata thus passed into legend as the incorruptible hero of the Mexican Revolution; with the great caudillo gone, the surviving Morelos leaders retreated in desperation to await a change of fortune.

Seven months later Carrancistas executed one of the revolution's most noble figures, Felipe Ángeles. Talented, highly cultured, a general whose sound advice Pancho Villa ignored time and again, Ángeles had supported himself in exile by washing dishes. He returned in 1919, ever convinced that he could somehow persuade Villa to lay aside his grievances with the United States and return to the righteous path of Madero. But events were too far gone for conciliation; Villa raided Ciudad Juárez in June, thereby keeping alive the fires lit at Columbus. Ángeles gave up on his peace plan and departed. Carrancista forces captured him in November and to prove the legality of the new order, they subjected him to a show trial in Chihuahua City. More than anything the trial allowed Ángeles to demonstrate once again his superiority to the Constitutionalist officers, and his execution on November 25 constituted one more stain on the first chief's reputation.

The ghosts of Zapata and Ángeles did not have to wait long for their revenge. Venustiano Carranza may have bested his military rivals, but he failed against the most dangerous foe of all, his own officer corps. Matters reached a head in 1920. Carranza had done all possible to contain radical changes, including those authorized by the constitution of 1917, whereas his military staff, younger and more in touch with the masses whom they had recruited and led, perceived that a coalition of progressive hacendados could not bring peace. Madero's revolt and martyrdom had established one sacred point—no reelection—a principle that holds true into the twenty-first century. This fact limited Carranza to one option: exercising indirect power by appointing a political nonentity. He chose as his successor Miguel Bonilla, who had served as Carranza's U.S. representative during the worst of the fighting. The officers, and above all Álvaro Obregón, had waded in blood for the Constitutionalist movement and now assumed that power was theirs by rights.

The selection of Bonilla thus instigated Carranza's downfall. Safe in Sonora, Obregón in April announced the Plan of Agua Prieta, which annulled Bonilla's election and identified Obregón himself as the country's legitimate leader. To set the seal, Obregón made extraordinary concessions to the remaining Zapatistas, granting them even more than they asked for. As his forces moved toward Mexico City they met with universal acclaim, and when Obregón entered the capital, in the car beside him sat prominent Zapatista leaders. Emiliano may have died, but the agrarian reform he demanded was to become a reality.

Carranza, meanwhile, found himself reduced to a hunted outlaw. After packing up what he could of the treasury, he followed the now-familiar tactic of retreating to Veracruz in order to await a change of fortune. But no better fortune came. He found the railroad destroyed in Puebla state; with a small group of loyalists he made his way to the village of Tlaxcalantongo, there to pass the night in a hut. His pursuers caught up with him during the night of May 10 and shot him to death: yet again the revolution, like the ogreish gods of Greek mythology, had consumed its own children. Incidentally, the man entrusted to escort the treasury back to the capital was a young lieutenant from Veracruz named Adolfo Ruiz Cortines, who many years later as president of Mexico conducted himself with the same scrupulous honesty that he exercised with Carranza's expropriated funds.

On June 1, 1920, Obregón associate Adolfo de la Huerta began an interim presidency, in the process initiating a political order that in some ways continues to the present day. Certainly one of the greatest achievements of his brief tenure was to reach out to Pancho Villa, now reduced to the status of guerrilla fighter. Carranza's death gave Villa the excuse he needed to make peace with the Constitutionalists. He accepted the gift of the hacienda Canutillo in Durango and there set up a fiefdom that, if highly armed and distinctly personalist, at least had sworn off the business of overthrowing governments. Neither Villa nor Obregón trusted one another, but for the moment, at least, a peace of sorts had arrived. The ultimate nature of the new order, however, remained anyone's guess, and the struggle among contending and seemingly irreconcilable visions was to consume the nation for the next twenty years and beyond.

The *Científicos* of Tomorrow
Struggles to Create a New Order,
1920–1946

What had changed? Porfirio Díaz was long gone, his federal army
and Rurales units had vanished, and the new government had
outdone itself in passing ad hoc decrees and philosophical statements.
To popular relief, Álvaro Obregón's triumph ended the revolution's most
violent phase. Armed irregulars slowly laid down their weapons and returned to their farms. But the question of Mexico's future remained. For
the next twenty years the new political order had to struggle for both
self-definition and simple survival.

Sonoran Dynasty

Post-1920 confusions drew directly from older uncertainties. For all its
plans and proclamations, the Mexican Revolution had lacked the sort of
controlling ideology that guided events in Russia and China. It variously
drew from the people's faith in the colonial-style agrarian village; from
their quest for representative democracy; from the glitter of national sovereignty; from the song of such amorphous sirens as anarchism and socialism; and from the fury of miners and factory workers over the abuses that
Porfirian growth had generated. Campesinos sought land, while men and
women of the cities invoked the middle-class reformism of American pro-
gressivism, with its emphasis on hygiene, efficiency, and uplift. This mish-
mash of ideals perhaps shielded the country from such doctrine-driven

calamities as Stalin's collectivizations or Mao Zedung's Great Leap Forward. But they also made for some confusing times, as post-Carranza Mexico groped uncertainly toward a functional national order.

At the center stood President Álvaro Obregón, who at last assumed power on December 1, 1920, ever after the date for Mexican presidential inaugurations. For all his talent, the new leader was neither an ideologue nor a theoretician. He shared the Porfiriato's fuzzy faith in progress and commerce, but he advocated for broader inclusion of young men of talent. For himself and others fitting that description, he proclaimed a manifesto of sorts: "We will be the científicos of tomorrow." Obregón understood with equal clarity that many of the generals wanted to take his place, and he retired as many officers as possible, either sending them to prestigious exiles as foreign ambassadors or buying them off with "cannon blasts of 50 million pesos," as he put it. But ambitious rivals persisted, especially in the form of the powerful zone commanders who controlled large chunks of the country. To meet that threat Obregón opted for pragmatism, allying with anyone who promised support. That fact created a government filled with contradictions and cross-currents.

Mexico's new president found one bulwark of support in organized labor. His alliance with the ill-fated Casa del Obrero Mundial had set precedent, and Article 123 of the constitution provided the legal framework for a more permanent relationship between the state and unions. In 1918 Mexico City–born electrician Luis Napoleón Morones (1890–1964) rose to the top of the newly created Confederación Regional Obrera Mexicana (Regional Confederation of Mexican Workers, or CROM). For the next ten years Morones tirelessly advanced the interests of Obregón and his successor, Plutarco Elías Calles, accepting solid benefits in exchange for men who would militate in favor of the Sonoran dynasty. Morones himself became a synonym for corruption, a man given to expensive suits and diamond stickpins, the very image of the union boss, but he was also an important voice for labor rights and national sovereignty.

Paradoxically, the regime's left emerged most stridently in the southeast, a region to which the revolution had come late. In Yucatán a dynamic young politician named Felipe Carrillo Puerto (1874–1924) picked up where Salvador Alvarado left off; using his command of Maya, he launched ambitious plans for land reform and tried to build a base of support through local organizations called *ligas de resistencia* (resistance leagues). Similarly, Adelberto Tejada rose to dominate state affairs in Veracruz. He championed land reform, ended the jefatura system, and on the urban front imposed a rent-control system that provided basic rights for renters.

Radicalism of a different sort gripped the state of Tabasco. A young politician named Tomás Garrido Canabal (1891–1943) came forward as the state's strongman, his position settled by his decisive opposition to the various anti-Obregón uprisings. In 1924 Garrido successfully switched loyalties to the rising star of Ernesto Plutarco Elías Calles and under his blessing remained the state's maximal leader until his untimely removal in 1935. Tabasco had relatively few large haciendas, while Garrido himself hailed from a modestly successful planter family; he consequently evinced little interest in land reform. On the matter of religion, however, he staked out an implacable position. He drove out all foreign priests and made life generally intolerable for those who remained. Saint-burnings became an all-too-common event here. Garrido may not have been a believer, but he was in other respects a bona fide Puritan, imposing state-level alcohol prohibition and discouraging smoking.

Mexican women comprised a group with a different agenda. Times had been changing for this half of the population, particularly for those females who had escaped the stagnation of the rural village. With greater disposable income, improved education, and more readily available news that carried currents of change from the outside world, women naturally began to chafe. As well they might: they could hold no political offices, could not vote, and for all the social advances of the eras of reform, mostly lived under some form of male supervision. The years since Madero's fateful call to arms had awakened their aspirations. Mexican suffragettes drew inspiration from the example of Sara Pérez, the energetic and devoted wife of the slain president, a woman who campaigned by his side from balconies and the cabooses of trains (and who lived a long, sorrowful widowhood in the capital after his assassination in 1913).

A watershed of sorts came in 1916 when the Alvarado government in Mérida sponsored the Primer Congreso Feminista (first feminist congress). From the beginning, educated and politically informed women established a unique agenda. Objectives centered around sex education, birth control, civil equality, voting rights, and overall integration into the professional ranks—hardly the sort of demands likely to interest Pancho

Villa. Attempts to follow U.S. feminists who joined their cause to that of temperance garnered little support, although prohibition was implemented (to little success) at the state level in Tabasco. The constitution of the following year in fact made some gestures in the feminists' direction, guaranteeing maternity leave and equal pay for equal work. But in this as in so many other things, the constitution did little more than establish philosophical principles; implementation lagged far behind. Meanwhile, conflicting paths hampered the nascent feminist movement. The revolutionary government and the emerging Partido Comunista Mexicano (PCM), both of which paid lip service to the cause, saw women as a bloc of support for their own agendas. Feminists themselves split between radical and reformist paths, and after 1926 the grinding Cristero War (discussed below) slowed progress on almost all other fronts. On gender issues, as on so many others, real change would have to wait.

Meanwhile, not all allies stood to the left. The early revolutionary government also spawned a new elite composed largely of zone commanders who discovered that their positions gave them unrivaled access to the public till. Zone commanders could charge protection money to propertied interests in their region of authority. They could work unoccupied land as their own, thereby taking advantage of the agro-export boom of the 1920s. Or they could form construction companies that operated through sweetheart contracts with the federal government, building roads, bridges, port facilities, and just about anything else the new order required. In certain ways the situation harkened back to the early national period, when generals were the only individuals with experience in large-scale management of humans and raw materials and hence had an almost exclusive claim to high office.

One former military leader who did not survive to challenge the regime was Pancho Villa. For three years the caudillo of Chihuahua kept to his minikingdom of Canutillo, sorting out his tangled love life and facing down attempts to restore the Terrazas-Creel empire. He understood how dangerous he was to the new order and kept an eye open for assassination attempts. Unfortunately, years of peace at last tempted him to let down his guard. On the morning of July 20, 1923, a group of gunmen ambushed him at an intersection in tiny Maturana, just outside of Parral, Chihuahua. The order to kill Villa evidently came down from either Obregón or Calles, although the details remain hazy. Following his death tributes flowed in from the international press; the *New York Times* commended, among other virtues, his "dog-like fidelity to Madero," but there could be no doubt that many people on both sides of the border felt relief. Only the common folks mourned. Villa the man had gone, but to them Doroteo Aranga became a lasting symbol of defiance to rule by a privileged elite.

Meanwhile, international alliances mattered almost as much as internal politics. Nationalist rhetoric notwithstanding, U.S. investors still held the bulk of finance capital at risk in Mexico, and no government was likely to remain in power without coming to some sort of understanding with them. Recognition therefore remained essential. To settle the problem, negotiators for the two nations met in the pleasant, tree-lined suburb of Bucareli in August 1923. They arrived at what are called the Bucareli Accords, in which Mexico agreed to recognize its foreign debt, pay damages on U.S. property, and not apply retroactively the controversial Article 27 (which among other things nationalized subsurface mineral rights). The United States, in exchange, granted recognition to the still-fragile government. In reality, neither congress ever ratified the treaty, and in later years Mexico withdrew from the deal altogether. Foreign investors screamed bolshevism, but the accords had given the new government breathing room.

And it would soon need that room. Madero's revolution had ended continuation in office; Obregón's own term concluded in December 1924, and since the unsettled conditions of the country made popular elections impossible, the sitting president had to choose a successor. Obregón selected Plutarco Elías Calles (1877–1945), a fellow Sonoran officer and close associate. A coterie of generals, alarmed over the president's new alliance with organized labor and stoutly opposed to a man they considered an operative and a poor general, proclaimed against the new president. As titular leader they recruited the somewhat reluctant Adolfo de la Huerta, Obregón's fellow Sonoran and one-time associate. The De la Huerta uprising drew in anyone who had a grievance against the government, and that list was long. The alliance included ambitious and unscrupulous generals, unreconstructed Porfirians, and a few principled revolutionary luminaries like Salvador Alvarado and Manuel Diéguez. Among the casualties of this uprising was Yucatán's radical governor, the Obregón-Calles ally Felipe Carrillo Puerto, who was executed along with close associates and two of his brothers in a public cemetery. The rebels actually enjoyed larger numbers, but by now Obregón had secured U.S. recognition and was able to import both money and arms. He defeated the Delahuertistas in the Battle of Ocotlán, Jalisco, in early 1924, then dedicated himself to mopping up the rebellion's surviving fragments.

The De la Huerta uprising had numerous consequences. Although a rural insurgency in western Mexico still awaited, the government had mustered enough strength to suppress a major army revolt, a pattern that would hold for the coming decades. Obregón executed as many commissioned officers as possible. Those purges probably benefited a nation suffering under the depredations of the zone commanders, but the government had to promote many others to take their places as a way of securing loyalty. Still, these replacements owed their careers to Obregón, and the crisis allowed some headway in subordinating regional zone commanders to national political actors. The December 1924 succession thus came off as Obregón had intended.

Beyond matters of mere survival, one of Obregón's most important initiatives was a dramatic expansion of the public school system, and for secretary of public education (la SEP, as it is known today) he made the fateful selection of José Vasconcelos (1882–1959). A man of extremely proper, late Porfirian background, Vasconcelos had belonged to a movement called the Ateneo de la Juventud, a gathering of elite writers and thinkers who proposed to counter Positivism with a return to the classical humanities. Vasconcelos (who later tarnished his legacy by turning conservative almost to the point of fascism) had served as director of the national university and had authored a famous essay championing, if not necessarily inventing, the mestizo raza cósmica (cosmic race) as the vanguard of humanity. Vasconcelos began Mexico's vast public school system, and he imagined a Mexico revitalized by thoughtful readings of Homer and Cervantes.

While today the SEP affects nearly every aspect of Mexican grade-school education, the revolutionary cultural project best known to foreigners was its art initiative. The muralist movement began with a quest for something else entirely. Vasconcelos had called for a new public art that would take revolutionary values—at least as he imagined them—to the illiterate masses, rather in the way that the counter-reformational church used Baroque paintings to win back the faithful. But when Vasconcelos contracted a young, Paris-educated painter named Diego Rivera (1886–1957) to create a public mural, the project took a far different direction. Rivera and fellow muralists, including luminaries José Clemente Orozco (1883–1949) and David Alfaro Siqueiros (1896–1974), often disagreed violently over politics and aesthetics, but all believed in the idea of taking art to the Mexican public. Their works included everything from historical figures to allegorical, even obscure, symbolisms, all bound together in dynamic colors and an often cartoon-like composition. Siqueiros, the most radical of the group, insisted on painting with mediums like industrial-quality paint used for automobiles. Early commissions included the old Jesuit Colegio de San Ildefonso and the Escuela Nacional Preparatorio, and nationalist murals eventually found their way into some of the most important buildings of government, culture, and education. Since 1930 the muralist movement has gone the way of all art trends: first opposed, then celebrated, then internalized as an approach before being rejected and periodically resurrected. The concept of public murals drenched in social and political commentary now seems so passé that it is easy to forget that Mexican art once hit the world with the force of an atomic bomb.

While most people associate revolutionary art with painting, the vibrancy of the 1920s reached into other mediums as well. One of the most important of these was music. In his youth the multitalented Carlos Chávez (1899–1978) had studied under some of Porfirian Mexico's finest musicians and composers, and he emerged as spokesman for an authentically American music that rejected the dictates of German romanticism. In 1928 Chávez simultaneously became director of the National Symphony Orchestra and the National Conservatory; a few years later he founded the Instituto Nacional de Bellas Artes, which continues to train world-class performing artists in such fields as music and dance. Beyond his work as an educator and molder of institutions, Chávez left behind an impressive body of compositions that continues to find venues.

A number of composers who came up under Chávez's influence carried even further the search for a music that was simultaneously modernist *and* Mexican. Silvestre Revueltas (1899–1940) was the older son of a Zacatecas family that included sister Rosaura (a famous dancer) and younger brother José (one of the leading novelists of Mexico's radical 1960s). In 1939 Revueltas composed a score for *La noche de los mayas*, at that moment the most lavish and costly film the country had ever produced and still notable for its arresting imagery and poetic vitality. Revueltas died the following year from heavy drinking, and the score for *Noche* sat gathering dust until it was rediscovered and adapted into a coherent suite in the late 1950s; it remains a standard of symphonic repertoires ever since. However, the palm for the finest incorporation of popular idioms into classical music goes to Mexico's single most frequently performed symphonic piece, José Pablo Moncayo's infectious *Huapango* (1956). Moncayo composed relatively little in his brief lifetime (1912–58), but this orchestral re-envisioning of mariachi and Huastecan *son* continues to rouse audiences and has been rearranged for such diverse formats as synthesizers and guitar quartets.

In terms of literature the revolution produced a sea change in themes, if not necessarily in styles. Mexican authors had already been moving toward social realism, with authors such as Manuel Sánchez Mármol and José López Portillo y Rojas raising questions about the deep problems of their society. The real florescence in Mexican novels lay years in the future, but for the moment aspiring authors tried to bring some sense to the terrible decade of the 1910s through literary renditions. Many of those first efforts reflect a late Porfirian disgust with popular movements, a contempt seen most visibly in Mariano Azuela's *Los de abajo* (1929). An only slightly more giving treatment of revolutionary fighting appears in Rafael F. Muñoz's ¡*Vámonos con Pancho Villa!* (1931), the tale of a group of young men who decide to join the Villista forces only to lose themselves amid the cruelty and senseless killings. However, the most memorable accounts of Porfirian and revolutionary times comes not from a Mexican national at all but rather from the pen of one B. Traven, a German expatriot writer whose actual identity remains uncertain even today. Traven was most likely Ret Marut, a Prussian anarchist who came to Mexico in 1924 and used his experiences to produce such lurid and gritty novels as *The Treasure of the Sierra Madre* (1927) and *The Rebellion of the Hanged* (1936). But whatever his real name, Traven's indelible accounts of human greed and exploitation, of jackbooted jungle overseers wielding whips and shotguns, still set the bar for popular understanding of Porfirian times.

At a more popular level, the Mexican Revolution also ushered in the great age of the *corrido*. A ballad composed of four-line stanzas, a form that descends from the romances of medieval Spain, the corrido typically celebrates great deeds, terrible tragedies, and famous persons and functions as a sort of folk memory that is as enduring as it is factually unreliable. The genre sank deep roots in northern and central Mexico (while being virtually unknown in the deep south and southeast). It proliferated exponentially during revolution's bumper crop of caudillos, shootouts, and bloody martyrdoms; indeed, there are more corridos about Pancho Villa than any other subject. Modern-day singers have kept the tradition alive through musical narratives of the great narcotraffickers: the *narcocorridos*.

If anything defined the changing tastes in popular art of the 1930s and 1940s, it was the rise of Mexican cinema. While feature-length films had existed since the 1910s, fans and film historians alike generally date the beginning of the golden age to 1936 with the appearance of the romantic comedy *Allá en el rancho grande*. (Sound films had begun five years earlier.) From that moment on the Mexican film industry launched a series of productions that matched motion pictures anywhere in terms of creativity and quality. In 1940 Mexico's unique comic genius Cantinflas (Mario Moreno, 1911–93) began his career with *Ahí está el detalle*, in which he unveiled his trademark verbal contortions that only speakers of Spanish, and especially Mexican Spanish, can truly appreciate.

Mexican cinema gave birth to other performers whose celluloid images shine as brightly today as they did in their heyday. Certainly the greatest of these was Sinaloan-born Pedro Infante (1917–57), who between 1939 and 1957 made dozens of films showcasing his versatile talents as comedian, singer, musician, athlete, motorcycle rider, and dramatic leading man. Charisma came easy to him: for an entire generation Infante defined Mexican masculinity, and when he died in a plane crash on the outskirts of Mérida in 1959, his fans, like those of Elvis Presley, refused to accept his death. His remains were burned beyond recognition, so who could say whether the death had not been a fake? After twenty-five years of working in Yucatán, this author has heard more than one story from individuals whose father, for some reason or another, was supposedly taken blindfolded to a remote ranch where he met the former matinee idol, alive and rakish as ever, who had fled the limelight in order to escape from gambling debts. Try as they might, great men never seem to die.

The rise of a national entertainment industry also fostered a veritable army of professional singers, composers, and musicians. Mexican movie casting drew heavily from a nightclub scene that featured diverse acts like balladeers, mariachis, Cuban mambo, and (for the period) strongly sexualized rumba dancers. The most enduring of these talents was certainly Agustín Lara (1897–1970). An impoverished piano player at Mexico City bordellos, a connoisseur of marijuana, and as thin as a tuberculosis patient, Lara invented an image for himself as a romantic crooner singing of languid Veracruz nights. In the process he composed many of the greatest works of the modern Mexican songbook. His career stands out for its extraordinary success, but like so many others, it drew from the gradual return of peace and the attendant rise of film, radio, recording, and urban consumerism.

New World, New Strongman

The Calles transition came at a supremely delicate moment. The new government's control remained tenuous, church-state frictions continued to build, the De la Huerta uprising had shaken the country, and most of the great issues that had ignited ten years of bloodletting remained unresolved. A wrong move in any direction threatened to drag Mexico back to 1914.

Fortunately, while Calles had lacked dash on the battlefield, he more than compensated as an administrator. The list of his accomplishments extends to some length. The new president got spending under control and established sound budgeting and tax collection (including the country's first income tax), so that by the end of 1925 the internal deficit had disappeared, while the immensely controversial $1.6 billion debt to the United States had fallen to a "mere" $890 million. The fiscal turnaround came in no small part from increased demand for Mexican goods during the robust 1920s. Calles also created the Banco de México, the first true national bank and an invaluable asset for later state-fostered development.

Nor did Calles neglect Mexico's tattered infrastructure. He launched a rural electrification campaign of far-reaching consequences. Meanwhile, the newly created National Roadways Commission began construction of such key arteries as Mexico City–Acapulco and parts of the Pacific coast's Pan-American Highway. Calles protected the rebirth of Monterrey's lucrative glass and steel industries. He was the first Mexican president to address the nation via wireless radio, a landmark in Mexico's communication history. Less commonly recognized, he also laid the groundwork for the landmark petroleum nationalization of 1938. The support of organized labor remained essential to social stability, and Calles promoted Luis Morones to cabinet level, where the former electrician's nationalist views began to mold policy. The world's foremost producer in 1921, Mexico's annual yield in barrels had fallen some 25 percent, in part the result of foreign companies' reluctance to invest. Under Morones's urging, Calles withdrew from the controversial Bucareli Accords, curtailed permanent private ownership of petroleum fields, and forced the oil companies to reapply for fifty-year concessions. At the same time Mexico tightened restrictions on foreigners purchasing coastal property, border property, and subsurface mineral rights.

The military also came in for reform. While Calles consolidated national power, his close associate General Joaquín Amaro professionalized what had been a heterogenous national army. Amaro created a formal process for promotions, set mandatory retirement ages, and above all reorganized the Colegio Militar, an institution that under his watchful eye taught officers to mind their soldiers and stay out of politics. Amaro was not always successful: the army remained both an instrument of rural repression and a political mischief-maker for some time. But the reforms of the 1920s and 1930s, the institution's updating during World War II, and the stability supported by increasing postwar prosperity cumulatively inculcated an ethic of civilian rule that paid dividends in the terrible 1970s, when military coups destabilized much of the rest of Latin America.

Calles also continued Obregón's push toward improving public health and welfare. As a precursor to the great epidemiological campaigns of the 1950s, the newly formed Departamento de Salud Pública (Department of Public Health) launched Mexico's greatest effort to date against such ancient scourges as smallpox. Although the new president and José Vasconcelos later became mortal enemies, Calles expanded the size and purview of the SEP by creating two thousand new primary schools, roughly seventy per state. The young and idealistic teachers who peopled these institutions saw themselves as soldiers of change for something that they called socialism. But instead of Soviet-style collectives, SEP activists usually preached a farrago of secularism, athletics, hygiene, and the fostering of national identity. Those who studied under SEP instructors adopted their ideas selectively: new sports such as baseball took the country by storm and national identity made lurching progress, while saint-burning died a quick death. But the SEP did effect lasting and profound changes on rural Mexico, bringing it out of its intellectual isolation *and* fostering the three Rs in a way that Benito Juárez would have endorsed.

The expanding role of federal education also forced policy makers to consider the situation of Mexico's indigenous peoples. Matters of Indian affairs undoubtedly strike U.S. observers as strange. In Mexico there have never been such features as government treaties or tribal sovereignty. In fact, with the exception of certain truly remote groups living in mountain ranges or along jungle rivers, tribal organization as such did not and does not exist. Colonialism had fragmented native groups down to the community level, each largely independent of the others but answerable to the Mexican state. No blood quantum or tribal rolls exist to allow formulas, however arbitrary and unsatisfactory, for group membership. In a contradictory way, Spanish colonialism had both exploited and protected, eroded and perpetuated, an older non-European world.

Mexican intellectuals had always nursed contradictory attitudes about the country's native peoples. Did they in some mysterious way embody national identity? Did their languages and cultures merit preservation? Or were their achievements best shelved in a museum, while the actual descendants of precontact Mayas, Nahuas, and others required complete assimilation? And if indigenous campesinos failed in Positivist measures of progress, was it because of biological inferiority or the result of cultural isolation? The answers to these questions varied, but at the level of policy, Mexican intellectuals had always inclined toward refashioning Indians into thrifty mestizos. And while everyone had their opinions, the actual business of doing something about the matter fell to the already overburdened SEP.

The first attempt came in 1925 in the form of the Casa del Estudiante Indígena, a Mexico City boarding school where male interns would wear shoes, speak Spanish, and adopt (in theory at least) the requisite Positivest attitude. Casa administrators hoped to turn the young men inside out and then send them back to their villages to act as beacons of progress. In practice the institute made only the faintest headway. The work was slow and costly. Relatively few interns actually graduated, and those who did so made less than optimal teachers, or at least in the way that Casa directors had hoped. The school closed in 1932, its grand mission of social transformation hardly dented.

Even as Mexico cobbled European shoes for Indian feet, another form of instability was brewing: the deepening conflict between church and state. Mexico's new leaders were mostly from Sonora, where church presence had been particularly weak. Having waded in blood to achieve their goals, the Sonoran generals had little patience for prim, middle-class church activists. They also drew around them a coterie of provincial allies who were even more willing to press the anticlerical agenda: men like General Francisco Múgica of Michoacán or Tabasco's flamboyant Garrido Canabal. Nor had the new revolutionary leaders forgotten that Catholic political parties had cooperated with Victoriano Huerta, the unforgivable sin, while the archbishop of Mexico steadfastly denounced the constitution of 1917 as morally inadmissible and forbade priests from swearing allegiance to the new order. These attitudes radiated outward to the laity, and Obregón sparred with banner-carrying *gremios* (guild members) intent on such demonstrations as coronating gigantic religious statues: "¡Viva Cristo Rey!" the marchers cried (Long live Christ the King!). Obregón actually tried to mollify disgruntled religious activists, but to little avail. A certain degree of Catholic support for the De la Huerta uprising sufficed to convince the Sonorans that a Catholic counter-revolution was in the offing.

The nation might have overcome these spats, but the inauguration of Calles reignited conflict once more. The new head of state nursed a deep, almost pathological hatred of the Catholic Church, an animosity that invites psychological speculation. Defiantly anticlerical, the new president launched a series of initiatives designed to end Catholicism as the molder of Mexican hearts and minds. In June 1926, when a newspaper reprinted some nine-year-old antigovernment comments by Archbishop José Mora y del Río, Calles seized the opportunity to enforce the constitution's anticlerical articles to their fullest. Measures included forcing priests to register, an unmistakable threat. A confrontation quickly ensued, and on July 31 the church proclaimed a suspension of religious services as a means of protest.

While groups like Juventud Católica agitated more or less peacefully in the cities, the conflict turned violent in the rural areas of western states like Jalisco and Michoacán. There an almost medieval religion flourished, the faith of an isolated Spanish-settler culture undiluted by indigenous syncretism or modern science. Seeing the world in starkly Manichean terms of good and evil, its adherents had no difficulty determining the side to which the president belonged.

Who were these Cristeros? Contrary to accusations of the time, the movement was not the handiwork of hacendados who somehow ginned up surrounding poor folk in order to halt agrarian reform. Nor, with some exceptions, did fire-breathing priests work the crowd; accustomed to waiting out political controversies, curas mostly advised their parishioners not to pick fights they could not win and preferred to administer church sacraments in private. Rather, the Cristero War was a showdown between a revolutionary state and a headstrong laity. It found its strongest base in places where Spanish-speaking settlers had taken over formerly Indian lands in the nineteenth century and where the organizational presence of the church was greatest.

The Cristero War raged from 1926 to 1929. The Mexican government at first underestimated the challenge and, rather like the British Army during the early Boar War, was caught off guard by their opponent's tenacity, local support, and knowledge of the territory. And like that other conflict, the Cristero War quickly turned into a grinding counterinsurgency campaign. History advances through ironies and contradictions, and the rebels found their best military leader in Enrique Gorostieta (1889–1929), an atheist and former Porfirian officer. Both sides descended into acts of extreme violence that neither the revolution's latter-day supporters nor the religiously faithful can today condone. Meanwhile, Catholics who attempted to drum up support in the United States met with frustration. By the time western campesinos took to the hills with their primitive firearms, Mexico had been wracked by some form of war for nearly two decades, and U.S. citizens could no longer distinguish between the various factions. Those Cristero representatives who spoke at masses came away with a warm reception and little more.

It was ultimately Dwight Morrow—the U.S. ambassador, corporate attorney, and father-in-law of international hero Charles Lindberg—who brokered a solution. The bishops agreed to accept the constitution of 1917, while Calles called off the persecutions. He also proclaimed an amnesty for Cristero combatants, who, significantly, had not participated in these negotiations. But the damage and bitterness lingered. The war had claimed some seventy thousand lives, agricultural production had plummeted, and the western states began a long-standing pattern of outmigration. Even so, minor outbreaks of the conflict recurred for the next ten years. The war also cost the life of Obregón, assassinated by a religious zealot in 1928. It was the last real war that Mexico ever fought, a pointless and unnecessary bloodletting whose residual venom lingers to the present day.

Calles survived the crisis but recognized the danger of hanging on to office. After all, "effective suffrage and no reelection" could easily be turned against him as well. He therefore relinquished the presidency in 1929 and declined further office for what was intended to be Mexico's first *sexenio*, or six-year presidency. His tenure was followed by a series of presidents often painted as mere Calles operatives: a highly competent lawyer and party stalwart who had negotiated the Bucareli Accords (Emilio Portes Gil of Tamaulipas, who presided from 1928 to 1930), a brigadier general who had served as both governor and cabinet minister (Pascual Ortiz Rubio of Michoacán, in office 1930–32), and a baseball player turned general and millionaire businessman (Abelardo Rodríguez of Sonora, 1932–34). Contrary to myth, Calles did not somehow run the country from a back room during this period. Rather, the actual center of power oscillated between the office of the presidency and the personalist influence that Calles brought to bear at certain critical moments.

Prior to 1934 the chief executives continued to rely heavily on the support of semi-independent provincial strongmen. These men varied greatly in both style and ideology. Tabasco's Tomás Garrido was if anything more radical than the federal government in matters of cultural revolution. Saturnino Cedillo governed the state of San Luis Potosí almost as a private feud, just as Román Yocupicio controlled Sonora. The federal government also tolerated the corruption of General Esteban Cantú, whose Tijuana-based empire of vice and gambling lives on in local legend. The times made it necessary to pact with these sorts of men, but Calles also understood the need for depersonalized institutions. To that end he oversaw the creation of the first national ruling party, the Partido Nacional Revolucionario (PNR), inaugurated in March 1929: this was an enormous step toward institutional government, albeit one taken in a political landscape still very much reliant on the goodwill of caudillos.

No sooner had the bleeding stopped from the Cristero War than a new problem struck: the Great Depression. The rotten fruit of overproduction, stock market manipulations, low farm prices, maldistribution of income, and the punitive reparations of the Treaty of Versailles (1919), the crisis originated in the United States in October 1929 and quickly spread to the rest of the world. It had several major effects on Mexico. Most immediately, the decline of disposable income and investment capital in the United States weakened the agro-export sector, which had profited so handsomely from the 1920s boom and whose interests ran counter to agrarian reform initiatives.

As if this were not bad enough, the political mood in the United States turned ugly; casting around for scapegoats, people settled on the Mexican migrant workers who performed so much of the basic labor of the national food system. Revolutionary violence and uncertain conditions had pushed many men out of their villages and into the fields, mines, and railroad projects of the north. By the time the Depression hit, cheap Mexican labor was adding billions each year to the U.S. economy. But a hysteria ensued after the stock market crash, and it resulted in mass deportations, mostly without legal process. In some cases the individuals returned to Mexico were actually U.S. citizens, second-generation Mexican Americans whose language and appearance tarred them as subversive foreign elements. Children in particular fell prey to illegal deportations, since many of them had been born north of the border and hence automatically qualified for citizenship. Between 1929 and 1939 nearly five hundred thousand men made their way back to Mexico, the largest repatriation in modern history. Some men were forced home, while others sized up the situation and opted to return on their own. The returns further stressed the Mexican economy, and the presence of the returnees further contributed to a mood in which the revolution's dormant promise of agrarian reform might at last awaken.

The Radical Wing Takes Charge

It was under these conditions that the next presidential transition occurred. Even in 1934, more than twenty years after Madero's death, the idea of holding some sort of mass election remained a practical impossibility, and succession therefore turned on intraparty politics. Calles himself may have settled into conservatism, but the Depression had created a worldwide climate favorable to activist governments: some benevolent, others anything but. The presidential transition of 1934 gave the left wing of revolutionary leadership its chance.

For the new presidential term Calles chose a man whom he considered one of his most reliable followers. Lázaro Cárdenas del Río (1895–1971) was born in the small town of Jiquilpan, Michoacán. He received a grand total of four years of schooling, and at the tender age of fourteen was apprenticed to a print shop; on the death of his father he assumed the role of head of family. But fortune had other ideas for this quiet, serious-minded young man. In 1913 he joined the Constitutionalist fight against Huerta, rising quickly in the ranks. He came under the wing of Calles, took part in the defeat of Villa, and became a brigadier general at twenty-five. Cárdenas brought to the table a truly unusual combination of talents and perspectives. He was simultaneously an idealist *and* a consummate politician, two traits seldom found together. Friends and enemies alike found him personally compelling. His own rather puritanical habits, which included early rising, regular exercise, no smoking, and only limited drinking, endeared him to a people raised to practice *buenas costumbres*, a combination of thrift, modesty, and respect for elders. Unlike most men of high office, Cárdenas enjoyed an ability to communicate with people of all walks of life, whether foreign diplomats or the serape-clad peasants whose quirks and attitudes he remembered from his father's country store.

The Cárdenas era began before his oath of office and for good and ill changed Mexico in ways no one had imagined. As a candidate he undertook a massive tour of Mexico, sitting in town squares where he sipped beer and talked at great length with locals about their problems. These visits, now legendary, had multiple ends. They fed the future president with facts about local conditions and provided a vast file of names and contacts, people who would repeatedly aid him over the coming years. They also put a human face on the federal government: from the days of Agustín de Iturbide, the president had always lived far away, enthroned on a kind of Mount Olympus, and for the first time even the poorest Mexicans sat face-to-face with their national leader. The personal visit gave Cárdenas one of his strongest weapons, and he would employ it repeatedly when his projects stalled.

The first great initiative, and one that began almost immediately, was Mexico's long-promised agrarian reform. Using a body of information that had been accumulating since the 1920s, the new president immediately began to award land titles. By the time he left office the government

Lázaro Cárdenas, who served as president from 1934 to 1940, brought fundamental changes: land reform, petroleum nationalization, and the corporate political structure that later became the PRI. Many features of his vision failed to live up to expectations, but they shaped Mexican life for over half a century. Cárdenas is seen here engaged in one of his most heartfelt causes, granting asylum for orphans from the Spanish Civil War. The mother country's loss was Mexico's gain. Courtesy of Alamy.

had redistributed some forty-four million acres. Combined with the work of predecessors and successors, it remains the largest land reform in Latin American history. The reform created an enormous class of small property owners, industrious rancheros who became faithful diehards of the new political order. More famously, it set up a complicated system of government-protected titles known as ejidos, after the old Spanish term for village lands.

The ejido remains one of the most poorly understood and consistently misrepresented of all revolutionary institutions. To begin with, ejidos do not constitute collective agriculture. The government simply guarantees the land titles, while establishing the basic conditions regarding how the land can be worked or to whom it can be passed down. Like the Indian village land titles of Hapsburg era, the land could be neither divided nor sold. The only collective dimension of the ejidos was the fact that the federal bureaucracy received petitions and dispersed funding to organized groups, not individuals, thus forcing a certain degree of cooperative behavior—and guaranteeing political support when needed.

Simultaneously, Cárdenas feared that peasant agriculture might shrink Mexico to a level of subsistence poverty. Dreading the loss of foreign credits derived from such well-capitalized enterprises as sugar, coffee, and henequen, he championed a cousin institution known as the cooperative ejido, several of which had existed and even prospered prior to his own inauguration. In this arrangement, the state appointed a technically trained managerial class, while the titular owners of the cooperative functioned more like underpaid and unconsulted employees. In a strange twist, then, the cooperatives became the least cooperative of all ejidos, and after an initial burst of enthusiasm, the titular owners quickly soured on state-appointed management, a preview of the response of Peruvian peasants under General Juan Velasco's massive land reform of the 1960s and 1970s. Almost without exception, the supposed beneficiaries of cooperativism eventually demanded the breakup of the properties; once this took place, so too went the advantage of the economy of scale.

State-run ejidos that did survive met an equally disappointing fate. Markets for henequen evaporated with the invention of combines, machines that simultaneously cut and threshed the wheat, hence obviating the need for binder twine. Mexican sugar and coffee, meanwhile, fell victim to massive global overproduction. In all cases, the government, concerned about the massive pain that would result from shuttering operations, met criticism from opposing sides: from the conservative opposition, who saw the cooperatives as fiscally wasteful voting machines; and from the ejidatorios themselves, who resented the arrangement as an infringement on their individual liberty.

At the same time, history demands lateral thinking, and a number of other perspectives argue for a more positive assessment of the ejido program. Life did improve for the first generations. Very much like Roosevelt's Works Projects Administration and Civilian Conservation Corps, the act of militating for, and engaging in, the early ejidos gave hitherto marginal citizens a sense of hope and participation. If the cooperative ejidos floundered, the more individually based sank deep roots. If many ejidal properties underproduced, a handful became grain baskets for hungry urban markets. And if children and grandchildren raised on the ejido gradually gave up and moved to the cities, that was at least a more palatable alternative than the shotgun dispossessions of the Porfirian era. The much maligned ejido system thus did play a role in finally concluding more than two decades of endemic violence.

The agrarian reform's close interaction with rural communities naturally forced a reexamination of the place of indigenous peoples in twentieth-century Mexico. A firm believer in progress with a mestizo face, Cárdenas set up the Departamento de Asuntos Indígenas (Department of Indian Affairs, DAI) to oversee assimilation. Unlike its predecessor agencies, from 1938 to 1947 the DAI worked more directly with communities on projects of local development. However, a familiar set of obstacles emerged. After four centuries of European colonization, it had become increasingly difficult to define and identify "real" Indians. The use of Spanish, for example, had grown remarkably since 1821, at a time when monolingual indigenous communities had become scarcer. Campesinos in their villages—not always as remote as Mexican intellectuals alleged—understood that they had to work with the DAI to obtain resources like funding and schoolteachers, but they found the department's representatives arrogant and overbearing, traits that they countered with passive resistance. A turn to political centrism and wartime priorities after 1941 rendered the DAI an inert body, and the entire program was definitively shuttered in January 1947. *Indigenismo*, with all its questions and barriers and contradictions, has lived on in Mexico, and quite surprisingly would raise its head again in the late twentieth century.

Cárdenas's second great achievement, one that occupied much of his time and energy, was the creation of the modern presidency and the political system that was to govern well into the twenty-first century. He was the first president to complete a six-year, nonrenewable term, and ever after the sexenio has served as the basic unit of Mexican political time. Since 1934 no Mexican head of state has ever been removed or assassinated, nor has any president resigned, died in office, or failed to complete his term.

Recognizing the need for unified support in the campaign to change and develop Mexico, Cárdenas organized three major blocs of the society: the rural sector, urban industrial labor, and the salaried middle class (essentially, government employees, including the growing army of teachers). Each had its own organization and its elected officials, and the idea ran that this three-legged machine would allow ideas and initiatives to issue from below. Cárdenas tried to incorporate the military into his complex balance of blocs, but he met no success: the institution accepted civilian rule but not its control for political benefits. Formally unveiled in March 1938, the new Partido de la Revolución Mexicana (PRM) was the forerunner of the later PRI, right down to the familiar tricolor logo.

As with so many features of Cardenismo, the arrangement functioned to some extent, but not always according to its intended goals. Regional caciques—by now a term for power bosses—clung stubbornly to their status and authority, and rule through *pistolero* gangs remained common enough in places such as Guerrero, Veracruz, and elsewhere. And for all his vision, the president had a deeply realistic streak and understood that he had to reserve his political capital for the battles that really counted. Against opposition from reactionary Yucatecans, he eventually succeeded in forcing a sweeping redistribution of the henequen plantations—even though former planters retained control of the defibrating machines that made the industry function. He also invested huge amounts of time and toil on the great Laguna cotton ejido, a showpiece of collectivization set in the heart of Madero country. All these projects forced him to make extraordinary concessions to political enemies and local power bosses, thus guaranteeing that in operation the PRM was far less radical than it might have been.

The populist political effervescence surrounding Cardenismo naturally rekindled hope among feminists that their time had at last come. The women who supported the president packed the same credentials as their predecessors: educated, middle-class urbanites. They held close to the agenda set a decade earlier at the Primer Congreso Feminista and lent their voices to the populist cause. Yet the old divisions remained. PRM leaders saw them as organized support, not as initiators of change or setters of agendas. Women did indeed make some professional gains, particularly as SEP teachers, in which capacity they charged into the rural world with all the fire and fervor of sixteenth-century Franciscans. Too often these idealistic educators found themselves trapped between Catholic women—who were bone-deep conservatives—and an inexhaustible legion of campesinas more attuned to traditional roles and the necessities of mere survival.

In political matters, too, this second wave of Mexican feminism met with only limited success. Even as activists were campaigning for suffrage, Cárdenas and others were sizing up the majority of Mexican woman as likely voters for Catholic causes and probable opponents to real change. As in the United States, Mexican women managed to gain voting rights at least at state levels: Guanajuato (1934) and Puebla (1936) led the change, although not coincidentally both states were deeply conservative regions where female votes could be counted on to uphold the status quo. In the larger sense, though, the move toward the PRM system, with its tripartite corporate structure, rendered individual voting less of a prize than it might have been elsewhere. Women's voting rights, like so many forward-looking reforms, stalled altogether during World War II, and full national suffrage did not become law until 1953, somewhat behind the curve of other major Latin American nations.

Throughout his presidency Cárdenas also jousted with Mexico's answer to European fascism, the Sinarquista movement. This exotic hybrid had both international and distinctly Mexican roots. Sinarquismo drew from a deep well of conservatism, an ultra-Catholic viewpoint that disdained pluralism, populism, and presidentialism in equal measures. But it also found inspiration in Spain's fascist Falangism. Sinarquistas had seen how Calles hammered the Cristeros, and they avoided armed confrontation, but from 1937 until the postwar years their militants were a perpetual nuisance to the government. Their ideology appealed to lower middle classes of the cities, to prosperous rancheros leery of would-be *agraristas*, and to campesinos who either had yet to savor the benefits of agrarian reform or else had found the taste disappointing. Sinarquista propagandists never tired of bashing the godless and communistic cabal they believed had hijacked the country. Despite their overwhelmingly Mexican orientation, the Sinarquistas did make some headway in proselytizing in cities like Los Angeles, where Mexicans and Mexican Americans alike felt the sting of marginalization.

The Sinarquistas came to various ends, none of them good. Failing to capture national power, some of the movement's leaders settled on the idea of separatist communities hidden away in the mountains of the Baja California peninsula. The federal government was only too happy to underwrite a plan that essentially quarantined perennial troublemakers. Baja may have offered splendid opportunities for whale-spotting, but it spelled a hardscrabble existence for the extremists, who ended their dreams with the usual squabbles and shattered hopes that attend utopian communities. The wartime draft of the early 1940s briefly heightened the movement's appeal, leading to a deranged member's unsuccessful attempt to shoot the Mexican president in 1944, but events eventually swung back in the state's favor, since the postwar global repudiation of fascism allowed the complete ban of the pesky organization in 1949. The Sinarquistas' more vociferous members drifted into the emerging National Action Party, where they took a back seat to conservative business interests and more mainstream political aspirants. However, while it may seem tempting to consign these New World Falangists to the overly referenced dustbin of history, anyone with extensive experience in Mexico, and particularly in homes and private circles in the more conservative states, sooner or later realizes that the attitudes of the original 1937 Sinarquista vision have by no means disappeared.

The final initiative of the Cárdenas years, and one that both defines and divides Mexico to the present day, was the nationalization of the petroleum industry. Troubles date back to the days when Don Porfirio chafed under the pretensions of the foreign oil companies. Carranza and the Sonoran presidents had negotiated with those same entities, but they had reached no definite conclusion. The problem at last boiled over in 1936, when Mexico's petroleum workers, with presidential blessing, formed a union and advanced a contract demanding such basic concessions as wage increases and a forty-hour work week. The companies balked, thereby throwing the entire issue to government arbitration. Cárdenas favored the unions; the Mexican supreme court upheld the government's ruling; and when the companies still refused to comply, they left the president with little choice. Taking advantage of decades of public and private investment in wireless radio, Lázaro Cárdenas addressed the entire nation on the evening of March 18, 1938, proclaiming the nationalization of the oil industry.

This daring move put Mexico in special company. Only the Soviet Union had done such a thing before, back in the days when Lenin still led and when a prostrate, war-torn Europe could scarcely resist. Bolivia had nationalized its oil in 1937, but the industry was quite small, nothing like the fields of southern Russia or northern Veracruz. In this case Cárdenas seized a prized sector of the economy, quite literally from under the nose of its extremely powerful neighbor to the north. His gamble paid off. The nationalization won nearly universal acclaim as Mexicans of all description came forward to support the president, a rare moment of unity for a people long torn by rival creeds and caudillos.

The creation of Petroleros Mexicanos (PEMEX) promised the nation much greater control over its internal development. Still, the prize to which Mexico laid claim was a rusting hulk. Foreign companies had ceased to invest in either exploration or in the upkeep of their decades-old refineries. Fearing precisely such a turn of events, they had focused on extracting and refining as much as existing terms allowed. The old Faro de Oro fields had long since declined from their peak production, and the development of the giant new fields off the southern Gulf Coast lay four decades in the future. For the time being the federal government enjoyed only modest benefits from PEMEX, and into the 1950s Mexico continued to import oil from Venezuela. The problem of refining and marketing known deposits continues to the present day, as does the challenge of balancing state revenues with consumer needs.

As with the great agrarian reform project, nationalization's success also planted the seeds of Cardenismo's decline. Sectors traditionally hostile to the revolutionary government, such as the Catholic Church, rushed to embrace the measure, for in so doing its leaders found a way reassert the institution into national life. Even more than the Second World War, it was the petroleum issue that allowed hitherto ostracized groups and individuals to wrap themselves in the Mexican tricolor and reclaim their place in public life.

Revolution from the Center

With the land reforms, the petroleum nationalization, and the construction of the great PRM machine and its king-like presidency, reformers of the 1930s had achieved all that they could. Had the president's populist system of corporate votes been allowed to work, there existed the strong possibility of nominating for the presidency General Francisco Múgica, one of Cardenismo's prime ideological architects and a man somewhat to the left of the president. But further changes risked significant resistance. Cárdenas therefore violated his own system by imposing his preferred choice, the more centrist General Manuel Ávila Camacho (1897–1955). The Mexican right responded by nominating General Juan Andreu Almazán, a Guerrero-born soldier who had risen with Madero, switched sides on multiple occasions, eventually made peace with Obregón, and grown extremely rich through federal construction contracts in the process. Like other Latin American conservatives, Almazán was known to speak admiringly of the Axis powers, whom he believed would prevail in a contest with the supposedly weak-kneed Western democracies. The election proved tight; even today a foundational myth of Mexican conservatives holds that a pack of revolutionary rascals stole the rightful election of Almazán. But legends notwithstanding, Ávila Camacho prevailed with a clear, if small, majority. Almazán turned out to be a lazy campaigner, and his opportunist past continued to dog him throughout the election (and ever after, for he had sided with Victoriano Huerta, the unpardonable sin). Indeed, not long after the election he made his peace with the new order; he died, rich if tainted, in Mexico City in 1965.

As chief executive during the war years, Ávila Camacho steered a centrist course. The last of the general-presidents, he suffered in comparison with the larger-than-life persona of Cárdenas and the strongman image of his own brother, Maximino Camacho of Puebla. An unkind journalist once described him as being as colorless as a slab of dead fish. The new president was no reactionary, but he manifested little interest in the populism of the 1930s. He was skeptical of further land reforms, ended the tumultuous "socialist education" program, and declined to perpetuate earlier antireligious campaigns. After two decades of military service, he operated far more comfortably in the political center. Ávila Camacho created Mexico's social security system (IMSS) and gave the PRM the name that it was to bear ever after: the Partido Revolucionario Institucional, or PRI.

The turn toward centrism partly reflected concerns about the situation in Europe and East Asia. Even before the 1940 election, Mexico had found itself caught between opposing considerations. Many right-wing Latin Americans looked admiringly toward Mediterranean fascists like Spain's Franco and Italy's Mussolini. The left, meanwhile, still idealized the Soviet Union. Cárdenas too felt torn. He had locked horns with the United States over issues of national sovereignty, but he bitterly opposed fascists like Franco and went out of his way to take in refugees from the defeated Republican cause. Spain's loss turned out to be Mexico's gain, and the huge Spanish influx—some twenty-five thousand people, many of them talented and educated—bolstered the university system, brought entrepreneurial skills, and contributed much-needed creative adrenalin. Both Sinarquistas and the Partido Acción Nacional (PAN) opposed admitting "reds," but Cárdenas stuck to his guns. Mexican relations with fascist Spain remained frosty until the death of Franco in 1975.

The new president shared Cárdenas's disgust for fascists, but unlike his predecessor he also saw cooperation with the Allied forces as a way of unifying Mexico politically and as a means of updating and professionalizing its armed forces. Events broke in Ávila Camacho's favor. Japan's December 1941 attack on Pearl Harbor exposed just how serious the threat to the United States' west coast really was. Of greater importance for the political scene, Germany's invasion of the Soviet Union in June 1942 immediately rallied Mexican leftists to the Allied cause. When German submarines sank two Mexican oil tankers off the coast of Florida that same year, even the most recalcitrant of rightists had to modify their views, and President Ávila Camacho quickly and unreservedly entered the war on the Allied side. For his secretary of defense Camacho chose Cárdenas himself, allowing him to tap into the ex-president's expertise and huge support base and to protect his own nationalist credentials.

World War II does not factor into national identity in Mexico in the way that it does in Russia or the United States. Still, war mobilization affected Mexico in many ways. Military cooperation with the United States, while never smooth, allowed Mexico to modernize its army; the old revolutionary generals gave way to younger and more professionalized officers, a momentous break with the country's past. But the public largely opposed the idea of sending troops to foreign soil. The national politics and psyche had always looked inward, and Mexicans had lost blood and treasure defending themselves against two of the powers—France and United States—with whom their national leader now proposed to ally. As Defense Secretary Lázaro Cárdenas pointed out, Mexican soldiers lacked the arms and equipment necessary for modern international warfare. The one exception was Squadron 201, an all-Mexican fighter-pilot unit trained and equipped by the U.S. Air Force. Though small in size, Squadron 201 conducted dangerous missions over the Philippines and Japan in the last year of the war, and newspapers covered their exploits in detail.

Meanwhile, internal dynamics changed to meet wartime concerns. The Secretaría de Gobernación (Office of Domestic Affairs) expanded its capacity for espionage and launched an all-out hunt for Axis spies, of whom there were actually a few. Following the example of the U.S. internment camps for Japanese Americans, Mexico relocated Italian and German residents to the dreary confines of the Perote fortress, impounding their property for the duration of the war. In the new spirit of unity, Mexican organized labor had to back down from its confrontational postures; the change put unions on a road to accommodation from which they have never escaped. And like most Latin American countries, Mexico contributed to the war effort by participating in, and profiting from, lucrative contracts to supply Allied forces with raw materials of every description.

Mexico's greatest contribution to the war effort, and one with far-reaching consequences for North American relations, had nothing to do with combat. The deportations of Mexicans in the 1930s, together with the mass conscriptions of men following Pearl Harbor, decimated the labor force in the western United States. Under pressure from growers, Washington treated with Mexico to allow a guest-worker program, whereby Mexican citizens could legally enter the United States, work for a period of months, then return home with their accumulated wages. Thus was born the Bracero Program, originally intended to run from 1942 to 1948. Mexico handled the recruitment of workers and their transportation to the border. Two renewals extended the life of the guest-worker program until 1964, a total of twenty-two years. All told, some 4.6 million men crossed the border as braceros, many of them repeat entries. They worked mainly but not exclusively in western states, and their economic input amounted to billions of dollars. (It bears mentioning that the U.S.-Mexican border was not actually patrolled until the First World War, and that throughout the history of the two nations, free transit has more often been the rule that the exception.)

Distortions, false promises, and the elegant smoke rings of a pipe dream surrounded the Bracero Program from the very beginning. Problems included humiliating health screenings and fumigations, lackadaisical protection for workers' rights, politicized recruiting, and grafting of workers' pensions; added to these was increasingly unilateral control on the part of the United States. Small wonder that leftists, right-wing Mexican nationalists, the Catholic Church, and labor organizations all

A worker harvesting celery in Florida. The Bracero Program, which underwent several incarnations between 1942 and 1965, sent thousands of Mexican workers under legal protection to the United States. Denounced by almost everyone at some point or another, it was highly popular with the workers themselves and remains a defining event of Mexican-U.S. relations. Bruce Roberts Photographic Archive, e_br_0058, Dolph Briscoe Center for American History, University of Texas at Austin.

blasted the arrangement. But for Mexican workers it was one of the most popular initiatives of the entire postrevolutionary era. They saw it as a chance to bring real material benefits to their lives. Many braceros signed up for second and third terms; employers happily accepted them; and Mexican archives contain examples of growers earnestly writing to their former pickers, urging them to return for a least one more season. The guest-worker arrangement was so attractive that it spawned a (probably equal) number of illegal entries. Men who had learned the ropes of U.S. farm work and who had grown tired of red tape simply crossed the border on their own initiative. But whether legal or otherwise, the money from transnational labor allowed rural Mexicans to endure hard times; they held on to their land, built new homes, educated their children, and generally improved their lives at a time when national priorities were shifting to favor urban industry. Seldom has a program so universally reviled been so popular among its purported victims.

The program finally ended in 1964, a victim of increasing mechanization and the crusading mood of the civil rights era. But the Bracero imprint lives on. The labor shortage caused by Mexican workers' brief disappearance in the mid-1960s allowed activist César Chávez to negotiate for better work conditions for his United Farm Workers organization. Mexican workers themselves returned soon enough. Millions of men had learned where to find work in the United States and had become accustomed to leaving their homes and crossing borders. The core of many key Hispanic communities in places such as Denver and Los Angeles originated with braceros wintering over until the next season. Growers and industry owners, meanwhile, regarded the low wages paid to migrants as indispensable to their own enterprises. In other words, the laws may have changed, but human beings kept doing what they had been doing, and the controversy surrounding the matter of undocumented workers has lasted into the twenty-first century. The questions, problems, and advantages that surround foreign workers have become permanent parts of the United States' social and political landscape. It is no exaggeration to say that in its own way the Bracero Program has been as foundational in U.S.-Mexico relations as the Treaty of Guadalupe Hidalgo.

Between 1920 and 1945 Mexico traveled vast distances. From the wartime dictatorship of Carranza, to the gradual birth of viable institutions reasonably autonomous from presidential power, to the radical reforms of Cárdenas and their partial adjustment under his successor, the nation no longer resembled Don Porfirio's elite planter society. The sun had set over the hacendado's golden age; roving armies no longer ravaged the land; the poor and the middle classes found their way into the public sphere; and the state experimented, sincerely if not always successfully, with new ways of fostering education, culture, and well-being. To the horror of holdover Porfirians, the nation reclaimed ownership of vast amounts of wealth and property, and all the decades of científico scorn notwithstanding, it looked as though the Biblical prophecy would perhaps come true: the poor might just inherit the earth after all. But of the many Mexicans who took heart in 1945, of all the die-hard Positivists, all the cynical operators who burrowed their way into the system: How many could have imagined the even greater changes that were to follow?

8

A Cigar, a Cadillac,
and a Ticket to the Bullfights
Postwar Mexico

T ime refashions all peoples, and the Mexicans who have lived after
the end of World War II have not escaped that rule. Little by little
the revolution receded into memory; its themes and heroes made grist
for historians, while new concerns, often the challenges born of the very
growth and prosperity that so many had sought, have occupied the public landscape. Mexicans have more than ever before in terms of goods,
services, opportunities, and expectations, yet public violence exceeds that
of the hardscrabble days of the early republic. The nation's people know
more than ever about the past, yet they are abandoning ways and beliefs
that once seemed as eternal as Olmec effigies. The impossibly ancient
shares space with the intensely cosmopolitan. So enormous is the social
distance separating 1946 and the early decades of the twenty-first century
that one can only wonder what Francisco Madero would make of this
new Mexico that he had preached, a world now transformed almost beyond recognition.

The Golden Age

In many ways the point of departure came with the presidency of Miguel
Alemán Valdés (1900–1983), who governed between 1946 and 1952.
The first civilian elected president since Lerdo de Tejada (even Madero
had briefly borne arms), Alemán cut a larger-than-life figure. Young,

handsome, gregarious, a *bon vivant,* and a wheeler-dealer, he contrasted sharply with the often-grim revolutionary generals who had held power for the preceding twenty-six years, and he dreamed of an affluent—even flashy—nation whose toils and bloodshed lay in the past. When asked what he wanted for his nation, the new president famously quipped that he wanted every Mexican to have a cigar, a Cadillac, and a ticket to the bullfights.

Alemán got his wish–or at least part of it. Perhaps the greatest change came in the form of a strategy known as import substitution industrialization, or ISI. The favored approach for Latin American economists in the 1950s and 1960s, ISI rejected the region's traditional role as supplier of agro-mineral exports and instead focused on producing manufactured goods for its own consumer needs. To jump-start the process, Mexico placed protective walls around key industries. The federal government provided easy credit, subsidized energy costs for entrepreneurs, kept union militancy in check, and lowered labor costs by enforcing low agricultural prices (joy for the hungry factory man, woe for the farmer). The idea was to start small, churning out cheap, disposable items for daily use, and then progress to durable goods such as automobiles. Consumers and manufacturers, the plan promised, would pull each other up by their bootstraps.

The Alemán years also steered priorities away from the countryside and toward the city, with all its promise and peril. ISI-generated industries clustered around Mexico City, where both labor and markets abounded and where political power in this highly centralized society ultimately lay. With ISI, then, came a whole new set of social concerns oriented toward producing functional, habitable cities. Housing remained in private hands, but the government poured money into schools and hospitals. As one of his most ambitious and costly projects, Alemán mandated the creation of the buildings and grounds of the new national university, Ciudad Universitaria, which consolidated on one campus the many buildings of UNAM. Opening in 1953, the university and its grounds reveal the influence of Swiss architect Le Corbusier and feature dramatic murals that offset their "boxy" style. The creation of the geographically remote university may have been an attempt to isolate politically strident students from the rest of the society; if so, it failed miserably, as events would show. But the designers of UNAM did succeed in creating an institution that bolstered Mexico's nascent professional class, providing the sort of integrated life and work that Le Corbusier had envisioned and allowing a platform for later growth into a world-class research institution.

Another landmark urban achievement of this period was the Museo Nacional de Antropología. Few nations on earth possess archaeological wealth on a scope equal to Mexico, and the excavation, preservation, and study of its treasures constitute a major academic discipline today as well as a cause for popular appreciation at both the national and international levels. Prior to the twentieth century private collections dominated the field, but in 1934 the revolutionary government passed a sweeping antiquities law that made ancient artifacts the property of the nation. Both archaeological training and museum curatorship have advanced remarkably since then. One sensational discovery after another transformed knowledge of the precontact past, and the nation's growing prosperity created a burgeoning body of educated urbanites and lovers of archaeology who demanded a showcase worthy of Mexico's immense wealth of antiquities. Designed by top-tier museum architect Pedro Ramírez Vázquez and inaugurated in 1964, the Museo de Arqueología houses one of the world's great collections and is complemented by high-quality secondary museums in such places as Mérida, Xalapa, Villahermosa, and Oaxaca City.

Any discussion of boom-era architecture must include Luis Barragán Morfín (1902–88). This Guadalajara-born genius blended Corbusier minimalism with an appreciation of Mexico's colonial vernacular to create buildings of startling originality. His designs emphasize space and simplicity, but they eschew the coldness that modernist constructions so often invoke. Barragán designed numerous private homes, the landmark Torres de Satélite sculpture, and the Cuadra San Cristóbal, an equestrian estate famous for its use of pastel colors and space-defining rectangles. His own residence in Mexico City's Tacubaya district remains a pilgrimage site for anyone interested in the history of architecture, Mexican or otherwise.

Another achievement came in the form of the Mexico City Metro, the capital's rapid transit system. Opened in 1969 and expanding operations even today, the Metro addressed a problem that had been growing since Porfirian times: namely, how to transcend the limitations of the "walking city." The facility's impressive technical features and ingenious system of logos (the work of New York–based designer Lance Wyman) means that passengers do not need to be literate to get where they needed to go: an aesthetic as well as a practical triumph. Each year its combination of overland and underground trains whisks over a billion passengers to their destinations. Smaller versions of the same exist in Guadalajara and Monterrey.

The expansion of education, print, and readerships birthed another triumph, one whose fruits remain as enriching today as they were in their moment: a literary renaissance known as the Boom. The movement's inaugural event came in the form of Juan Rulfo's bombshell novel *Pedro Páramo* (1948). Seldom has a single work exerted so remarkable an influence over the entirety of Spanish-language literature. This imaginative tale of caciques, corruption, madness, and violence in Rulfo's native Jalisco moved Latin American writing much closer to the English-language version of modernism, with its fragmented narrative and consciousness, but Rulfo also infused his novel with what has come to be called magical realism, a creation that achieves Franz Kafka's vision of the radical violation of reality through its emphasis on Latin America's often confusing social contradictions. Among the other Mexican novelists who followed Rulfo's path was Carlos Fuentes; his *Where the Air Is Clear* (1958) and *The Death of Artemio Cruz* (1962) explore the deceits and paradoxes of Mexican society: sometimes cruel, sometimes amusing, but always compelling. Through the works of Fuentes and others, the Boom continued into the 1980s, when the collapse of Mexico's developmental economic model met with the often-harsh realities of neoliberal reform; this, combined with the simple exhaustion of Boom techniques, forced writers onto different paths.

The visual arts diversified alongside literature. While muralism survived (and continues today), younger artists demanded a break from what they considered a worn-out approach tainted by association with the state and its ruling party. By the 1950s some Mexican painters, notably Justo Rufino Tamayo, had moved in the direction of symbolism. In the early 1960s José Luis Cuevas (1934-2017) spearheaded the Generación de la Ruptura, an art movement so named because its adherents rejected the politics and often cocksure didacticism of the muralists in favor of a more introspective, often abstract, approach. One wing of la Ruptura, a group that called itself the Nueva Presencia, began with the premise that artists cannot change society; instead they focused on inward reactions to a corrupt and dissatisfying world. Ruptura artists rejected such muralist hallmarks as indigenismo and historical reportage and instead drew from such eclectic sources as surrealism, abstract expressionism, and even seventeenth-century Spanish portraiture, most notably in the work of Rafael Coronel.

Meanwhile, a very different form of visual arts—television—made its entry. The technology has Mexican roots, given the fact that a Guadalajaran engineer named Guillermo González Camarena (1917–65) actually invented the basis of the color television in the 1940s. The first transmissions in Mexico, and in Latin America as a whole, came in 1946. Prior to the 1980s broadcasts remained limited to only a few channels. Televisa, the multitentacled entertainment conglomerate created by Emilio Azcárraga, began in 1973, the result of a merger of several smaller channels. From the start Azcárraga aimed at lowbrow tastes, and he found them: crude comedies, inane game shows, and soccer on Sunday. Above all, Televisa pioneered the *telenovela*, a serial drama in soap opera format, but one that offers a discreet beginning and end and only runs for one season. In terms of the global entertainment industry, Televisa has exerted an influence exceeding that of the muralist movement. Competition entered the marketplace in 1993 in the form of TV Azteca, although its programming and format adhered closely to the Televisa model. Real competition came with the advent of cable, satellite, and streaming services; these mediums bring modern Mexicans into contact with a world that is far removed from most people's daily experience and at times make it hard for society to perpetuate the conservative values that nineteenth-century Catholics had fought so passionately to maintain.

Skylines shot upward, students matriculated, and the roads whirred with contented motorists: ISI had produced real and visible changes. The strategy elevated consumer spending, and urbanization, literacy, cultural advances, and overall standards of living grew accordingly. Many of the old barriers against female advancement began to tumble, and society jettisoned the more visible signs of racism and oppression that the científicos would have accepted as necessary conditions of life. This same pattern appeared in varying degrees throughout the major Latin American nations. ISI, it seemed, had won the day.

But the ISI ointment had its fly. While early industrialization—for example, the manufacture of such articles as shoes and sheet metal—came easily, the transition to more sophisticated products required design and technology, plus financing and education, that were simply unavailable. ISI countries also suffered from product duplication: they were all producing the same things and hence had only limited success in breaking into export markets. Government-guided development also required a huge concentration of wealth in order to create an entrepreneurial class: that is, money first had to accrue among the few before it could trickle down. Even today Mexico suffers from a highly regressive tax structure, the direct legacy of the Alemán years. That fact, in turn, creates a perpetually underfunded state and a debilitated consumer class incapable of generating demand for arts and industry. Finally, in Mexico as elsewhere, those who govern the developmental state eventually become an inbred, privileged elite who generate little gratitude, only cynicism and contempt.

It is easy to explain ISI limitations to historians and economists, but not to a voting public. Because the changes happened over the course of decades, and because the immediate benefits were so attractive, most people were initially willing to overlook hidden problems. Much to the grief of ruling parties, the boom years had fostered a swelling body of expectations. People grew accustomed to improvement. Better living conditions, together with the rhetoric of democracy that had infused the war effort, led many to expect a better and more inclusive tomorrow, and when ISI stalled in the 1980s, social unrest naturally followed.

While urban growth persisted, albeit in checkered fashion, rural Mexico struggled. True, increasing fiscal solvency allowed Alemán to rein in much of the pistolero governance that had prevailed in the countryside. But the ejidos, once the favored children of federal policy, languished in a state of abandon that only deepened with time. Three factors eroded the benefits and the appeal of the Cárdenas land system. First, the population quadrupled between 1934 and 1980. Simple health programs that provided vaccinations, antibiotics, and improved sanitation lowered infant mortality rates, but natality changed only grudgingly, for limiting birthrates involves birth control and sex education, both touchy topics in a land strongly influenced by rural machismo and religious norms. Births per woman in Mexico began to plummet in the early 1970s as a result of government programs and the cost of a middle-class lifestyle and education. And while the current birthrate is almost identical to that of the United States, the effects of three decades of exploding population continue to be felt in a demand for land that the Cárdenas-era reforms simply could not accommodate. Younger sons of ejido families typically solved the matter for themselves by leaving for the cities or by embracing the itinerate life of the bracero.

Second, ejidos suffered by their limited ability to partake in the so-called Green Revolution, as new techniques brought modern science to agriculture: hybrid crops, mechanization, chemical fertilizers and pesticides, irrigation on a massive scale, and mechanization produce vast yields, but in addition to other severe problems they require considerable outlays of capital. Mexico's private commercial farmers, who controlled the broad, flat farmlands on which Green Revolution techniques best function, have prospered; the underfunded ejidos, often based on poor and irregular plots of land, have not. Ejido farmers focus on traditional crop strains that, if less productive in terms of volume of grain, also require less pampering and are more certain to produce something.

Finally, the ejido system has always struggled with the problem of funding. In market-driven agriculture, farmers mortgage their land and future crops in order to pay for the planting, and in the process they are able to factor in the costs of such improvements as irrigation and technology. Ejidatarios have no such ability, since their lands cannot be alienated: without the possibility of repossession, no commercial bank would ever loan them money. Only the government can provide credit, but such lending, in turn, depends on political priorities. After 1940 federal policy-makers grew skeptical of campesino agriculture and gave priority either to urban industry or to footing the bill for the irrigation projects necessary to large-scale commercial export agriculture.

Under these conditions Mexico has developed a dual agricultural system: one tier is privately owned, highly capitalized, and oriented toward supplying the lucrative U.S. market. The second tier consists of underfunded peasant producers using far more traditional farming methods and whose crops are geared mainly toward domestic markets. Most ejidos are not terribly productive, but a few have shown themselves extremely efficient. The administrations of the 1950s and 1960s struggled with the Cárdenas legacy of land to the tiller. Presidents such as Adolfo López Mateos (who led from 1958 to 1964) and Gustavo Díaz Ordaz (in office from 1964 to 1970) gave out more land than Cárdenas, although much of that land was of marginal quality. But none of this could satisfy the needs of an exploding population; nor could mere possession, even with the available systems of credit, somehow elevate campesinos' standard of living in a world of increasing technology, urban amenities, and education requirements. One way or another, people had to leave the countryside.

Prosperous and Unhappy

The Cold War period of 1945–89 stands as one of the darkest moments in all of Latin American history, a time in which naive hopes collided with naked repression and when ancient enmities of class and ethnicity operated under the essentially foreign masks of pro- and anti-Communism. As it went, Mexico's own taste of this period was mild. Economic growth remained robust until the early 1980s, civilians retained the upper hand over a depoliticized military, and the political apparatus born of the revolution purred with contentment, dodging succession crises and populist demagogues as if they were so many slow-moving beasts. Political repression certainly took place, and protestors and armed insurgents alike met violent deaths, but at least these nowhere approached the levels of such pariah states as post-Perón Argentina, Augusto Pinochet's Chile, or the death-squad nightmares of El Salvador and Guatemala.

In Mexico these postwar conflicts interacted with a crisis of the one-party system. The PRI ultimately met the fate of most developmental states: namely, death by success. As industry and urbanization grew, they produced a middle class impervious to the old mechanisms used to control campesinos and industrial workers. Nowhere was this truer than in the nation's universities. Conflict between the government and Mexico City's volatile college students boiled over in 1968 as part of a global trend. At that moment a demographic bulge stemming from the baby boom of the immediate post-1945 years was reaching its peak, and more persons than ever enjoyed education, social awareness, communication skills, and leisure time. China's Cultural Revolution (1966–76), now dismissed as a tragic aberration, in its moment inspired many people to think that student street rallies could change the world. Such movements had already rocked the political systems of France and the United States, so why not Mexico? Finally, the non-Communist world's Cold War alliance with some of the globe's most outrageous human rights abusers—including several Latin American nations—made U.S. moral leadership ring hollow and by extension discredited an authoritarian Mexican government that had long ago ceased to pose a nationalist challenge.

Problems came to a head in the fall of 1968. Youth protests that grew originally out of gang warfare and complaints about police brutality fused with demonstrations by radical student organizations in a series of huge antigovernment rallies. These events escalated as Mexico City prepared to host Latin America's first-ever Olympic Games. On the night of October 2, 1968, security forces opened fire on the protestors at the Plaza de Tlatelolco. Some protesters perished, while others were either arrested or driven off, and a state of siege enveloped the capital for days. Tlatelolco became a dividing line in Mexican history. In the decades since it has become clear that long-accepted numbers of student deaths were greatly exaggerated, overestimates made all the more believable by the secrecy with which the whole affair was smothered. Instead of tens of thousands, or even the commonly cited 350 (a number whose actual source has never been determined), it is likely that fewer than fifty protestors perished. However, in the final analysis, killing three people may be as bad as three thousand. No official explanations or public apologies could salve the matter, and the October tragedy became a bloody shirt to wave for anyone with an ax to grind against the Mexican government. And there were many.

The 1970 presidential transition raised to power one Luis Echeverría Álvarez, a longtime party member and the secretary of gobernación during the Tlatelolco massacre. But instead of bringing down the iron fist that many expected, Echeverría set out to win back the left and recapture the lost populist laurels of the Cárdenas era. Although the subject of the usual jokes, the new president (born in 1922 and still alive at time of writing) was a man of high intellectual caliber and endless energy. To the surprise of his detractors, Echeverría embraced what might be called the "old left" coalition of campesinos, labor unions, and nationalist intellectuals. He adopted a populist style, jettisoning double-breasted and peaked-lapeled suits in favor of white Yucatecan guayabera shirts. Far from sealing himself off in the luxurious Los Pinos presidential residence, Echeverría was everywhere: in meetings with protestors, in public demonstrations, in remote ejidos. Aided by his socially conscious wife, María Esther Zuno, he radically upped presidential visibility and embraced popular causes. It was as if the calendar had rolled back to 1935.

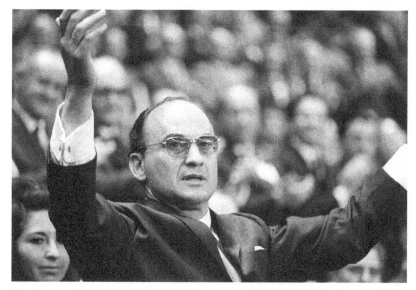

The luster of the revolution had begun to dim by the late 1950s, giving rise to unrest even as urban Mexico expanded and prospered. President Luis Echeverría Álvarez (who held office from 1970 to 1976) tried to win back lost credibility by embracing populist positions, but he ended up antagonizing as many people as he satisfied. The perpetually dynamic Echeverría is seen here in a characteristic pose. Courtesy of Associated Press Images.

But the Echeverría moment involved far more substantive changes as well. Convinced that entrenched hacks had eroded party prestige, he purged the PRI of its old guard and replaced it with a younger generation whose claim to leadership rested not on militancy but on education and technical expertise. Indeed, few other choices presented themselves. In the 1960s Mexico had become a society dominated by an urbanite majority: large cities had complex utility and service needs; combined with the need to keep pace with international standards of technology and training, they spelled the rise of a technocracy. But the change also signaled the return of the class divisions that had bedeviled Porfirio Díaz. On one side were the party stalwarts, now derisively tagged "Dinosaurs," who had risen from lowly positions as student militants, coffee boys, and leafleteers. Opposing them were the notably younger "Technocrats," who had attended elite foreign schools and who, with no political experience whatsoever, moved directly and comfortably into cabinet-level positions;

Echeverría identified these latter men as the party's future. Meanwhile, a parallel change took place in the military. Realizing that he would require the loyalty of the armed services in order to suppress dissent, the president retired a large number of aging officers and promoted younger ones in their place, sweetening the deal with a new military college.

In characteristic style, Luis Echeverría also tried to recapture the lost Cárdenas mantle of agrarian reformer. However, Mexico was no longer prostrate from civil war and global depression. Export agriculture now thrived, and prosperous ranchers and growers, most of them beneficiaries of government largesse, knew only too well how to protect themselves. Private security forces known as *milicias blancas* (white militias)—groups reminiscent of the regulators of the Johnson County War in nineteenth-century Wyoming—moved aggressively to prevent peasant land occupations. A singularly nasty encounter in rural Sonora in October 1975 resulted in the deaths of nineteen campesino activists: a body count negligible by the standards of modern narcoviolence but shocking to a nation that had put the revolution behind it. The San Ignacio Massacre forced Echeverría to reconsider his strategy. Presidential prestige was on the line, so he forced through the promised land titles in San Ignacio but halted further redistributions. Thus ended four decades of agrarian reform; the massive tangle of lawsuits and backlogged cases and the constitutional framework that had enabled the reform would require another four decades to undo.

Meanwhile, Mexico's young protestors went the way of the other remnants of the global student movement of 1968. A certain number of the former radicals now entered government service as directors and advisors, shedding their earlier politics in favor of income and influence. Both Echeverría and his friend and successor José López Portillo (who held office from 1976 to 1982) understood that much of the discontent centered in student communities, and as a result they dramatically expanded the numbers of universities and centers, thus decentralizing the radicals. (In fairness, we have to recognize that far from being some massive feather-bedding project, many of these new institutions went on to perform heroic feats of research and publication.) An even larger number of those who militated in 1968 simply returned to their studies or else joined the workforce. A still smaller subset became Mexico's nascent counterculture, which rejected politics and instead sought out alternate lifestyles often involving a potpourri of drugs, rock music, and indigenous culture. The movement known as La Onda (the wave) lasted only a brief while and flourished mainly among metropolitan youths and their echoes in the provincial capitals. La Onda was amorphous, as countercultural movements tend to be; at varying moments it embraced virtually any value that the mainstream despised. Its most loyal followers came from the capital, where the national university system, together with the anonymity of the big city and its tendency to draw artists and writers along with everyone else, exposed people to new ideas. Provincial youths, meanwhile, remained rooted in a more static, conservative world, and at most produced smaller echoes of La Onda. Like the Beats of the United States or the post-1965 counterculture, much of what La Onda generated in the way of art and literature has not endured—such being the fate of popular culture everywhere—but a few gems in these and other genres remain. The movement's defining moment was the 1971 Avándaro concert, held in Mexico state. Echeverría made political hay out of trashing La Onda, appealing to an older, explicitly nationalist left; at the same time, attacks on radical or alienated youths provided the president with useful cover against the conservatives on his right. Still, Mexico's version of the 1960s global youth movement left an indelible imprint on the social memory, just as hippies—a phenomenon equally difficult to define—have lingered in the minds of U.S. citizens.

An even smaller nucleus decided that Tlatelolco had shown the folly of peaceful reform. The more successful radicals stayed true to the old formula of rural insurgency. Following the example of the Cuban Revolution (1959), disillusioned rural teachers Genaro Vázquez and Lucio Cabañas created guerrilla groups in dirt-poor Guerrero state, and while predictably falling victim to repression or the simple hazards of underground life, they assumed a folk-hero status far out of proportion to anything they actually achieved. At the same time, a new vogue was sweeping Latin America: the urban guerrilla strategy. Shortly before his death at the hands of Brazilian security forces, Communist revolutionary Carlos Marighella authored a highly influential book called *Minimanual of the Urban Guerrilla* (1969). Drawing on the cases of the Irish Republican Army, the French underground, and Che Guevara, Marighella moved the locus of revolution to young urban radicals, whom he encouraged hide out in the concrete jungle while surreptitiously working to bring down an authoritarian state.

Seldom has a strategy failed so consistently, or so catastrophically. Mexico's urban cells, with such overblown names as the Fuerzas Revolucionarias Armadas (revolutionary armed forces) and the Movimiento Nacional Revolucionario (national revolutionary movement), shared the trajectory of their Brazilian, Uruguayan, and Argentine counterparts: at first ignored, then winning an unexpected success born of surprise, then crossing a line and triggering a repression for which the idealistic warriors were simply unprepared. They went so far as to kidnap and execute Eugenio Garza Sada, a member of a prominent Monterrey family, and later attempted to kidnap the sister of president José López Portillo. These ill-advised strikes invited serious repression in the form of paramilitary groups that received funding from the government and army; their role was to kill anyone perceived as subversive. Surviving fragments of the revolutionary cells retreated deep into remote corners of places such as Guerrero and Chiapas, where all problems were local and where the collapse of the socialist bloc remained unknown to most. Their revolutionary descendants would return to surprise the Mexican public in the mid-1990s, at precisely the moment when everyone had pronounced their movements dead and buried.

The neopopulist presidents also changed government policies relating to indigenous peoples. The creation of the Instituto Nacional Indigenista (INI) in 1948 had marked the culmination of more than twenty years of governmental dabbling in some sort of bureaucratic interface with Mexico's Indian peoples. INI itself grew out of the 1940 Interamerican Indigenous Conference, organized under Cárdenas. Although it did not actually open its first station until 1957, it thereafter became a long-lived actor in rural affairs. Under the direction of the capable Alfonso Caso, the starkly assimilationist INI fanned out into the countryside, opening its first station (in Chiapas) in 1957, and quickly establishing counterparts throughout the length and breadth of the republic. Theoretical underpinnings notwithstanding, the first years of INI left a complex legacy. For all its assimilationism, it provided a series of benefits unimaginable in previous times. Campesinos may have politely tolerated the INI's pilot programs of experimental crops, but they loved the dental care, sewing machines, electric corn mills, and water pumps that the stations provided. In some places INI became a useful counterweight to a local gentry who had long seen campesinos as a personal resource.

Unfortunately for the INI idealists, the agency, along with indigenismo itself, became mired in tragedy. In 1967 the federal government began a project on the Papaloapan River, a plan to generate hydroelectricity for much of southern Mexico by erecting the Miguel Alemán Dam in northeast Oaxaca. It fell to INI to relocate the thousands of Mixe, Mazatec, and Chinantec Indians who inhabited the river basin. The haphazard way in which this was carried out led to the spectacle of internal refugees, victims of an insensitive and self-satisfied mestizo government moving around native peoples for its own benefit. The scandal fed into the larger critique of Mexican society that was emerging in the late 1960s. More radical anthropologists now mounted a withering attack on the accommodating tendencies of the INI bureaucracy. As a response, Echeverría and López Portillo moved in the opposite direction, embracing the preservation of indigenous culture. For a brief period money poured into the agency as it began to develop educational materials in some forty different indigenous languages.

These and other social programs were only possible because of a sudden rush of petroleum wealth. After years of limping by on low production and Venezuelan imports, Mexico came into its own in the late 1970s through the opening of the Cantarell oil fields, just off the coast of Tabasco. This great new field began production at precisely the moment that OPEC had briefly driven crude prices to record highs and when the United States was feeling the pinch of gasoline shortages and inflation. For once, it seemed, the historic tables had turned: the United States' loss would be Mexico's gain. U.S. banks, then brimming with deposits from Saudi Arabia's windfall oil profits, competed to loan money to Mexico. By 1982 Mexico's foreign debt had climbed to a record US$80 billion, but few worried, for everyone assumed that continued high petroleum prices would make repayment a fairly routine matter.

Throughout the 1970s it was all too easy to be swept up in the heady excitement of the petroleum boom. López Portillo spent grandly, and the government assumed massive social commitments. The federal government now dedicated itself to PEMEX expansion, price subsidies, agricultural subsidies, new institutions of education, social programs for indigenous peoples, support for the arts, expanded credit for businesses, and an ongoing campaign of bettering infrastructure. But López Portillo learned the hard way that prices can go down as well as up. Producers seldom dictate global markets in the long run, and OPEC's brief triumph provoked determined searches for new petroleum sources. These materialized in Alaska, Alberta (Canada), and Britain's North Sea, and by 1982 global oil prices had tumbled back to a mere $8 a barrel. Mexico thus found itself saddled with an $80 billion foreign debt. It was a modest sum by comparison with today's $611 billion, but unpayable by the revenue structures of 1982. The predicament had repercussions far beyond national borders. Large segments of Latin America—including South American military dictatorships anxious to conceal their illegitimacy beneath a patina of prosperity—had contracted huge amounts of foreign loans. Mexico's debt default of August 1982 caused U.S. and European banks to suspend further loans to Latin America, resulting in the so-called "lost decade" of the 1980s, when credit was hard to come by and austerity penetrated into many features of daily life.

The predictable reactions followed. Mexican entrepreneurs, who had always distrusted the neopopulist presidents, sent their capital out of the country. (Even today, at US$80 billion, Mexico leads Latin America as the chief depositor in U.S. banks; this money has a significant impact on stabilizing our financial system.) López Portillo desperately tried to staunch the bleeding by nationalizing the banks, but the law of political influence dictated that those closest to the president stood the strongest chance of getting around restrictions, making his friends and relatives the greatest offenders. As his sexenio drew to a close, López Portillo found himself forced to take the humiliating step of devaluing the peso. The man who had hoped to preside over a historical role-reversal between Mexico and its northern neighbor thus went out a victim to inequalities that had prevailed since the days of Porfirio Díaz.

Back to the Porfirian Future

With the exit of López Portillo in 1982, Mexico had nowhere to go but rightward. The incoming president, Miguel de la Madrid Hurtado (who held office 1982–88), was chosen for his financial and administrative expertise: that is, as a cleanup man for a crisis that threatened to drag Mexico back to the Great Depression. Thus began a prolonged period of austerity. De la Madrid and his successors gradually scaled back state commitments, sold off money-losing state companies, and allowed prices for key commodities to adjust to market levels. Overall, the 1980s were years of hardship and were made even worse by a terrible earthquake that rocked the Mexico City center in 1985.

One of the most important post-1982 changes was the liquidation of state-owned industries. Over the course of the previous decades, the Mexican government had assumed control over some four hundred enterprises, including high-profile sectors such as petroleum, railroads, and telecommunications; these also included a wide range of less-significant businesses such as the paper industry. Some of these industries had fared better than others, but in the worst instances they encountered the same problems as the state-owned industries of socialist-bloc nations: politically driven mismanagement, undisciplined labor, lack of technological innovation, and failure to discern or respond to market demands. Under the presidencies of de la Madrid and his successor, Carlos Salinas, the federal government reprivatized huge swaths of the state sector.

The reprivatized enterprises met diverse fates. The newly independent banks struggled; some were temporarily returned to state control only to sold off again, while others passed into the hands of international competitors from Spain and the United States. In the case of the telephone company, however, the privatization greatly improved the country's communications system and in the process made entrepreneur Carlos Slim one of the richest men in the world.

The neoliberal governments also reversed revolutionary policies by opening Mexico to foreign investment. President Carlos Salinas de Gortari (who presided from 1988 to 1992) at first tried to partner with European investment groups, but he found that the entire continent was absorbed in the emerging European Union. That left only the United States. Gradually, the older restrictions were cast aside. When Salinas signed the North American Free Trade Agreement (NAFTA, or, as it is called in Mexico, the Tratado de Libre Comercio) in 1994, he laid the groundwork for large-scale entry of U.S. and Canadian enterprise. Within twenty years manufacturing grew from about 8.5 percent of Mexico's GNP to nearly 40 percent. In a rush to conquer hitherto protected markets, multinationals quickly established bases of operation throughout major Mexican cities. The most successful of these companies, Walmart, is now the largest private employer in Mexico. Moreover, Mexican nationals dominated the high-paying upper- and midlevel management positions, thereby guaranteeing an important base of support for the new model.

Among other effects, easing restrictions on foreign capital produced the dramatic expansion of the *maquiladora* sector. Originally a Mexico-devised project for employing the thousands of men returned home at the termination of the Bracero Program, maquilas took their name from an old Spanish practice whereby those who brought wheat to be milled paid for the services by leaving a portion of the flour. The approach had already sunk some regional roots as U.S. industry began to denationalize in the late 1960s; companies such as Playtex and Texas Instruments operated in San Salvador, for example, while Spaulding produced its baseballs in Haiti in the 1970s. The idea was to ship prefabricated parts to the Mexican border, where assembly costs were cheaper, then ship the finished products to the country of origin. Over the next twenty years maquilas swamped the border cities, bringing the usual boomtown cocktail of better wages, easy money, and social havoc. Though eventually undersold by China in the twenty-first century, maquilas briefly dominated the economic and social landscape, penetrating into remote places like the Yucatán Peninsula.

Little change in agrarian policy took place under De la Madrid, given the pressures of the international debt crisis. But Carlos Salinas broke with older ejido policies. First, in 1992 Salinas formally announced that Mexico would no longer assume the responsibility for guaranteeing land for everyone—a decision decried both in Mexico and abroad but at bottom a concession to reality that informed policy-makers had understood since the 1970s. Salinas's program of tribunals to clear up the backlog of ejido disputes won considerable popularity and helped untangle the morass of rural legal conflicts. Finally, the Salinas government allowed for the privatization of ejidos, pending majority consent. This arrangement itself produced mixed results. Ejidatarios had been illegally renting and selling their land for years, so in that sense the law simply regularized what had become widespread practice. In some places ejidos disappeared quickly: the first to go were those lands that lay just outside large urban areas, thus becoming part of a global conversion of farmland to suburb. But the majority of ejidos still remain with their original owners, and if such a change does come, it will happen not as a bursting dam but rather as slow seepage.

In places where the cooperative model survived, it also tended to outlive its profitability, as happened with the henequen processing plants of Yucatán. The state kept these operations on artificial life support because the economic hurt of privatization (or in this case, simple closure) would have been too great. By the time that overall social and economic changes finally shuttered its doors in the 1990s, the great henequen processing company and its related rural input stations had become relics of an era that few Yucatecans today even remember.

Neoliberal policies also had the unintended effect of eroding the one-party system. Mexico's technocratic reformers understood that the older elements of the PRI, with their reliance on patronage, would oppose or subvert many of their reforms, so they consequently developed ways around the Dinosaurs' reach. The most famous of these devices was the Programa Nacional de Solidaridad (PRONASOL), better known by its bumper-sticker name of Solidaridad. Under this arrangement rural communities could petition directly to the executive branch for assistance: the presidential office provided the money and resources, while communities committed themselves to providing manpower. Solidaridad won immense popularity, and its ubiquitous logo became a symbol of the late 1980s and early 1990s. (While virtually any sort of public works qualified, the single most common project was the basketball court, hundreds of which now dot the republic.) It also eroded support for the Dinosaur element that President Salinas and his cabinet distrusted, and it greatly weakened the party's strength, ultimately contributing to its transition to a multiparty arrangement. To frame the matter in a way to which U.S. readers might relate, once there were no more potholes to fill, no more taxes to slash, and no more government contracts to award, the old political class lost its appeal for voters and contributors.

For anyone who remembers the Mexico of the 1970s and 1980s, the changes have been nothing short of amazing. Use of personal vehicles has exploded, to consequences both good and destructive, as major cities now host oozing rivers of vehicles. Shoppers now find international merchandise readily available. Interminable lines for banking services and bus tickets have given way to computerized inventories and online purchases. Today, Mexico has the highest number of Internet users of any Spanish-speaking country (although in terms of percentage of total population, it still lags behind Argentina, Chile, Costa Rica, and Uruguay). Anyone who remembers waiting interminably to make an international call can only marvel at the country's digitized phone system, its widespread connectivity, and its almost religious conversion to the cell phone.

There are innumerable ways to slice and dice economic statistics, and the case of Mexico offers no exception. Viewed from where it stood a hundred years ago, the country has traveled immense distances, for its GNP now ranks as the fifteenth largest in the world. In 2020 as in 1910, Mexican rich is world-class rich; at the same time, though, the size of the middle class has expanded, and more people have left behind the conditions of extreme poverty. But several major drags continue to hamstring economic growth. Banks are reluctant to loan money to small- and medium-sized businesses. Even many of the larger firms continue to operate (and not always efficiently) as family concerns, while widespread crime acts as a disincentive for investment.

One important way of analyzing the economic health of a nation is to review its foreign exchange structure: how it obtains foreign money that in turn can be used for the purchase of much-needed foreign goods and services. In this regard Mexico has perhaps not traveled as far as might be hoped. In terms of known oil reserves, Mexico has fallen from its privileged position to nineteenth, behind such lesser-known producers as Angola and Ecuador. Still, 7.9 billion barrels in proven reserve is no mere gas station, and petroleum sales continue to account for some 40 percent of national revenue. With a production of nearly 4 million barrels per day, Mexico remains the United States' third largest supplier, behind Canada and Saudi Arabia. After petroleum, the next largest sources of foreign credits are remittances, manufacturing (actually a highly diverse body), and tourism. Of course, oil wealth carries its own problems. In many ways, and despite an attempt to impose a more realistic income-tax system in the 1980s and 1990s, Mexico remains caught in a low-tax model. The extremely wealthy pay little tax, while the poor have nothing with which to pay, leaving only an oversoaked, and insufficiently large, middle class.

Perhaps the neoliberal agenda was necessary, given the extravagant costs and diminishing returns on state-run industries. Gazing from the windows of the Palacio Nacional, presidents had seen the need for greater private-sector participation since the early 1960s. But the spectacle of a Mexican plutocracy, wealthier and more insensitive than ever, inadvertently laid the conditions for an entirely unexpected challenge.

It came about through a long series of unplanned, almost fortuitous circumstances. During the brief flourish of urban guerrillas in the early 1970s, one of the groups who took up arms was the Movimiento Nacional Revolucionario (MNR), in the almost proverbially commercial and conservative city of Monterrey, Nuevo León. After losing many members in a raid on their safehouse, survivors relocated to the most remote part of Mexico imaginable: the Selva Lacandona of southeastern Chiapas. Here they encountered a world straight out of the Wild West. The federal government had homesteaded small farmers, mostly indigenous, here since the days of Echeverría; undercapitalized and focused mainly on subsistence farming and a few small trade crops, they invariably came into conflict with cattle and coffee entrepreneurs who saw the Chiapan frontier as an export opportunity. Attempts to establish grassroots, community self-help programs failed repeatedly, leaving a deep disillusionment with legitimate strategies. The arrival of Liberation Theology in the person of Bishop Samuel Ruiz heightened expectations; their failure to be met was followed by frustration and anger.

All the while the MNR continued to recruit members from the Mexico City universities. One of those contacted was Rafael Guillén Vicente, an industrial design instructor who hailed from Tampico. Following the Tlatelolco massacre, Guillén had adopted increasingly radical views, and he eventually left his position in a posh metropolitan university to become part of the Lacandona nucleus. Under the nom de guerre Subcomandante Marcos, he modified the original movement in two basic ways. First, he brought a personal charisma lacking among the initial leadership. Second, he shifted away from textbook Marxism, with its emphasis on urban proletariats, in favor of the indigenous rights issues that hit any Chiapas resident squarely in the face. Thus was born the Ejército Zapatista de Liberación Nacional (EZLN). A dawn assault on Chiapan cities on January 1, 1994, caught the country by surprise, and while it failed to generate a wider uprising, the Zapatista challenge did set off a far-reaching debate about the direction and future of Mexican society.

For Mexico the years 1994–95 challenged even the steadiest of nerves. Not only had the Chiapas uprising caught the nation off guard, but in March 1994 an alienated loner assassinated the recently unveiled PRI candidate Luis Donaldo Colosio at rally in Tijuana, leading to his replacement by the relatively unknown Ernesto Zedillo, hitherto secretary

By the 1990s Mexican leaders had reversed many revolutionary policies. Their decisions benefitted manufacturing and urban consumers but hurt the rural sector. Much to the surprise of both the Mexican public and the world, the country's indigenous past reasserted itself in 1994 in the form of the Zapatista rebellion of southeast Chiapas. Courtesy of Alamy.

of education. Six months later assailants yet unknown shot the PRI's secretary-general, José Francisco Ruiz Massieu, outside a posh hotel in downtown Mexico City. Zedillo himself struggled as a campaigner, and though he ultimately proved himself a responsible president (holding office from 1994 to 2000), his devaluation of the overvalued peso in 1995 precipitated a brief financial crisis. He declined to invoke the old party mechanisms that favored PRI success at the ballots, and in 2000 Vicente Fox Quesada, a Guanajuato rancher and Coca-Cola executive who had risen in the conservative Partido Acción Nacional (PAN), at last broke the single-party monopoly over the presidency.

However, the PRI's loss of national office affected Mexico far less dramatically than one might suspect. PAN suffered the fate of long-denied opposition parties whose chance finally comes: it fell victim to its own inflated rhetoric. The new Fox administration took office saddled with a burden of impossible expectations that Fox himself had stoked. The track record for outsider chief executives coming to "clean house" is poor indeed, and for all his electoral bravado, Fox proceeded timidly. Failed initiatives included an attempt to carve a new airport out of ejido lands east of the Distrito Federal: politically feasible in 1950, but not a half-century later. His own wife operated a thinly disguised influence-peddling arrangement called Vamos México, in which entrepreneurs paid cash contributions in exchange for access. Fox spent huge amounts of political capital in a failed attempt to oust Mexico City's leftist mayor, Andrés Manuel López Obrador. Nor did the president appreciate the devastating impact of the immense narcotrafficking problem that was growing under his nose and that had infiltrated his own administration.

Fox's PANista successor, Felipe Calderón Hinojosa, managed to squeak past the PRI's López Obrador in the 2006 elections by a margin so tiny that it left a permanent asterisk beside the victor's legitimacy. Both he and Fox made headway in bringing about greater transparency and in moving Mexican governance into the online age. Calderón also instituted a form of health care for low-income sectors, Seguro Popular. But he soon confronted far greater headaches in the form of a spiraling drug war that inflicted unprecedented casualties on traffickers, law enforcement, and bystanders alike (a topic treated below). High petroleum prices obscured the weaknesses and limitations of the two PANista sexenios, but beginning in June 2014 an eighteen-month slide cut oil prices by some 75 percent and the return to earlier highs has yet to happen. The 2012 elections returned the PRI, in the person of Enrique Peña Nieto, to power.

Mexico beyond the Millennium

The present day is dangerous ground for historians, but we can offer a few observations. Certainly one of the most shocking changes of the last two decades has been the wave of narcotrafficking wars that have brought levels of public violence not seen since the days of Pancho Villa.

Drug trafficking has a long history here, one that extends back to the days when the United States first banned morphine (1905) and cocaine (1914). Mexico really hit its stride as a supplier of illegal substances to the United States during the Prohibition years (1919–33). The trade declined thereafter, only to explode again in the 1970s, when Drug Enforcement Agency (DEA) initiatives closed off the heroin routes from Europe, the famous "French Connection," together with cocaine shipments via the Caribbean. Both campaigns inadvertently turned Mexico into the favored point of entry. Colombians ran the first operations and merely paid Mexican counterparts for use of routes and the promise of protection. Within fifteen years, however, Mexicans took control of distribution and relegated Colombians to the role of suppliers. In addition to Andean-produced cocaine, the new Mexican organization, controlled by Sinaloa-born Miguel Ángel Félix Gallardo, added marijuana and poppy-derived opiates. (Both crops have enjoyed a long history in the Mexican northwest.) Meanwhile, the ingrained tradition of an underfunded state—itself the legacy of Spanish colonial practices and the difficulties of building a tax-based fiscal system in a world of profound inequalities—left Mexico with underprepared police enforcement.

In 1989—following the kidnapping and sadistic murder of DEA agent Kiki Camarena, in which his killers drilled a hole in his head after nearly three days of continual torture—Mexico came under intense political pressure, and Mexican federal police arrested Félix Gallardo. Today El Padrino remains behind bars, but to better protect his operations, he divided his kingdom into multiple cartels, each with its own plaza (a territory ranging from an individual city or cities to entire states), and each controlled by a chief known as a capo. By 2000 profits from the trade had grown immense. Inevitably, the various cartels fell into a war for control of any plaza whose management seemed weak. A cartel's assassination of Cardinal Juan Jesús Posada in 1991, albeit possibly by accident or mistake, gave an unmistakable sign that the old PRI order was losing control over narcoviolence. In 2001 Sinaloan-based Joaquín "El Chapo" Guzmán escaped from a penitentiary in rural Guadalajara and launched a full-scale campaign to take over the Juárez plaza, setting off a war among the cartels that continues to the present day. PANista president Calderón's determination to fight the cartels through military means increased the body count, but his interventions failed to end the underlying problems.

In terms of its larger influence, narcotrafficking defies easy evaluation. It enjoys a certain widespread support, as capos can purchase loyalty by providing basic services to remote, capital-starved communities. Moreover, the decline of small- and midsized enterprises, one of the consequences of the Mexican *perestroika*, expanded the pool of otherwise unemployed men. Indeed, the lowering of tariff protections and subsidies

Even narcotraffickers could use some help from above. Long-standing practices of popular religion led to the emergence of shrines devoted to San Malverde. This one resides in a chapel in Culiacán, Sinoloa. In exchange for prayers and offerings, he keeps his devotees out of jail and away from the bullets. Courtesy of Alamy.

for Mexican agriculture made small-scale farmers NAFTA's principal victims, causing over two million men to abandon their fields in search of better opportunities. Trafficking employs a relatively small percentage of the population, while the actual amount of money involved pales the revenue generated by legitimate agriculture, industries, and services. Yet that same traffic exerts a negative effect far beyond numbers, undermining the rule of law and generating a deep sense of personal insecurity. Drug operations long ago branched off into such areas as illegal logging and mining. Moreover, the industry itself selects brutal men, because being a leader is dangerous business. Mexican capos typically have about three years at the top before ending up dead or in jail. To guard against either fate, a successful chief must be prepared to use ruthless tactics.

Meanwhile, a far greater percentage of the population is involved in money laundering, often without even being aware of it. Hiding vast amounts of illicitly obtained cash generates a need for false bank accounts, bogus investments, and splashy businesses and nightclubs that often correspond to no evident demand for their services and that disappear as quickly and as mysteriously as they arose. National drug consumption is increasing as well. For generations it was possible to dismiss the drug problem as something belonging to a decadent United States, but more Mexican-produced narcotics now remain in the country. Between 2002 and 2016 the percentage of Mexicans aged twelve through sixty-five who consumed illegal substances more than doubled, rising to nearly 10 percent and placing the country's drug use on par with that in the United States.

Behind these tales and statistics looms three inescapable facts. First, the U.S. market drives, and has always driven, the Mexican side of the industry. Drug use remains counterintuitive, in that societies with the highest levels of education and opportunity actually have the highest levels of drug consumption. Equally contrary to what one might expect, the bulk of cartel profits come not from the more compact heroin or cocaine but rather from bulky shipments of marijuana; in recent years the focus has shifted to smuggling ingredients for methamphetamines. Second, the massive entry of U.S. agribusiness into Mexico has driven millions of rural Mexicans out of farming, while the corresponding growth of urban jobs has failed to compensate: the attraction of illicit but highly profitable activities thus grows all the stronger. Third, forces within the U.S. supply the cartels with their firepower. The United States' strong culture of gun ownership rights and its huge firearms industry have made it easy for Mexican smugglers to arm themselves against law enforcement and each other. Between 2010 and 2012 alone, a staggering quarter of a million U.S. guns entered Mexico. (In contrast, legal access to private gun purchases in Mexico remains next to impossible, the legacy of a nation intent on curbing revolutionary mayhem.) The long and involved history of arms in the United States is beyond the scope of this study, but suffice it to say that a practice born out of tradition, ideology, practicality, political appeal, and simple profit-seeking exerts a terribly negative effect on our southern neighbor. As of 2020 neither the demand for illegal substances nor the current permissive gun atmosphere show any signs of abating. Accepting blame is never popular, and the U.S. role in bringing about the international narcotics problem shows little sign of entering either the public consciousness or political discourse any time soon.

Another feature that defines daily experience in the early twenty-first century is the transfer of populations. In the case of Mexico, most people probably equate that phenomenon with immigration to the United States—an immigration that has steadily declined over the last fifteen years. Increased globalization and greater diversity activated a backlash movement in the United States, one that found a banner in anti-immigration sentiments and policies.

We less commonly recognize that Mexico has long been a destination for people fleeing other countries, including the United States. Mexico showcases a variety of immigrant success stories. For example, the Mennonites, an offshoot of the sixteenth-century Anabaptist movement, began coming here in the 1920s, when the patriotic fervors of World War I raised conflicts between themselves and the Canadian government. Mennonites were exactly the sort of thrifty yeomen that Obregón liked, and he only too happily admitted them. Their communities stretch from Chihuahua to Quintana Roo, and despite making their peace with cars, air travel, and cell phones, the Mennonites stand out for their distinctive clothing and language. (Many continue to speak either standard or Low German.) Those who live in areas close to the Mennonites admire the industrious habits that have given this scant population of a hundred thousand people a level of economic success that eludes many Mexican small rancheros and milpa farmers.

Asia has long influenced Mexico, and that fact holds true in the twenty-first century. In colonial times the Philippines provided New Spain with its gateway to Asian (principally Chinese) goods, and Asians have always formed a part of Mexican society. Chinese and Japanese settlements in Sonora stoked nativist anger during the revolution, but these days it is Asia's commercial gravity that exerts the greatest influence, as China has become a major destination for Mexico's agricultural and mineral exports. South Korea has made significant inroads as well, and Mexicans have embraced Samsung electronics, tae kwon do, and the Korean Wave with a fervor bordering on the devotional.

In terms of economic success, few can match the Lebanese, or as they are known here, sirio-libaneses. In the mid-nineteenth century, missionary schools lifted education levels among Christians in Lebanon while hospitals also brought on a population boom as more infants survived to adulthood. Latin America, including Mexico, became a popular destination for those seeking a better life. Political instabilities since 1945 have perpetuated a Lebanese brain drain. Not only do Lebanese descendants occupy a disproportionate share of the entrepreneurial class, but Lebanese foods such as *kibis*, *labni*, and tabouli have all become standard fare, particularly in the cities. Mexico's wealthiest citizen—Carlos Slim, CEO of the privatized Telmex—and some of the dominant figures of the Mexican entertainment industry have strong Lebanese roots. (It is worth mentioning that one of the most commercially successful films in Latin American history, *Nosotros los nobles* [2012], is directed by Gary Alazkari, who is of Middle Eastern descent; it makes numerous references to Mexico's Lebanese culture.)

Mexico also continues to draw people from other Latin American countries. An echo of the Spanish Civil War occurred in the 1970s and 1980s, when South America's horrendous political persecutions caused intellectuals from such places as Argentina, Brazil, and Chile to flee to Mexico, entering the ranks of writers, journalists, and university professors. A far different fate has awaited another immigrant group: Central Americans. Poor, balkanized, and in many instances dominated by foreign companies, places like El Salvador, Honduras, and above all Guatemala have long sent migrant workers seeking better wages. Guatemalans have historically handled such work as coffee picking in Soconusco, toiling cheaply and often in the face of nationalist resentment. The terrible Guatemalan civil war of the 1970s and 1980s created refugee camps in states like Campeche and Quintana Roo. The communities born of those camps endured dislocation, poverty, and raids by Guatemalan security forces, but they have survived and even thrived in their new homeland. The question of the status of Central American migrants, many but by no means all of them en route to the United States, continues to the present day.

But all of these immigrant groups fail to compete in numbers with U.S. citizens who have chosen voluntarily to live as expatriates in Mexico. Over a million U.S. citizens, overwhelmingly retirees, currently reside here, and while they may not generate concern over jobs, they do occupy broad swathes of blue-chip property, including such scenic communities as San Miguel Allende, Lake Chapala's Ajijic, and Cholul, just outside of Mérida. Drawn by low taxes and warm weather, these expatriates have little interest in returning to the land of their birth. They resist assimilation and live in cultural enclaves that re-create as closely as possible their old lives, only without the astronomical health-care costs.

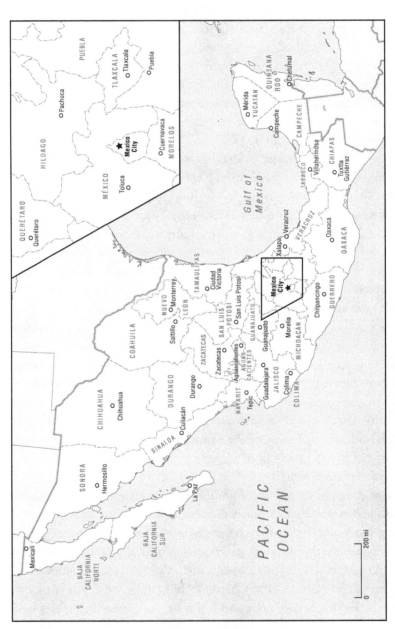

Political map of modern Mexican states and main cities. Map by Erin Grib Cartography.

Beyond narcotrafficking and immigration lies the simple fact that contemporary Mexicans live differently than did their parents and grandparents. Long a bastion of religious unity, Mexico is now only 80 percent Catholic. This is a far cry from places such as Chile and Honduras, where Catholics barely account for a majority, but it is nothing that the bishops of old would have accepted. The nation even boasts a religion of its own creation: Luz del Mundo, founded by Eusebio (later Aarón) Joaquín González in Monterrey in 1926 and now strongly rooted in the state of Jalisco. Luz del Mundo's tendency to messianic leaders has led some critics to label it a cult; indeed, the founder's grandson, Naasón Joaquín García, is currently in jail in Los Angeles on charges of child pornography and sexual trafficking of minors. But its strict adherence to traditional gender roles draws directly from the roots of colonial society.

Perhaps no group has felt the changes of recent decades more keenly than women. Indeed, the advances of the twentieth century have utterly transformed female education, professional expectations, and personal relationships. Women lead men in terms of university enrollment, even though the latter still dominate in terms of employment. Social mores for women have also loosened, and most females now expect to make the key decisions regarding their own lives. The days when Mexican parents could tell their daughters whom to marry walked away a long time ago. Birth control is available and widely used. Since 2007 abortion is legal under certain circumstances (in Mexico City only, and only for the first trimester); ironically, the nation as a whole has an abortion rate higher than that of the United States, a relatively common feature of societies that outlaw the procedure altogether.

In politics, too, the landscape has shifted. Women currently occupy 45 percent of the seats in the Cámara de Diputados (as compared to only 24 percent of the seats in the U.S. House of Representatives at time of writing), and 17 percent of the seats in the Mexican Senate. The 2012 elections saw the first-ever female presidential candidate from a major party: economist and author Josefina Vázquez Mota, representing the PAN. Though her candidacy polled third, it did strike a blow against barriers that had prevailed until a mere forty years earlier. At this point the greater divide may not be so much between men and women but rather between women of different backgrounds. Rural women suffer far higher rates of poverty, illiteracy, and disempowerment than their urban counterparts.

The survival of old attitudes among marginal sectors became tragically apparent with the unsolved murders of over three hundred women, most of them young employees of the maquila system, in Ciudad Juárez between 1993 and 2013.

Attitudes toward sexuality have also changed remarkably. As with all societies, homosexuality is nothing new here. Pre-Columbian societies demonstrated considerably more permissive attitudes toward same-sex relationships than did their European contemporaries. Despite extremely powerful religious and social taboos, colonial and national-era society often tolerated gays and lesbians who maintained discretion in their personal lives. To give only one example, Manuel Palafox, a key advisor to Emiliano Zapata, was gay. Under the influence of the Napoleonic Codes, Mexico decriminalized adult consensual sex in 1871, long before this same step was taken in the United States. But further change came slowly. Religious attitudes, a predominantly rural population, and an overall cultural conservatism relegated gay life to a demimonde of bars and clubs, their patrons alternately harassed and ignored. Indeed, at various periods in modern Mexican history, police persecution of homosexuals went so far as to deport "offenders" to a prison island. It was only in the 1970s and 1980s that Mexican activism, global changes, and the AIDS epidemic brought discussion of homosexuality into the open. In 1997 Patria Jiménez became the first openly lesbian woman to be elected to the Cámara de Diputados. A 2010 law—passed, ironically, under a conservative Catholic president—requires all states to recognize gay marriages performed in Mexico, even though performing said marriages is only legal in Mexico City and fourteen states. However, President Enrique Peña Nieto's attempt in 2016 to make same-sex marriage universal stalled, and while the overall legal direction of the matter appears settled, real change has been a forward-then-back-again process.

Sadly, modern Mexico is also overweight. Doubtless the famished peasants of 1848 would have found it difficult to imagine their descendants struggling with chronic obesity. And yet it is true. Per capita, Mexico consumes more sugary soft drinks than any country in the world. The advent of fast foods, easily abundant processed foods, a higher consumption of sugar and carbonated beverages, and an increasingly sedentary lifestyle have resulted in a society only slightly trimmer than its notoriously plump northern neighbor. Almost a third of all Mexican children now suffer from obesity. The changes have manifested themselves in significantly higher rates of diabetes and heart problems.

Like so many other nations, Mexico has had to confront its many environmental sins and recognize that the expanding human presence has had often dire consequences for the natural world. For most of its history the nation prioritized economic development, including widespread ranching, strip mining, and plantation agriculture. Moreover, the revolution's land programs came into being in a world where environmental concerns did not even exist. But by the late twentieth century the negative consequences of development had become too great to ignore. Uncontrolled logging, urban sprawl, water contamination, species loss, reef destruction, and border-region chemical dumping have been among the greatest concerns. In 1994 the government responded to increasing environmental concerns by creating what is now called Secretaría del Medio Ambiente y Recursos Naturales (Secretariat of Environment and Natural Resources, SEMARNAT). Since 1976 Mexico has created no fewer than forty biospheres, environmentally sensitive areas that receive special protection. Finally, private conservation groups like PRONATURA encourage sustainable use of forests.

Nevertheless, commercial interests and popular usage still outstrip corrective measures. NAFTA's promotion of large-scale agribusiness brought an unbridled use of chemical fertilizers and pesticides. Home to one of the greatest concentrations of biodiversity in the world, Mexico also suffers one of the highest deforestation rates; at least half a million hectares succumb to commercial logging or land clearance each year. Habitat destruction has made the future of such creatures as the monarch butterfly uncertain. Endangered species also include the Mexican wolf, the jaguar, the manatee, and the scarlet macaw. In some cases, particularly in the Yucatán Peninsula, protection of maritime species has succeeded: as a boat captain in Cozumel once explained to me, "It would be better for the Coast Guard to catch you with a dead body than with a sea turtle." And anyone who has had the privilege of diving Cozumel's underwater marvels—places such as Columbia Reef and Palancar Gardens—can only hope that underwater park management and informed usage somehow averts the worst of the coral reef destruction that has already hurt so much of this fragile ecosystem.

The future is dangerous territory for the historian, whose analytical powers rest on a thoughtful consideration of facts carefully gathered from the past. But we can still underline a few basic realities likely to condition Mexico's future. It seems unlikely that the country will ever be free of its massive foreign debt, and that means that the government will always channel off a certain amount of the GNP for debt servicing. Nor does it seem probable that the population will return to the land in any significant way; if the previous history of the human race provides any indication, migration to the cities permanently redefines people. In addition, the United States will always embrace a ready supply of cheap labor, and consumers will not tolerate the abrupt price increases that would come with the end of that labor. It is certain that the U.S. demand for narcotics will continue, and interdiction has its limits—as do awareness and treatment programs—but far greater impact is likely to ensue from legalization, as is currently happening with marijuana. Legalization of more dangerous substances such as cocaine and methamphetamines remains unlikely and far less defensible. And barring some radical shift of the political landscape, guns and ammunition are almost certain to remain readily available.

At the time of writing, Mexico is experiencing the backlash against a governing class seemingly insensitive to the consequences of its forty-year campaign of liberalization. In 2018 public resentment castigated both the PRI and the PAN, and by a level of consensus overwhelming in terms of the nation's fragmented political landscape, the elections favored Andrés Manuel López Obrador. Besides holding the presidency, his newly formed party, Movimiento de Regeneración Nacional (MORENA), enjoys absolute majorities in both upper and lower houses of the legislature, a startling if perhaps temporary implosion of old party structures. It remains to be seen whether the parties born of the revolution have permanently imploded or whether these organizations and their constituencies can somehow reconstitute themselves. Equally unclear is the degree to which AMLO can actually achieve his promise of restoring economic sovereignty and driving out entrenched corruption—as is the question of whether political systems can exist without something resembling corruption.

Mexico's startling evolution of the past half century has happened as part of a growing crisis of the nation-state. Too large to satisfy some interests, too small for others, the national sovereignty that Lázaro Cárdenas so urgently demanded now has to make its peace with ethnic and cultural minorities, foreign multinationals, globally based religions, and digital communications networks that know neither bounds nor taboos. Examined from almost any angle, it seems that when and if Mexicans finally complete their golden project of national creation, it may take place in a world that no longer has much use for the sort of rules and limitations that nations provide.

This tension between past and present, between the intensely local and the vastly global, informs so much of the Mexican epic and even features in the prophetic Maya writings of the *Chilam Balam*. As one of its dark passages shrewdly remarks about the burden of history, "It is not we who did it; it is we who pay for it today." The *Chilam Balam* speaks of terrible times, the culmination of what happened long ago bearing down upon those who live in the here and now: of war, famine, invasions, pestilence, and even the final eradication of the human race from this ancient scene of first civilizations.

"But," as that same book adds in one of its occasional sprinklings of hope, "perhaps God will not desire all the things which have been written to come to pass."

Suggested Reading

Chapter 1. First Peoples

Adams, Richard E. W. *Prehispanic Mesoamerica*. 3rd ed. Norman: University of Oklahoma Press, 2005.

Berdan, Francis F. *The Aztecs of Central Mexico: An Imperial Society*. Belmont, CA: Thomas Wadsworth, 2005.

Carrasco, Davíd. *Religions of Mesoamerica*. 2nd ed. Long Grove, IL: Waveland Press, 2014.

Coe, Michael. *The Maya*. 8th ed. New York: Thames and Hudson, 2011.

Davies, Nigel. *The Toltecs, until the Fall of Tula*. Norman: University of Oklahoma Press, 1977.

Diehl, Richard A. *The Olmecs: America's First Civilization*. London: Thames and Hudson, 2004.

Kepecs, Susan, and Rani T. Alexander, eds. *The Postclassic to Spanish-Era Transition in Mesoamerica: Archaeological Perspectives*. Albuquerque: University of New Mexico Press, 2003.

Kowalski, Jeff Karl, and Cynthia Kristan-Graham, eds. *Twin Tollans: Chichén Itzá, Tula, and the Epiclassic to Early Postclassic Mesoamerican World*. Washington, DC: Dumbarton Oaks Research Library and Collection, 2007.

Pollard, Helen Perlstein. *Tarícuri's Legacy: The Prehispanic Tarascan State*. Norman: University of Oklahoma Press, 1993.

Quezada, Sergio. *Maya Lords and Lordship: The Formation of Colonial Society in Yucatán, 1350–1600*. Translated by Terry Rugeley. Norman: University of Oklahoma Press, 2014.

Chapter 2. Colonial Crown Jewel

Couturier, Edith Boorstein. *The Silver King: The Remarkable Life of the Count of Regla in Colonial Mexico*. Albuquerque: University of New Mexico Press, 2003.

Hassig, Ross. *Mexico and the Spanish Conquest*. Harlow, UK: Longman, 1994.

Knaut, Andrew L. *The Pueblo Revolt of 1680*. Norman: University of Oklahoma Press, 1995.

Lockhart, James. *The Nahuas after the Conquest: A Social and Cultural History of the Indians of Central Mexico, Sixteenth through Eighteenth Centuries*. Stanford, CA: Stanford University Press, 1994.

Restall, Matthew. *The Maya World: Yucatec Culture and Society, 1550–1850.* Stanford, CA: Stanford University Press, 1997.

———. *Seven Myths of the Spanish Conquest.* Oxford, UK: Oxford University Press, 2003.

Ruiz Medrano, Ethelia. *Mexico's Indigenous Communities: Their Lands and Histories, 1500–2010.* Translated by Russ Davidson. Boulder: University Press of Colorado, 2010.

Tayor, William B. *Drinking, Homicide, and Rebellion in Colonial Mexican Villages.* Stanford, CA: Stanford University Press, 1979.

Townsend, Camila. *Malintzin's Choices: An Indian Woman in the Conquest of Mexico.* Albuquerque: University of New Mexico Press, 2006.

Chapter 3. Blue Skies, Blood-Stained Land

Frasquet, Ivana. *Las caras del* águila*: Del liberalismo gaditano a la república federal mexicana (1820–1824).* Xalapa, Mexico: Universidad Veracruzana, 2010.

Hamnett, Brian R. *Roots of Insurgency: Mexican Regions, 1750–1824.* Cambridge, UK: Cambridge University Press, 1985.

Henderson, Timothy J. *The Mexican Wars for Independence.* New York: Hill and Wang, 2009.

Peraza-Rugeley, A. Margarita. *Llámenme "el mexicano": Los almanaques y otras obras de Carlos de Sigüenza y Góngora.* New York: Peter Lang, 2013.

Taylor, William B. *Magistrates of the Sacred: Priests and Parishioners in Eighteenth-Century Mexico.* Stanford, CA: Stanford University Press, 1999.

Tutino, John. *From Insurrection to Revolution in Mexico: Social Bases of Agrarian Violence, 1750–1940.* Princeton, NJ: Princeton University Press, 1986.

Van Young, Eric. *The Other Rebellion: Popular Violence, Ideology, and the Mexican Struggle for Independence.* Stanford, CA: Stanford University Press, 2001.

Voekel, Pamela. *Alone before God: The Religious Origins of Modernity in Mexico.* Durham, NC: Duke University Press, 2002.

Weber, David. *The Spanish Frontier in North America.* New Haven: Yale University Press, 1994.

Chapter 4. Time of Triumph, Time of Troubles

Anna, Timothy. *Forging Mexico, 1821–1835.* Lincoln: University of Nebraska Press, 1998.

Fowler, Will. *Santa Anna of Mexico.* Lincoln: University of Nebraska Press, 2007.

Guardino, Peter. *Peasants, Politics, and the Formation of Mexico's National State: Guerrero, 1800–1857.* Stanford, CA: Stanford University Press, 1996.

Lira, Andrés. *Comunidades indígenas ante frente la Ciudad de México: Tenochtitlán y Tlatelolco, sus pueblos y barrios, 1812–1919.* Mexico City: Colegio de México, 1995.

McArdle Stephens, Michele. *In the Land of Fire and Sun: Resistance and Accommodation in the Huichol Sierra, 1723–1930.* Lincoln: University of Nebraska Press, 2018.

Perry, Laurens Ballard. *Juárez and Díaz: Machine Politics in Mexico*. DeKalb: University of Northern Illinois Press, 1979.

Rugeley, Terry. *Rebellion Now and Forever: Mayas, Hispanics, and Caste War Violence in Yucatán, 1800–1880*. Stanford, CA: Stanford University Press, 2009.

———. *The River People in Flood Time: The Civil Wars in Tabasco, Spoiler of Empires*. Stanford, CA: Stanford University Press, 2014.

Sinkin, Richard N. *The Liberal Reform, 1855–1876: A Study in Liberal Nation-Building*. Austin: University of Texas Press, Institute of Latin American Studies, 1979.

Chapter 5. The Strongman of the Americas

Altamirano Piolle, María Elena. *José María Velascao: Paisajes de luz, horizontes de modernidad*. 2nd ed. Mexico City: DGE Ediciones, 2006.

De Vos, Jan. *Oro verde: La conquista de la Selva Lacandona por los madereros tabasqueños, 1822–1949*. Mexico City: Fondo de Cultura Económica, 1988.

Guerra, Francois-Xavier. *México: Del antiguo régimen a la revolución*. 2 vols. Translated by Sergi Fernández Bravo. Mexico City: Fondo de Cultura Económica, 1985.

Hale, Charles A. *The Transformation of Mexican Liberalism in Late Nineteenth-Century Mexico*. Princeton, NJ: Princeton University Press, 1989.

Kourí, Emilio. *A People Divided: Business, Property, and Community in Papantla, Mexico*. Stanford, CA: Stanford University Press, 2004.

Mora-Torres, Juan. *The Making of the Mexican Border: The State, Capitalism, and Society in Nuevo León, 1848–1911*. Austin: University of Texas Press, 2001.

Saka, Mark Saad. *For God and Revolution: Priest, Peasant, and Agrarian Socialism in the Mexican Huasteca*. Albuquerque: University of New Mexico Press, 2013.

Vanderwood, Paul. *The Powers of God against the Guns of Government: Religious Upheaval in Mexico at the Turn of the Nineteenth Century*. Stanford, CA: Stanford University Press, 1998.

Chapter 6. A Confusion of Armies

Ávila Espinosa, Felipe Arturo, and Pedro Salmerón Sanginés. *Historia breve de la Revolución Mexicana*. Mexico, D.F.: Instituto Nacional de Estudios Históricos de las Revoluciones de México, Secretaría de Educación Pública, Siglo Veintiuno Editores, 2015.

Brunk, Samuel. *Emiliano Zapata! Revolution and Betrayal in Mexico*. Albuquerque: University of New Mexico Press, 1995.

Castro, J. Justin. *Radio in Revolution: Wireless Technology and State Power in Mexico, 1897–1938*. Lincoln: University of Nebraska Press, 2016.

Gilly, Adolfo. *Cada quién morirá por su lado: Una historia militar de la decena trágica*. Mexico, D.F.: Ediciones Era, 2013.

Hart, John M. *Empire and Revolution: The Americans in Mexico*. Berkeley: University of California Press, 2012.

Katz, Friederich. *The Life and Times of Pancho Villa.* Stanford, CA: Stanford University Press, 2000.

Knight, Alan. *The Mexican Revolution.* 2 vols. Cambridge, UK: Cambridge University Press, 1986.

Lear, John. *Workers, Neighbors, and Citizens: The Revolution in Mexico City.* Lincoln: University of Nebraska Press, 2001.

Lomnitz-Adler, Claudio. *The Return of Comrade Ricardo Flores Magón.* New York: Zone Books, 2014.

Meyers, William K. *Forge of Progress, Crucible of Revolt: The Origins of the Mexican Revolution in the Comarca Lagunera, 1880–1911.* Albuquerque: University of New Mexico Press, 1994.

Womack, John, Jr. *Zapata and the Mexican Revolution.* New York: Knopf, 1968.

Chapter 7. The *Científicos* of Tomorrow

Buchenau, Jürgen. *Plutarco Elías Calles and the Mexican Revolution.* Lanham, MD: Roman and Littlefield, 2006.

Dawson, Alexander S. *Indian and Nation in Revolutionary Mexico.* Tucson: University of Arizona Press, 2004.

Dormandy, Jason H. *Primitive Revolution: Restorationist Religion and the Idea of the Mexican Revolution, 1940–1968.* Albuquerque: University of New Mexico Press, 2011.

Dwyer, John J. *The Agrarian Dispute: The Expropriation of American-Owned Rural Land in Postrevolutionary Mexico.* Durham, NC: Duke University Press, 2008.

Escamilla Torres, Rogelio Javier. *La formación de una nación y el sinarquismo de Michoacán, 1920–1941.* Morelia, Mexico: Universidad Michoacana de San Nicolás de Hidalgo, 2011.

Fallaw, Ben. *Religion and State Formation in Revolutionary Mexico.* Durham, NC: Duke University Press, 2013.

Jones, Halbert. *The War Has Brought Peace to Mexico: World War II and the Consolidation of the Post-Revolutionary State.* Albuquerque: University of New Mexico Press, 2014.

López Ulloa, José Luis. *Entre aromas de incienso y pólvora: Los Altos de Jalisco, 1917–1940.* Ciudad Juárez: El Colegio de Chihuahua, Universidad Iberoamericana, Universidad Autónoma de Ciudad Juárez, 2013.

Lucie-Smith, Edward. *Latin American Art of the Twentieth Century.* London: Thames and Hudson, 1993.

Martinez Assad, Carlos. *El laboratorio de la revolución: El Tabasco garridista.* Mexico City: Siglo Veintiuno Editores, 1979.

Olcott, Jocelyn. *Revolutionary Women in Postrevolutionary Mexico.* Durham, NC: Duke University Press, 2005.

Overmyer-Velázquez, Mark, ed. *Beyond La Frontera: The History of Mexico-U.S. Migration.* Oxford, UK: Oxford University Press, 2011.

Smith, Benjamin T. *Pistoleros and Popular Movements: The Politics of State Formation in Postrevolutionary Oaxaca.* Lincoln: University of Nebraska Press, 2019.

Chapter 8. A Cigar, a Cadillac, and a Ticket to the Bullfights

Alexander, Ryan M. *Sons of the Mexican Revolution: Miguel Alemán and His Generation.* Albuquerque: University of New Mexico Press, 2016.

Avina, Alexander. *Specters of Revolution: Peasant Guerrillas in the Cold War Mexican Countryside.* New York: Oxford University Press, 2014.

Barmeyer, Niels. *Developing Zapatista Autonomy: Conflict and NGO Involvement in Rebel Chiapas.* Albuquerque: University of New Mexico Press, 2009.

Flores Caballero, Romeo Ricardo. *México, desde la revolución social a la revolución liberal, 1910–2014.* Monterrey, Mexico: Universidad Autónoma de Nuevo León, 2015.

Gillingham, Paul. *Cuahtémoc's Bones: Forging National Identity in Modern Mexico.* Albuquerque: University of New Mexico Press, 2011.

Padilla, Tanalís. *Rural Resistance in the Land of Zapata: The Jaramillista Movement and the Myth of the Pax Priísta, 1940–1962.* Durham, NC: Duke University Press, 2008.

Soto Laveaga, Gabriela. *Jungle Laboratories: Mexican Peasants, National Projects, and the Making of the Pill.* Durham, NC: Duke University Press, 2009.

Wood, Andrew Grant. *Agustín Lara: A Cultural Biography.* New York: Oxford University Press, 2014.

Zolov, Eric. *Refried Elvis: The Rise of the Mexican Counterculture.* Berkeley: University of California Press, 2009.

Index

Index

CPSIA information can be obtained
at www.ICGtesting.com
Printed in the USA
LVHW041524130722
723342LV00004BA/204

9 780806 167077